Measuring Global Migration

This book focuses on how to improve the collection, analysis and responsible use of data on global migration and international mobility. While migration remains a topic of great policy interest for governments around the world, there is a serious lack of reliable, timely, disaggregated and comparable data on it, and often insufficient safeguards to protect migrants' information. Meanwhile, vast amounts of data about the movement of people are being generated in real time due to new technologies, but these have not yet been fully captured and utilized by migration policymakers, who often do not have enough data to inform their policies and programmes. The lack of migration data has been internationally recognized; the Global Compact for Safe, Orderly and Regular Migration urges all countries to improve data on migration to ensure that policies and programmes are "evidence-based", but does not spell out how this could be done.

This book examines both the technical issues associated with improving data on migration and the wider political challenges of how countries manage the collection and use of migration data. The first part of the book discusses how much we really know about international migration based on existing data, and key concepts and approaches which are often used to measure migration. The second part of the book examines what measures could be taken to improve migration data, highlighting examples of good practice from around the world in recent years, across a range of different policy areas, such as health, climate change and sustainable development more broadly.

Written by leading experts on international migration data, this book is the perfect guide for students, policymakers and practitioners looking to understand more about the existing evidence base on migration and what can be done to improve it.

Frank Laczko is former Director of the IOM Global Migration Data Analysis Centre in Berlin. Prior to this, he was Head of Research at IOM HQ in Geneva. He was the Co-Chair of the UN Expert Group on International Migration Statistics (2018–2022). He has acted as an adviser to several international agencies including WHO, UNHCR, ILO and OECD. His current research focuses on migration from and to China. He has published extensively on a wide range of migration topics and is also an expert on social policy issues relating to poverty, labour markets and ageing. He is the co-author of *Changing Work and Retirement* (1991).

Elisa Mosler Vidal has worked in migration policy and research for eight years, most recently for the International Organization for Migration (IOM) at its Global Migration Data Analysis Centre (GMDAC) in Berlin. There she led work focusing on migration data for development and data for the Sustainable Development Goals (SDGs). She has authored numerous research reports and technical guidance documents on migration and co-authored *IOM's Migration Data Strategy* (2020–2025). She is currently working towards a DPhil in Migration Studies at the University of Oxford, exploring the links between migration, development and health.

Marzia Rango has over ten years of experience working in migration data, research and public policy. She is currently a Migration and Human Mobility Specialist at the UN Operations and Crisis Centre (UNOCC) in the UN Secretariat in New York. Previously, she led work on responsible data innovation and data capacity building for governments at the Global Migration Data Analysis Centre (GMDAC) of the International Organization for Migration (IOM) in Berlin. She was the co-convenor of the Big Data for Migration Alliance (BD4M) and is co-editor of *Harnessing Data Innovation for Migration Policy* (IOM, 2023) and *Migration in West and North Africa and across the Mediterranean* (IOM, 2020).

Routledge Key Issues in Global Migration

Routledge Key Issues in Global Migration investigates the rising number of challenges and opportunities linked to the movement of people around the world. Migration is a growing global phenomenon, with factors such as climate change, poverty, humanitarian crises, demographic changes, and labour competition and shortages suggesting that mobility will continue to increase over the coming years. This series brings together a collection of accessible yet authoritative overviews of the key issues in global migration. As well as providing researchers, students, think tanks, NGOs and policy makers with the latest evidence and analysis, it also highlights real-world applications to help to inform policy responses.

Series Editor
Frank Laczko was the Co-Chair of the UN's Expert Group on Migration Statistics and founder and Director of the International Organization for Migration's first Global Migration Data Analysis Centre. He has over 25 years of experience of working on international migration issues.

Measuring Global Migration
Towards Better Data for All
Frank Laczko, Elisa Mosler Vidal and Marzia Rango

Measuring Global Migration
Towards Better Data for All

Frank Laczko, Elisa Mosler Vidal
and Marzia Rango

LONDON AND NEW YORK

Designed cover image: Getty Images

First published 2024
by Routledge
4 Park Square, Milton Park, Abingdon, Oxon OX14 4RN

and by Routledge
605 Third Avenue, New York, NY 10158

Routledge is an imprint of the Taylor & Francis Group, an informa business

© 2024 Frank Laczko, Elisa Mosler Vidal and Marzia Rango

The right of Frank Laczko, Elisa Mosler Vidal and Marzia Rango to be identified as authors of this work has been asserted in accordance with sections 77 and 78 of the Copyright, Designs and Patents Act 1988.

All rights reserved. No part of this book may be reprinted or reproduced or utilised in any form or by any electronic, mechanical, or other means, now known or hereafter invented, including photocopying and recording, or in any information storage or retrieval system, without permission in writing from the publishers.

Trademark notice: Product or corporate names may be trademarks or registered trademarks, and are used only for identification and explanation without intent to infringe.

British Library Cataloguing-in-Publication Data
A catalogue record for this book is available from the British Library

ISBN: 978-1-032-20952-4 (hbk)
ISBN: 978-1-032-20951-7 (pbk)
ISBN: 978-1-003-26607-5 (ebk)

DOI: 10.4324/9781003266075

Typeset in Galliard
by codeMantra

Contents

List of figures ix
List of tables xi

1 Introduction: Why migration data matter 1

PART I
The state of migration data 15

2 International migration data: An overview 17

3 How international migration data are managed: Challenges and solutions 43

4 Big data: How much can they tell us about migrants and migration policy? 72

PART II
Data availability on key migration topics 103

5 Migration and sustainable development: Measuring progress 105

6 Data on migration and climate change: Making sense of the numbers 134

7 Improving data on migration and health after the global pandemic 157

8 Way forward: Four key recommendations 183

Index 205

Figures

2.1	International migrant stocks, 2020	25
3.1	Censuses and migration data	46
4.1	Sources of data for measuring migration and human mobility	73
5.1	Average percentage of countries reporting migration-related SDG data by indicator, 2023	120

Tables

2.1	Selected categories of migrants: definitions, trends, summary of the data and key global actors	33
2.2	Characteristics of migrants	36
5.1	Sustainable development indicators directly referencing migration	117
6.1	Highest IDP stock numbers linked to disasters in 2021	149
7.1	Health Inclusivity Index: countries with policies of exclusion against migrants and asylum-seekers	171

1 Introduction
Why migration data matter

> *The fact is: counting is hard. Collecting data and using it properly is hard, but we have to try to do better. Doing nothing is not a neutral option. It has a cost.*
>
> (Sturge, 2022, p. 231)

Migration is a topic of huge interest to policymakers around the world, but counting migrants and measuring migration from one country to another, and globally, are difficult endeavours. Individuals responsible for producing migration statistics must consider many factors, including the purpose of the movement, the length of stay in a country and change in residence, before deciding whether to count someone as a migrant. Migration status can often change in response to shifts in government policies. Some migrants may enter a country irregularly and gain legal status only after a shorter or longer stay within a country. Some may be in vulnerable situations and may not wish to be counted.

Traditionally, statistics about migration have come from censuses, surveys and administrative records, but in the digital age, vast amounts of information about the movement of people can potentially be captured through the use of digital devices. We live in an era where due to new technologies, more data are being collected than ever before. At the United Nations General Assembly in September 2022, countries were informed that the "world is in the middle of a data revolution" as data are being generated at previously unimaginable rates (UN, 2022).

It is often said that good data are essential for designing, implementing and evaluating migration policies and programmes (IOM, 2020). Availability of timely data is especially critical when fast changes occur and urgent action is required, for example, in humanitarian crises. Decision-makers need timely data not only to help them understand current migration trends, but also to anticipate and prepare for potential future migration, such as migration linked to climate change. States also need good data if they are to report on the progress that they are making in reaching globally agreed targets, such as those linked to the Sustainable Development Goals (SDGs) (IOM, 2022a), among others. Indeed, most countries agree that better data on all aspects of migration could help them leverage migration for national development objectives, respond to the challenges and plan for migration more effectively.

DOI: 10.4324/9781003266075-1

2 Introduction: Why migration data matter

Countries need data on both international migration and migrants (IOM, 2022b). International migration refers to all movements of people into or out of a specific country. Migration data might, for example, include data on the emigration of a country's citizens or the return of their citizens after a period of residence in a different country. Thus, policymakers are not only interested in collecting data on migrant populations living in countries, whether they be defined in relation to place of birth (foreign-born) or nationality (foreign citizenship), but also migratory movements, or "flows", in and out of their countries. Data relevant to migration can also include data on public attitudes to migrants, remittances (the money sent home by migrants) and data on the impact of migration policies and programmes. Migration data can also refer to past, present or future trends and forecasts, different migrant groups and their characteristics.

However, simply collecting more migration data does not necessarily mean that the data will be used to improve the lives of migrants. Data are often required to inform policy responses, but ultimately policymakers make decisions based on their political priorities, not always using data as a basis for those, using information selectively, or again shaping data collection to follow preconceived political priorities. For example, some policymakers may wish to know more about the drivers of migration and the profiles of undocumented migrants in order to implement more restrictive migration policies. Evidence to support policy decisions consists of more than just data and includes understanding and interpretation of data and statistics. Robust analysis of data is critical, as the same data can be interpreted in different ways depending on the policy priorities of decision-makers.

The global number of international migrants, defined as those living outside their country of birth for at least a year, has increased from 102 million in 1980 to an estimated 281 million by mid-2020 (UN DESA, 2018; 2021). Although, based on these estimates, the share of migrants in the global population has been relatively constant over the past four decades, remaining at approximately 3.6 per cent, human mobility dynamics overall have become much more significant and varied, with people moving temporarily or being displaced from their homes due to disasters, conflict or political instability. International migration and human mobility have become major global issues which present both challenges and opportunities for countries around the world.

Despite widespread agreement on the importance of data to design, implement and evaluate migration programmes and policies, the current availability of reliable and comparable data on many different aspects of migration is still very limited. We know surprisingly little about the 281 million international migrants and the many more who move temporarily or are displaced – who they are, why and how they decided to migrate, what their needs are and what the impact of their migration is on communities of origin and destination (a brief summary of some of the main facts about global migration can be found in Box 1.1). Data on some aspects of global migration tend to be better than others. Box 1.1 shows that global migration statistics often refer to only certain aspects of international migration, such as migrant stocks, remittances and the demographic profile of migrants. Data on other aspects of global migration, such as the scale of irregular migration, the health of migrants or indicators of the well-being of migrants, are more difficult to find.

For more than 60 years, the UN has been issuing recommendations to encourage countries around the world to improve migration data and ensure their comparability across countries (UNSD, 2021). But still, today the term "international migrant" is not fully defined in international law. Also, there is practically no global-level agreement on how migration should be measured, and UN-recommended standards are not equally applied across all countries (IOM, 2021). As discussed in Chapter 2, international definitions of migration and migration data used by countries can vary very widely in practice.

The former Special Representative of the UN Secretary-General on Migration, Peter Sutherland, summed up the situation in 2017:

The global community is still struggling to establish basic facts, such as who migrants are, where they are, where they come from, and where they have moved to.

(Sutherland Report, 2017, p. 25)

For example, due to lack of data, it was not easy for many countries to answer the basic question – how many migrants need to be vaccinated against COVID-19? Many countries do not have an up-to-date register of the number of migrants residing in their country or accurate data on the number of migrants who may be in an irregular situation in their country. In its first-ever global report on the health of refugees and migrants, the WHO highlighted the paucity of data on health and migration:

Although the world has well-established international survey instruments that are constantly improving, the largest datasets currently yield relatively little robust, comparable information about the health of refugees and migrants, and these data are from only a small number of countries and for only a small number of indicators.

(WHO, 2022, p. 297)

For several countries, there is an acute lack of even basic data on international migration. For example, 17 per cent of countries in Africa and 12 per cent in Asia have not produced official statistics on the number of international migrants since 2005 (UN DESA, 2018). Only 45 of the 193 UN Member States report statistics on migration flows – or migratory movements from one country to another over a certain period (typically a year). In summary, international migration statistics are not produced frequently enough, are often not comparable between countries and do not provide enough information to be able to identify the profiles and needs of specific migrant groups (Dumont et al., 2018).

4 Introduction: Why migration data matter

> **Box 1.1 Snapshot of global migration trends: global data and trends**
>
> - 281 million persons lived outside their country of birth by mid-2020. This means that 3.6 per cent of the global population in 2020 were international migrants.
> - At the end of 2020, 35.5 million children, 1 in 66 children globally, were living outside their country of birth.
> - In 2019, there were more than 169 million migrant workers in the world.
> - During the 2015–2020 period, the net flow of migrants moving from lower-income to higher-income regions was estimated at 2.8 million annually.
> - The pandemic may have reduced the global number of international migrants by around 2 million by mid-2020.
> - Since 2014, more than 50,000 deaths of migrants on migratory routes have been recorded globally.
> - In 2020, officially recorded remittances sent to low- and middle-income countries were amounted to an estimated USD 549 billion.
>
> *Source*: adapted from United Nations Report of the Secretary-General, Global Compact for Safe, Orderly and Regular Migration, 27 December 2021 and (IOM, 2022b)

1.1 Aims of the book

This book aims to contribute to the global discussion about how best to improve the collection, analysis and use of data[1] on international migration while protecting the rights of migrants. The book provides an overall assessment of the state of data on global migration while also looking in-depth at data on some key global issues linked to migration sustainable development, climate change and health. Specific chapters of the book are devoted to a discussion of data strengths and weaknesses on each of these topics. The book discusses more generally the key sources of data available on global migration and the potential for addressing data gaps using new data sources.

In recent years, the international community has begun to focus much more on how to improve international migration data, as high-profile calls for better migration data have gained momentum (IOM, 2021). For example, in the landmark 2018 Global Compact for Safe, Orderly and Regular Migration (GCM), the first-ever inter-governmentally agreed document on international migration globally, most countries around the world recognized that much more needs to be done to improve data on migration, if countries are to manage migration effectively. Indeed, improving data on migration is the first of

23 objectives of the GCM. However, no agreement exists yet on how to meet this objective, monitor progress on it and build on the remarkable examples of data innovation which already exist in many parts of the world. The GCM provides few examples of good data practice, and there is no systematic global monitoring framework in place to understand how far data on migration and migrants are actually improving.

In this book, we consider examples of innovative approaches that have been developed to improve migration data. This means not simply considering technical innovation in terms of new methods for gathering data. Innovation can also lie in how data are used and in the development of new strategies to collect, analyse and protect their confidentiality. It can mean innovation in capacity-building, data sharing, data communication and visualization or data literacy. In short, by "data innovation" we mean not only closing data gaps or collecting more data, but also innovation in sharing, protecting and using data in a responsible manner (UNDP/Global Pulse, 2016).

The book also aims to show that investing in migration data can make a huge difference in the lives of migrants. Take, for example, the case of human trafficking. In the United States, the National Human Trafficking Resource Center (NHTRC) operates a national hotline for human trafficking. Between 2007 and 2015, the hotline received more than 122,000 calls. Information from each of these calls was originally stored in independent files, making it difficult to identify trends and develop a coordinated local response. The creation of a new data analytics trafficking platform managed by the non-profit Polaris Project transformed the way the NHTRC operates and responds to trafficking cases. The creation of a trafficking database has not only enabled NHRTC to better understand trafficking trends but also made it easier to provide rapid assistance to victims of trafficking. In an emergency situation, the difference between responding in eight minutes versus ten minutes can be critical. When a caller contacts the NHTRC, their location can be immediately identified, and the platform automatically maps out local resources in that location, from critical emergency response to social services for recovery (ART, 2016; Grove and Bedi, 2019; Galez-Davis et al., 2022). Looking beyond the United States, the "Counter-Trafficking Data Collaborative", the world's first human trafficking data portal, was created in 2019. This portal, described in more detail in Chapter 7, has also contributed to building the evidence base for policymaking and programming on counter-trafficking (Galez-Davis et al., 2022).

1.2 Obstacles to improving migration data

Despite decades of calls and international recommendations to enhance migration data around the world, considerable differences remain in the ways countries define and measure international migration, as explained in Chapter 2. For example, censuses are a key source of data on international migration, but these tend to collect data on individuals' country of birth, and not always on citizenship, as internationally recommended. Further, only approximately half of countries collect data on the date or year of arrival of the migrant, making it difficult to understand and contrast the characteristics of more and less recently arrived migrants. Few censuses include questions on the reasons why someone has chosen to migrate, making it difficult to distinguish between migration for work, family reasons, education or asylum and tease out the impact these may have on societies of origin and destination.

Counting who is a migrant is not a straightforward exercise. Definitions of migration often refer to movement across an international border followed by a certain duration of stay or change of residence. But how long should that duration of stay be before someone is counted as a migrant rather than a visitor? Migration is often defined in relation to a change in "usual residence", which raises questions about how this residence should be defined. What happens when someone has more than one residence? Counting migrants implies movements across borders, but sometimes it is the borders which move, not the people. Overnight, for example, many people in the Common of Independent States (CIS) found themselves foreigners in countries that they had lived in for years.

Migration is often defined in relation to foreign birth or foreign citizenship, but some migrants who return to their own country after many years living abroad might not fit easily into either of these two categories. As argued in a joint United Nations, Department of Economic and Social Affairs (DESA), Organization for Economic Co-operation and Development (OECD) and International Organization for Migration (IOM) submission to the GCM Secretariat (Dumont et al., 2018), while some key migration concepts have been well defined for purposes of statistical measurement, some terms relevant to migration policy discussions such as return migration and re-integration, integration and diaspora remain poorly defined at the international level – "defining and understanding basic concepts employed in measuring migration is essential for an informed, fact-based discussion of realities of migration" (ibid).

Another challenge for those counting migrants, as explained further in Chapter 2, is that some of those who enter or stay in a country do not do so through legal or regular channels. Some migrants may be in transit and may not be easily included in official state-led data collection exercises, such as censuses and surveys. Insufficient capacity and a lack of resources can be key obstacles to effective migration data governance. Although most primary data are collected at the national level, many countries may not have the resources or technical capabilities to do so in a systematic way. Problems may lie with the collection and aggregation of data from several sources, as a lack of intragovernmental coordination and systematic sharing of data collected by different parts of governments is a common issue (IOM, 2021). Lack of comparability and interoperability of migration data collected by different actors, due to different terminology or methodology used, and often linked to differing national priorities and legislation, is another major challenge. These issues stand in the way of integrating data collected by states and that produced by other stakeholders. In addition, as political sensitivities loom large, states may be reluctant to share the data on the movement of people they do have. Further, addressing critical data protection and privacy considerations can be challenging in data sharing (Laczko, 2017).

The challenge is not simply a lack of collected data or a lack of technical capacity or tools: data need to be analysed and shared effectively to have an impact. In other words, data do not speak for themselves. They have to be properly analysed, carefully interpreted, communicated and used to have an impact. Data may be regularly collected, for example, but may not be fully shared or utilized by policymakers, or may be communicated in ways that skew public perceptions of migration (IOM, 2021). For example, some studies show that despite the existence of accurate data on the number of migrants living in a country, host populations often believe that the number of migrants is two or three times higher than the actual figures (IOM, 2011). Statisticians across the globe are sometimes subject to political pressures to conceal data or present figures in certain ways to appease policymakers (Harford, 2020). One data expert put this bluntly – "around the world, the pressure to fiddle the figures is real and widespread" (Harford, 2020, p. 204). Official statistics are often politically and financially sensitive. For example, if the latest figures for inflation or economic growth are poorer than expected, financial markets might react badly, and governments might become less popular. In the case of migration, some data can be highly politically sensitive. For example, few countries collect or release official statistics about the number of migrants who die trying to cross their borders (Brian and Laczko, 2014).

Measures also need to be taken to ensure confidentiality of the information, as well as ethical and responsible handling of the data, as explained in more detail in Chapter 4 (IOM, 2020). For some, more data means more risks, as well as more potential benefits. Some experts argue that having more migration data will lead to better lives, while others are more sceptical about the value of having more information. "Data sceptics" rightly ask whether we can trust the data that are being produced, and whether safeguards are in place to ensure that data are not used to undermine individual security or the rights of migrants (IOM, 2020). The growth in the volume of big data has increased the potential risks of data falling into the wrong hands due to cyber security breaches, or being re-used for a variety of different purposes, without the full consent of migrants (Sievers et al., 2022). There can also be problems with the algorithms that are used to analyse big data, which can unconsciously discriminate against migrants (ibid). As Harford notes, "if algorithms are shown a skewed sample of the world, they will reach a skewed conclusion" (2020, p. 161).

8　*Introduction: Why migration data matter*

1.3　Harnessing the potential of new data sources

Unlike in the past, when most data came from national authorities, data relevant to migration and human mobility today are increasingly being collected by private actors. Huge amounts of data are continuously generated through the use of mobile devices, electronic financial transactions or web-based platforms, mainly owned and maintained by private entities. By 2025, it is expected that the world will generate 175 zettabytes of data, up from 33 zettabytes in 2018. Much of these data are being generated in real time and have the potential to inform many different aspects of migration policy, provided they are used ethically and responsibly. New technology has also made it easier and faster to process and analyse data. Numerous studies have shown that "big data" can be used to monitor people's displacement, short-term migration, remittance flows, migratory movements and efforts to reduce human trafficking (Laczko and Rango, 2014).

The recent global pandemic made policymakers and practitioners more aware of the potential of using such data sources. As many countries were forced to postpone or cancel traditional data collection through censuses and surveys, policymakers turned to alternative data sources for timely information.

There are many challenges associated with using these new data sources, which will be discussed in detail in Chapter 4. For example, there are significant risks associated with using novel data if there are insufficient safeguards to protect the rights of migrants against data misuses (IOM, 2023). These data may also not be fully representative of migrants, because they only represent those who use digital devices. It is well established that a "digital divide" exists and that some population groups do not have access to computers, phones and an internet connection, meaning they may still be uncounted in this context. While investments in new technologies increase across high-income countries, there is also a risk of a widening gap between information-rich and information-poor countries, with implications for global migration governance. Other significant challenges and complexities include ethical and privacy considerations; concerns about the reliability and integrity of the information derived from new data sources; problems of accessibility and cost; continuity and sustainability considering the fast-changing nature of the space, data and actors involved and a persistent lack of governing standards and frameworks.

Still, the potential for using these data to better understand migration dynamics has yet to be fully explored. How far could this type of data be used to inform migration policies and practices around the world? How can such data be used ethically, ensuring that individual privacy and fundamental rights are respected? How to overcome the bias in such data and standardize the use of concepts?

This book discusses ongoing efforts to leverage "Big Data" to inform migration policy, drawing upon examples of initiatives identified in IOM's Data Innovation Directory – a repository of migration data initiatives launched in 2020 (IOM, 2023). The chapter also discusses the concept of "data collaboratives" and suggests ways to enhance public-private data cooperation and accelerate ethical re-use of private data for public policy purposes. The book argues that we need both "Big Data" and "Small Data", and that the challenge is to effectively integrate and combine data from various sources, traditional and non-traditional.

1.4 Notes on scope and terminology

The UN's International Organization for Migration (IOM) defines migration data broadly, in relation to different forms of human mobility:

> *Migration data includes all data that support the development of comprehensive, coherent, and forward-looking migration policies and programming, as well as those that contribute to informed public discourse on migration. This includes data on different forms of population movement, whether short or long-term, forced or voluntary and cross-border or internal, as well as data concerning characteristics of movement and those on the move, and the reasons for and impacts of migration.*
>
> (IOM, 2020, p. 2)

While this book takes a broad definition of migration, the main focus is on international migration. The above definition of who is a migrant includes internal migrants. Together, internal migrants are a considerably larger population than international migrants. Figures on the number of internal migrants tend to be highly imperfect, but in 2013 it was estimated that there were at least 763 million internal migrants worldwide (Lucas, 2016; Hirani et al., 2022). Discussing issues related to collecting data on internal migration is beyond the scope of this book, given the size of this population and the different challenges associated with collecting information about population movements within countries.

Refugee statistics are also not the main focus of this book. Refugees are often included in broad UN statistical definitions of the global stock of migrants, but they are recognized as a special category of persons who cross borders and who are covered by a separate international legal regime. In 2020, for example, refugees accounted for approximately ten per cent of the persons counted as international migrants (26 million refugees compared to 258 million migrants; UN DESA, 2021). There is a separate and distinctive Global Compact for Refugees and several ongoing initiatives specifically designed to improve refugee statistics (see, for example, Chapter 2, which describes the work of EGRISS, the Expert Group on Refugee, IDP and Statelessness Statistics).

1.5 How this book is organized

The first part of this book provides an overview of the overall state of migration data, explaining why there is often a lack of reliable, timely, comparable disaggregated data in countries around the world.

10 *Introduction: Why migration data matter*

Chapter 2 seeks to answer the following questions: What is meant by migration data? What are key topics within migration on which data are available, and what is known based on these data? After introducing key concepts and definitions, this chapter shows for a few key areas - migrant stocks and flows, as well as others relating to specific migrant groups, for example labour migrants, displaced populations and others - what migration data tends to be available, and outlines key trends.

Chapter 3 aims to answer the following questions: How are migration data usually collected and managed? What are common sources of migration data? The chapter examines typical migration data governance structures in countries, and introduces major sources of data along with their key advantages and disadvantages. Next, it presents common methodological issues, including uneven adherence to official statistical definitions and high levels of data fragmentation, several practical challenges, such as poor coordination across government, and key considerations related to ethics and data protection. Finally, the chapter discusses capacity development initiatives to strengthen migration data and how these could be improved, exploring common approaches and statistical capacity efforts.

Chapter 4 focuses on how to harness the potential of data innovation linked to new technologies and the use of "Big Data". The chapter explores how far big data could be used to better inform migration policy and practice. It discusses the advantages and disadvantages of using new data sources and suggests ways in which these data, if used in an ethical and responsible manner, could contribute to our understanding of global migration.

The second part of this book focuses on a series of case studies spanning key migration-related themes, such as sustainable development, climate change and the environment and health. These broad topics were selected as they are of enduring and growing relevance to all countries around the world, regardless of their migration patterns or income levels. Each of these chapters highlights both data gaps and challenges and showcases examples of data innovation, demonstrating some of the progress made in recent years in addressing migration data gaps and analysing, sharing and using data in specific areas. Overall, data on the movement of people are still incomplete and fragmented – but that is not the whole story of this book. In fact, much progress has been made in improving migration data over recent years. Innovation in migration data has grown considerably, but these "success" stories have not been fully captured and shared.

Chapter 5 explores challenges and opportunities related to data on migration and development. It begins by introducing what is usually meant by this in practice and why it is especially significant today, before placing this in the wider context of fast-evolving migration and development debates over the years. The chapter discusses the state of data on selected topics traditionally associated with migration and development such as remittances and diaspora populations, and introduces other relevant topics. It discusses key practical challenges related to producing such data and examines key opportunities in this context, including new commitments at global level linked to global frameworks such as the 2030 Agenda for Sustainable Development (2030 Agenda), and to what extent these have created new data reporting requirements and can be linked to data progress. Finally, it presents several examples of innovative initiatives to improve data on migration and development.

Chapter 6 focuses on one of the major global issues of our time – climate change. Policymakers are interested in knowing how many people may be forced to move in the future due to climate change, and how many may migrate to facilitate adaptation to climate change. The chapter discusses what kinds of data are being collected on different aspects of "climate migration" and what these data reveal about current patterns of migration linked to climate change. The chapter concludes with suggestions on how to improve data on migration and climate change in the future.

Chapter 7 focuses on a theme which has received a huge amount of attention in recent years due to the global pandemic – the health of populations around the world. The chapter reviews key sources of data on migration and health, relating to both migrants' access to health services as well as data on their health status. It includes a special analysis of the data relating to COVID-19 and its impact on migrants. The chapter presents examples of innovative data practice and suggests ways in which the collection, analysis and use of migration and health data could be improved in the future.

Chapter 8 focuses on the way forward and discusses what changes and investments in migration data could be taken to significantly improve our understanding of global migration. The final chapter of the book proposes four key recommendations, which, if implemented, could help to improve the collection, analysis, sharing, use and positive impact of international migration data. These recommendations include concrete measures which could be taken by any country, many in the short-term, and at relatively low cost, to enhance the availability and use of data on migration. The book concludes with a discussion about the way forward and presents a global agenda for improving data on migration and human mobility, building on concrete examples of data innovation. It also outlines a possible framework for monitoring the global state of migration data on a regular basis.

Note

1 Like the "Economist" magazine, we will be using data in its singular form alongside the plural. "Specifically when considered as a concept – as in data is the new oil – the singular will be acceptable, as well as when the data in question is considered as a mass (the data on this mobile phone plan is insufficient)". The plural should still be used when data points are considered as a group of pieces of information; data from the National Oceanic and Atmospheric Administration *indicate* the hottest summer of all time. (Economist, August 13th, 2022).

References

Art, A. (2016). Tracing a web of destruction can big data fight human trafficking?, November 18, Harvard University, Technology and Operations Management, MBA student perspectives.

Brian, T. and Laczko, F. (2014). *Fatal Journeys*. Geneva: IOM.

Dumont, J.C., Hovy, B., Osaki Tomita, K., and Laczko, F. (2018). Improving data for safe, orderly and regular migration. In Laczko, F., Borgnas, E., & Rango, M. (Eds.), *Data Bulletin Series: Informing the Implementation of the Global Compact for Migration*. Geneva: IOM, 15–19.

Economist. (August 11th, 2022). Should "data" be singular or plural?. *Economist Magazine*, London.

Galez-Davis, C., Cook, H., Laursen, S., and Jasi, P. (2022). Leveraging administrative data to fight human trafficking. In Mosler-Vidal, E., & Laczko, F. (Eds.), *The Sustainable Development Goals and Migration: Measuring Progress*. Geneva: IOM.

Grove, B. and Bedi, A. (2019). *It's time we harnessed Big Data for good*. Geneva: World Economic Forum.

Harford, T. (2020). *How to Make the World Add Up*. London: Bridge Street Press.

Hirani, P., Costanzo, J., and Sullivan, D. (2022). Internally displaced persons and internal displacement data in the SDGs. In Mosler-Vidal, E., & Laczko, F. (Eds.), *The Sustainable Development Goals and Migration: Measuring Progress*. Geneva: IOM, 63–71.

IOM (International Organization for Migration). (2011). *World Migration Report: Communicating Effectively About Migration*. Geneva: IOM.

IOM (International Organization for Migration). (2020). *IOM Migration Data Strategy: Informing Policy and Action on Migration, Mobility and Displacement, 2020–2025*. Geneva: IOM.

IOM. (2021). *How Countries Manage Migration Data*. Geneva: IOM.

IOM. (2022a). *The Sustainable Development Goals and Migration: Measuring Progress*. Geneva: IOM.

IOM. (2022b). *The World Migration Report*. Geneva: IOM.

IOM. (2023). *Harnessing Data Innovation for Migration Policy: A Handbook for Practitioners*. Geneva: IOM.

Laczko, F. (2017). Improving data on migration: A 10-point plan. In Ardittis, S., & Laczko, F. (Eds.), *Migration Policy Practice. Vol. VII, Number 1 (January–March 2017)*. Geneva: IOM/EurAsylum, 18–23.

Laczko, F. and Rango, M. (2014). Can big data help us achieve a "migration data revolution"? *Migration Policy and Practice*, IV(2), 20–29, April–June, Geneva.

Lucas, R. (2016). Internal migration in developing countries. *Geopolitics, History and International Relations*, 8(2), 159–191, London: Addleton Academic Publishers.

Sievers, N., Griesmer, L., Rango, M., Trigwell, R., and Jusselme, D. (2022). *Ethical Considerations in Re-Using Private Sector Data for Migration-Related Policy: A Practioners' Perspective*. Geneva: IOM.

Sturge, G. (2022). *Bad Data: How Governments, Politicians and the Rest of Us Get Misled by Numbers*. London: The Bridge Street Press.

Sutherland, P. (2017). Report of the UN special representative of the secretary-general for migration Peter Sutherland to the UN secretary-general, 2017, United Nations General Assembly, A/71/728, 3 February.

United Nations (UN). (2022). Concept note, "Unlocking Impact: Data with Purpose", 77th Session of the United Nations General Assembly, 22nd September, United Nations, World Bank, Global Partnership for Sustainable Development Data, New York.

United Nations Department for Economic and Social Affairs (UN DESA). (2018). *International Migrant Stock*. New York, NY: UN DESA.

United Nations Department for Economic and Social Affairs (UN DESA). (2021). *International Migrant Stock 2020*. United Nations Database. Available at http://un.org/development/desa/pd.content/international migrant stock.

United Nations Development Programme (UNDP) and UN Global Pulse. (2016). *A Guide to Data Innovation for Development*. New York, NY: United Nations.

United Nations Statistics Division (UNSD). (2021). "Revised overarching conceptual framework and concepts and definitions on international migration produced by the Expert Group on Migration Statistics. Background document", Fifty-second session, 1–3 and 5 March 2021, UN Statistical Commission, New York. Available at http://unstats.un.org/unsd/statcom/52nd-session/documents.

World Health Organization (WHO). (2022). *World Report on the Health of Migrants and Refugees*. Geneva: WHO.

Part I
The state of migration data

2 International migration data
An overview

2.1 Introduction to migration data

As underlined in Chapter 1, policymakers around the world need timely, reliable, accessible and comparable data to make informed policy decisions on migration. The current lack of such data makes it difficult to understand ever-evolving migration dynamics today. But what exactly do we mean by "migration data", and how much can existing data actually tell about migration?

While information on migration appears across global media every day, we know much less than we ought to about migration. From a global perspective, relatively few quality statistics on international migration are collected. While data on migrant stocks and remittances are frequently cited, less is known about many other aspects of migration, such as how many migrants enter and leave countries each year, the working and living conditions of migrants, and the scale and dynamics of return migration. Further, there are significant data gaps with respect to topics that require data from different sectors, such as migrant health, or migrant integration. Even when data are available, they may not be of high quality or be equally available around the world. Overall, today, collection, management and analysis of quality migration data are highly imperfect at local, national, regional and international levels.

Several high-level international frameworks and processes have underlined the urgent need to improve migration data. In 2015, the 2030 Agenda for Sustainable Development (2030 Agenda) was adopted, a blueprint for global development, which includes several mentions of migration. This has increased migration data needs around the world and provided impetus to improve migration data (see Chapter 5). Improving migration data is also the first objective of the Global Compact for Safe, Orderly and Regular Migration (GCM), which calls on countries to "commit to build a robust global evidence base on international migration by improving and investing in the collection, analysis and dissemination of accurate, reliable, comparable data, disaggregated by sex, age and migration status" (UNGA, 2018). Within this objective, the GCM lists suggested actions at national, regional and international levels to improve data, including harmonizing migration data methodologies on collection, analysis and dissemination, increasing efforts to build national capacity on migration data, establishing and strengthening regional migration observatories, and others. The Global Compact on Refugees (GCR) similarly recognizes the importance of data and commits that "States and relevant stakeholders will, as appropriate, promote the development of harmonized or interoperable standards for the collection, analysis and sharing of age, gender, disability, and diversity disaggregated data on refugees and returnees" (UNHCR, 2018). While the GCR has a set of agreed indicators to assess its implementation, this is not yet the case for the GCM, meaning that it is not totally clear how to measure progress against each of the 23 objectives. Other high-level international frameworks also have implications for migration data; for example, the Sendai Framework for Disaster Risk Reduction 2015–2030 makes several references to migrants and 38 indicators are designed to monitor progress against it.

Although the need to improve data on migration has been the subject of global-level discussions for a long time, progress has been relatively slow. There are many reasons for this. Some of these relate to the way that migration data are collected and managed at national level. For example, different types of migration data tend to be collected by different parts of government, with low levels of coordination. This means that often, particular ministries do not know what migration data – often of high relevance to them – are held by other ministries, much less have access to these. Other reasons relate to specific migration topics, data collection instruments or data sources. For example, it is particularly challenging to count undocumented migrants; several important statistical instruments used regularly in countries, such as Demographic and Health Surveys (DHS), do not include basic questions on migration; and often data collected through administrative sources are not effectively used. Further, issues related to countries' financial, technical or other capacity to address many of these challenges are common, particularly in low- and middle-income countries. While the UN has been producing recommendations for decades to encourage countries to produce better and more comparable statistics on migration, it remains difficult to compare key migration trends across countries due to differences in data. UN recommendations on migration statistics are not binding, and over the years relatively little funds have been made available to implement these.

This chapter seeks to answer the following questions: what is meant by migration data? What are key topics within migration on which data are available, and what is known based on these data? After introducing key concepts and definitions within migration data, this chapter briefly discusses data by migration topic, showing for a few key areas what information tends to be available and providing an outline of overall trends. These areas include migrant stocks and migration flows, generally considered basic migration statistics, as well as others relating to specific migrant groups and migration topics, for example migrant workers, displaced populations and others.

2.2 What are migration data? Key concepts and definitions

What exactly is meant by migration data? Here, "migration data" refer to "all types of data that would support the development of comprehensive, coherent and forward-looking migration policies and programming, as well as contribute to informed public discourse on migration". This encompasses data concerning "different forms of population movement, whether short or long-term, forced and voluntary and cross-border or internal, as well as data concerning characteristics of movement and those on the move, reasons for and impacts of migration" (IOM, 2021a). In practice this can mean a very wide range of data, from data on the number of migrants forced to move due to climate change, to data on the number of highly educated migrants in a country or data on migrants stranded in a country during a humanitarian emergency. Migration data can also be, but is not limited to, "migrant data" or data on migrant populations. Policymakers need data on the movement of people to or from their countries, as well as data on the status of persons who may be considered to be "migrants" living in their country. Some countries, for example, want to know more about emigration trends and why their citizens are leaving their country. Policymakers interested in harnessing the benefits of migration for development need data on both the status of *migrants* in the receiving country and on *migration* itself, i.e. migratory movements between countries. For example, many return migrants are citizens of the countries they are returning to; this movement has implications for many policy areas beyond reintegration, such as housing, education, employment and health policies, and policymakers will be interested in understanding the scale of these migratory flows as well as the characteristics of those returning. Migration data does not solely involve the movement of people; it can also mean collecting data on the total amount of remittances sent to family members around the world every year, or quantifying the trade benefits of migration. Migration data can include data on migration policies and programmes or monitoring public attitudes to migration. It can also include data relating to migrants and migration from other sectors, such as the labour market, education or health. For example, the unemployment rate of a country, with a breakdown of who is a non-migrant and who is a migrant, would here be considered migration data.

While the spectrum of migration data can be very broad, at the centre of it are individual migrants. How is a migrant conceptualized and defined statistically? UN efforts to do this at the global level have a relatively long history. The UN published its first set of recommendations on this, *International Migration Statistics,* in 1953. In 1976, it adopted *Recommendations on Statistics of International Migration* to encourage countries to collect quality and comparable data on migrants. In 1998, these were revised and expanded to include special guidelines on data on asylum seekers. Today countries are encouraged to follow these non-binding recommendations, and these inform most global initiatives to improve migration data.

The 1998 recommendations define an international migrant as

> *"any person who changes his or her country of usual residence", distinguishing between "short-term migrants"* – those who change their country of usual residence for at least three months but less than a year – *and "long-term migrants"* – those who do so for at least one year.
>
> (UNSD, 1998)

One of the main benefits of having an internationally recommended definition is that it helps to generate comparable information. Having most countries use the above definition of who is a migrant helps policymakers, researchers and others alike be able to know the number of migrants worldwide or compare migrant numbers from different countries side-by-side. This is also important to agree on basic facts and to try to limit political misunderstandings: clashing or confusing data coming from different sources based on differing concepts or definitions produce different results.

However, even with existing migration data definitions, accurately assessing and counting who a migrant is not a straightforward exercise. There are many difficulties and open questions involved in defining who a migrant is; many are contained in the above definition through its terminology. For example, migration is defined in relation to a change in *usual residence*. According to the 1998 recommendations, a person's country of *usual residence* is defined as "that in which the person lives, i.e., the country where the person has a place to live where he or she normally spends the daily period of rest" (UNSD, 1998). But what happens when someone's residence is not clearly defined, or someone has more than one residence? The concept of *duration of stay* or how long an individual is in a country until they should be classified as a migrant is often contested by experts. The definition of a migrant refers to movement across an international border, followed by one year (*long-term migrant*) or three months (*short-term migrant*): are these the right parameters for someone to be counted as a migrant rather than a visitor, and a long- rather than short-term migrant? Further, counting migrants implies movement across borders, but sometimes it is the borders which move, not the people. Overnight, for example, after the Soviet Union dissolved, over 25 million ethnic Russians living in 14 non-Russian republics suddenly found themselves classified as migrants as a result of border changes, becoming foreigners in countries they had lived in for many years (Heleniak, 2002). Where do such examples fit within the official definition? Further, there are significant challenges associated with operationalizing these definitions. For example, many of those who enter or stay in a country do not do so through legal channels for different types of migration and do not officially change their country of usual residence. This means they will not always be registered by a country's official data collection instruments, such as censuses and surveys, and will not often be included in migrant stock figures. Further, some migrants may be in transit for longer periods of time and would similarly not change their country of usual residence or be included in official data collection. These are just some of the methodologically difficult questions and challenges involved in defining and measuring who is a migrant that the statistical community, including the Expert Group on Migration Statistics, continues to try to answer.

Thus the 1998 recommendations do not necessarily reflect many nuances related to migration, and it has become clear they do not fully respond to more complex emerging human mobility dynamics. Increasingly, practitioners speak not only about migration but also about "human mobility". *Mobility* is typically used as a concept wider than migration, involving those who move but do not classify as migrants according to the 1998 definition – for example, those regularly undertaking cross-border movements for study or work, travelling for periods under three months or living across different countries. In this context, a process is underway to update the 1998 recommendations, and a revised conceptual framework on migration and mobility, reconceptualizing the way that migrants are defined and counted, has been proposed. See Box 2.1 for more.

Additionally, as will be explored in Chapter 3, despite work at global level to officially define and standardize concepts, definitions and methodologies around migration data, these are not always operationalized evenly by different actors, and migration statistics produced by different stakeholders can reflect varying concepts or definitions.

Box 2.1   The Expert Group on Migration Statistics and revision of the 1998 recommendations

The Expert Group on Migration Statistics established by the United Nations Statistical Commission in 2018 aims to improve statistics on international migration. It is composed of academic experts, UN representatives across agencies working on migration data and several country representatives from National Statistical Offices (NSOs) and other national bodies, and functions both to set standards, as well as convene regular dialogue on migration data.

The Group recently revised the *1998 Recommendations on Statistics of International Migration*. To inform this, a global consultation was held to assess national migration data practices and needs. 103 national agencies from 79 countries took part, providing a useful insight into specific migration data challenges and opportunities. For example, countries used varying cut-off periods for duration of stay to classify migrants, ranging from 4 to 12 months, or even longer in some cases. Countries were more likely to produce statistics on labour migration than on return migration. The consultation also revealed key data gaps and needs, as many countries referred to some areas of policy interest for which there were no or few statistics – for instance, irregular migration and citizens living abroad. Based on this and ongoing discussions and efforts of the Expert Group's members, a new conceptual framework was developed, with concepts and definitions on international migration, to form the basis of revised recommendations. This was endorsed by the United Nations Statistical Commission (UNSC) in 2021 (UNSD, 2021a; 2021b). Further, the Expert Group developed a set of core and additional indicators related to migration, to support the operationalization of the revised conceptual framework. The indicators correspond to six key policy areas that are relevant for international migration, in line with the 2030 Agenda and Global Compact for Migration, to monitor progress in each area. These indicators were approved by the UNSC in 2023 (UNSD 2022; 2023).

Recognizing the need to not only align and harmonize global statistics on migration but also ensure these remain responsive to trends today, the Expert Group also aimed to include concepts of mobility in its considerations. Thus, responding to several of the challenges discussed above, the new conceptual framework includes definitions of different types of mobility, including temporary mobility. For example:

- *International mobility*: all movements that cross international borders within a given year.
- *International migration*: all movements resulting in a change in the country of residence (a subset of international mobility) within a given year.
- *International migrant*: a person who has changed his or her country of residence and established new residence in the country within a given year. International migrant can be either 'immigrant' or 'emigrant' and include those with national or foreign citizenships or stateless persons.
- *Temporary (non-resident) population*: all persons who stayed or intend to stay (or granted to stay) in the country for less than minimum duration required for residency in a particular year.
- *International temporary mobility*: all movements that cross international border that do not result in a change in the country of residence (UNSC, 2021; UNSD, 2021a; 2021b).

The framework represents a significant step forward in conceptualizing and measuring modern migration. Work in this area is ongoing; the framework will be accompanied by information on plans for its implementation around the world and available assistance for countries in doing so (ibid.).

There are significant data gaps around refugees, asylum seekers and internally displaced persons (IDPs), where information is urgently needed to inform policy and programming responses around the world. Several efforts are also underway to continue conceptualizing and defining different types of "forced migrants". This chapter focuses predominantly on data on migrants who cross borders and who are not displaced by conflict, violence or disasters, and in line with IOM's broad definition of a migrant, categorizes displaced individuals within the definition of a migrant (IOM, 2019). However, it is important to acknowledge that the established dichotomy between forced and voluntary migration is increasingly contested, in particular as phenomena including mixed migration flows show how migrant categories are becoming progressively more blurred (IOM, 2022). Responding to these challenges, there are several proposed new concepts and categorizations, including, for example, that of "survival migration" (Betts, 2013). Despite its focus on migrants as defined above and recurring use of the term "migration", to contextualize wider discussions on migration and human mobility data and to provide a deeper understanding of this, the book introduces key statistical definitions and concepts related to forced migration, as it has been traditionally conceived. It also signposts to relevant further resources, including some interrogating existing categorizations of migrants and furthering new conceptions of human mobility. See Table 2.1 for more information.

The 1998 recommendations do not address large movements of refugees and related populations or internal displacement (EGRISS, 2018). To address this, notable recent work has been undertaken at the global level on data on refugees and IDPs. The Expert Group on Refugee, IDP and Statelessness Statistics (EGRISS) was established in 2016 and – similar to the Expert Group on Migration Statistics – includes representatives from national, regional and international authorities, among others. The 1951 Convention and 1967 Protocol define a refugee as a person who

> *owing to a well-founded fear of being persecuted for reasons of race, religion, nationality, membership of a particular social group, or political opinion, is outside the country of his nationality, and is unable or, owing to such fear, is unwilling to avail himself of the protection of that country.*
>
> (UNHCR, 2010)

Nevertheless, this definition contains some challenges when it comes to measuring such populations. For example, the concept of usual residence can be difficult to measure and does not indicate clearly how to measure other refugee-related populations, such as those in refugee-like situations, those under different types of temporary protection, and many others (EGRISS, 2018).

Moreover, the refugee data landscape grapples with the question of how to develop countries' statistical capacities to generate quality and timely data. The *International Recommendations on Refugee Statistics (IRRS)* were published by EGRISS to help improve quality of national data on refugee and refugee-related populations by providing detailed guidance on definitions (EGRISS, 2018; for further information on data on refugees, see UNHCR, 2001; 2015).

To date, available IDP data are often based on operational data collected by humanitarian actors, and relatively little international guidance exists on IDP statistics (EU and UN, 2020). The *Guiding Principles on Internal Displacement* define IDPs as

> *persons or groups of persons who have been forced or obliged to flee or to leave their homes or places of habitual residence, in particular as a result of or in order to avoid the effects of armed conflict, situations of generalised violence, violations of human rights or natural or human-made disasters, and who have remained living in the country's internationally recognised border.*
>
> (UN Commission on Human Rights, 1998)

However, this does not state how long a person must be displaced to be an IDP or advise on how to classify children of IDPs (EC et al., 2020). There are many further open questions in the IDP data world – for example, how to statistically treat the concept of durable solutions, and again how to approach statistical capacity development (ibid.). EGRISS continues to work on these and many other issues related to IDP data, convening dialogue and publishing international guidance on the topic, such as the *International Recommendations on Internally Displaced Persons Statistics (IRIS)*, which outline an internationally agreed framework for countries and international organizations to improve the production, coordination and dissemination of high-quality official statistics on IDPs. See Table 2.1 for more on refugee and IDP data.

Having explored some basic concepts and definitions, the chapter next explores available data on different types of migrants and migration phenomena.

2.3 The state of migration data: what do we know?

2.3.1 Migrant stocks

2.3.1.1 Key definition(s)

International migrant stocks indicate how many migrants live in each country and can be defined as "the total number of international migrants present in a given country at a particular point in time" (UNSD, 2017).

2.3.1.2 Global trends

Available statistics on migrant stocks show that there were an estimated 281 million international migrants worldwide in 2020 (UN DESA, 2020a). Figure 2.1 shows an overview of stock figures around the world that year by continent. More than 52 per cent of international migrants counted lived in Northern America and Europe (58.7 million and 86.7 million, respectively). 85.6 million lived in Asia and 25.4 million in Africa.

There are more international migrants today than there used to be in absolute terms – the total stock figure has increased since first being recorded in 1990. This increased from 153 million in 1990 to 173 million in 2000, to 220 million in 2010 (UN DESA, 2020a). However, while in the last two decades migrant stocks have grown by an average of 2.4 per cent per year (UN DESA, 2020a; Batalova, 2022); the share of international migrants in proportion to the world's population has remained relatively stable. Between 1990 and 2020, this increased only from 2.9 to 3.6 per cent (UN DESA, 2020b; IOM, 2021b).

These estimates of migrant stocks are regularly produced by the UN Department of Economic and Social Affairs (UN DESA, Population Division) and are based on available national statistics taken usually from censuses. These figures mainly reflect the number of individuals across countries who are "foreign-born" – living in countries other than those they were born in.

Migrant stocks are a central and vital area of data on migration, and yet act as a good example of the lack of clarity surrounding migration data. For example, while the given UNSD definition has been endorsed by the UN Statistical Commission, and cited UN DESA figures widely globally accepted, many actors at different levels continue to conceptualize and measure migrant stocks differently (see Box 2.2; see also IOM, 2021d).

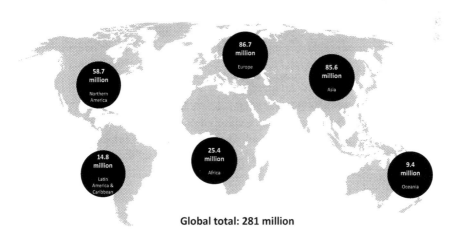

Figure 2.1 International migrant stocks, 2020.
Source: UN DESA (2020a).

Box 2.2   Differences in global migrant stock figures

In 2023 the World Bank released its *World Development Report 2023: Migrants, Refugees and Societies*, which places the total number of international migrants around the world at 184 million. The estimates are constructed from different data sources, including available census data, the EU Labour Force Survey, adjusted UN DESA stock estimates and UNHCR data (World Bank, 2023, p. 45). In the report, migrants are defined as people who live outside of their country of nationality, in contrast to UN DESA's conceptualization which includes those who live outside of their country of birth *or* nationality. The World Bank excludes as migrants those who are citizens of the countries they live in but who were born elsewhere. This dramatically reduces the number of those who are considered migrants, as seen in the difference between the World Bank's 184 million and UN DESA's 281 million estimates. In effect, the World Bank classification of an international migrant could be considered a subset of the UN-accepted classification of an international migrant.

This shows that while there are internationally accepted standards surrounding migration data, these are not always agreed on in practice, and often different actors use alternative, technically non-compliant, definitions. Often the differing conceptualizations and definitions have different backgrounds, theoretical frameworks or motivations behind them. The existing statistical definitions and figures of migrant populations, especially of migration flows, are linked to concepts around demography and are born out of dialogue on international demography statistics. However, the World Bank definition, hinging on the concept of citizenship, can be indirectly linked more to policy dialogues and ideas around individuals' inclusion, integration, rights and entitlements in a modern state and to questions about who around the world enjoys access to different types of living standards. To put this simply, the UN's 1998 recommendations on migration statistics were developed in large part to measure the number of people who changed their country of residence. The World Bank, by contrast, focuses on those with foreign nationality to help stress the specific challenges that stem from lack of citizenship. Data relating to the percentage of foreign-born who are citizens of the country they reside in are very useful when considering to what extent migrants may be integrated in a society and have access to the same entitlements as the native population. However, from a comprehensive migration policy perspective, it is also useful to have quality data on all the foreign-born. For example, even when they become citizens, many of the foreign-born may continue to remit money to their country of origin or support trade links with that country; information on this would be useful for policymakers.

Arguably, the World Bank estimate concerns a sub-category of migrants who are most directly implicated by discussions about international migration around the world today, and who may face the biggest challenges in destination countries, and who policymakers are most interested in. However, by excluding being foreign-born as a component of being a migrant, the estimates have some drawbacks. The World Bank count includes some individuals who may not usually be considered migrants, such as those who have citizenship of a country, for example, through their parents but have never lived in that country. However, more importantly, it excludes many individuals, who would usually be considered migrants, such as citizens returning to their country of origin – return migrants – and potentially those with more than one citizenship. Citizenship rules vary across countries, making the World Bank definition contingent to an extent on national or regional policies, as opposed to on country of birth, which is fixed and unchanging. Further, the World Bank approach makes several indirect assumptions about how most countries operate, namely that having citizenship is related to better access to services or has other benefits, and fundamentally, that there is a state apparatus strong enough to guarantee this. However, this is not always the case. In some countries, having a type of recognized permanent or other type of residence is key to accessing services and contributing to the economy (such as in the UK), or there may be an equivalent at the local level, such as in sanctuary cities, making the holding of citizenship a much less relevant data point. In other cases, there may not be a welfare system, formal economy or sufficiently strong governance system where these concepts are relevant at all or directly correlated to a migrant's living standards or ability to contribute to a destination country. Having citizenship of a country is not a guarantee of full access to services, labour markets or other potential factors affecting living standards. For example, many naturalized migrants, or those holding another citizenship, may be subject to different types of discrimination and issues accessing a country's services.

Further, the operationalization of this definition based solely on citizenship has one key challenge that limits its robustness – many developing countries do not produce statistics on the number of foreign citizens but only on the foreign-born living in their country. As seen elsewhere in this chapter, censuses around the world are more likely to collect data on country of birth, than citizenship, making it more challenging to produce a global migrant stock figure based on counting foreign citizens residing in a country. For example, during the 2010 census round, 25 per cent of the 149 countries for which data are available in the UN Statistics Division database did not ask respondents about their country of citizenship (Juran and Snow, 2017).

> Overall, the World Bank conceptualization of who is a migrant has advantages and disadvantages and provides a good case study of the implications of using different definitions. Use of competing definitions among actors will likely continue, as discussed further in the capacity development section. While capacity development activities at the national level will continue to try to improve data harmonization, the issue also highlights the importance of presenting migration data with clear accompanying explanations, definitions, data sources used and other relevant metadata to avoid confusion and to help users interpret figures.

The migrant stock figures mentioned above relate to the global level and are based as seen on national statistics. At the local level, it can be difficult to estimate migration populations due to fast changes of inflows and outflows; usually census data are used to understand local migrant stock populations, but these are only conducted every five or ten years. In some cases, administrative data can be used instead to estimate migrant stocks (Oxford Migration Observatory, 2011).

2.3.1.3 Summary of data

While migration policymakers are often severely constrained by the information available to them, there is one area of existing data they often start with: migrant stocks. Information on migrant stocks is available at global level – there are estimates available for 232 UN countries/areas – meaning that these statistics are available for most countries in the world on a regular basis and can be compared across them. Data on migrant stocks are an important starting point to understand migration in any country and are of ever-green relevance to migration policymakers, as they can help inform a wide range of programmes and policies, such as within public service provision.

Typically, NSOs collect data on migrant stocks through population censuses. Censuses usually collect information on the country of birth of each respondent and/or on their country of citizenship; the resulting data on how many people in a country are foreign-born and/or of foreign citizenship are used to understand migrant stocks. Commonly, some countries use other data collection instruments to collect information on stocks; for example, population registries, administrative records or others. The United Nations Statistical Division (UNSD), within UN DESA, is mandated to collect migrant stock data from countries through its Demographic Yearbook data collection system. Based on this, the UN Population Division provides regular global estimates of international migrant stocks. In this way, the global statistics on stocks – including the 281 million figure in the introduction of this book – are based on national statistics. While UNSD compiles and disseminates this information at global level, there are some bodies that perform a similar function at regional level. For example, Eurostat reports migrant stock statistics for EEA Member States, and the OECD for its member countries (OECD, 2022; Eurostat, 2023). Finally, there are some innovative efforts to generate estimates of migrant stocks based on big data sources (see Chapter 4).

While statistics on migrant stocks are generally widely available globally, there is significant regional variation. For example, 43 per cent of Central and Southern Asian countries do not have updated information on the total number of international migrants since the 2010 census round, while in Eastern and South-eastern Asia, Oceania and Northern America, almost 90 per cent of countries have updated data on migrant stocks, by age and country of origin (UN DESA, 2020b).

Even though global migrant stock statistics are presented as harmonized and directly comparable, the national data they are based on often look quite different initially. Technically this information – the total number of people residing in a country other than their country of birth and/or citizenship – may not exactly be in line with the official statistical definition of a migrant and is therefore a widely accepted proxy for migrant stocks. However, not all countries collect data using the same recommended questions – on country of birth, citizenship and year or period of arrival – and many employ different methodologies. If data from different sources are used, they may not have the same coverage or may have different characteristics. Sometimes data from different countries are based on the same recommended methodology but cover different time periods, as the census date may vary. The UN harmonizes the national statistics it receives as best it can. For example, it uses interpolation and extrapolation techniques to estimate stocks for countries with data for two or more points in time. For those with only one data point available since 1990, stocks are estimated using the change in stocks within the region, similar area or country (UN DESA, 2020b). For this reason, sometimes estimates of migrant stocks shared by the UN do not match exactly with those published by an NSO. Further, the World Bank example above shows how even at global level, different definitions may be used.

Aside from differences in measurement, there are other common issues with existing migrant stock data. For example, migrants in an irregular situation are often not included or easily identified in a country's censuses (see GMG, 2017; UN SD, 2017; with notable exceptions such as the U.S. census), as are other migrant groups who may be of special policy interest, such as homeless migrants or unaccompanied migrant children. Globally available stock data are not categorized by type of migrants or reason for migration, meaning that they tend to include, for example, labour migrants, family migrants, refugees and other groups together (global estimates exist on migrant workers, refugees and other sub-groups, as seen below, but these are produced separately to the stock estimates, by other actors). Therefore, while useful, globally presented migrant stock figures may not include all migrants in countries and may not give any information on reasons for migration. However, at national level, there may be further information available, depending on how the data were collected.

Thus, despite some limitations, publicly accessible, quality statistics are available on how many international migrants live in all countries around the world, and these represent one of the most significant areas of migration data availability globally (for further reading on migrant stock data, see Bilsborrow et al., 1997 and UNSD, 2017).

While estimating total immigrant populations in a particular country is possible, it is much harder to get a picture of emigration from a country. Effectively and systematically counting emigrant populations – a topic of high policy interest, particularly in countries with high emigration rates – presents key methodological challenges. One key reason for this is that as emigrants are no longer present in their home countries, they cannot be easily included as respondents in population censuses or household surveys in those countries. Some countries ask census or survey respondents whether somebody else in their household has emigrated, and if so for further details, to estimate emigrant stocks. Other countries use migrant stock data on their own native-born or citizens residing in those countries. While useful, this is an imperfect measure: some countries may define or collect this information differently, meaning it is not always directly comparable. Further, these estimates may not be comprehensive, as data categorized only either by country of birth or by citizenship may not capture an individual's migratory status. For example, an emigrant may have naturalized in their destination country, meaning that if that country collects stock data by country of citizenship instead of by birth, this individual will not be counted as a migrant. There are various further challenges, as well as potential solutions to address this data gap (see UNSD, 2017), including by leveraging data from population registers and specialized surveys, or using innovative methodologies. For more information on counting emigrant and/or diaspora populations, see Chapter 5.

2.3.2 Migration flows

2.3.2.1 Key definition(s)

Migration flows indicate how many migrants move across borders and are defined as the "number of migrants entering and leaving a given country during a given period of time, usually one calendar year" (UNSD, 2017).

2.3.2.2 Global trends

Due to a lack of comparable data, it is very difficult to accurately describe trends in migration flows around the world. In 2015, 45 countries from around the world shared national data on flows with UN DESA (UN DESA, 2015). These data show national trends in migration flows in detail, but they do not make it possible to draw meaningful conclusions about global trends.

Instead, examining regional data can help elucidate some trends on different types of movements. For example, data from the OECD and its 38 Member States show that OECD countries received 4.8 million new permanent-type immigrants in 2021, an increase of 22 per cent after lower levels in 2020 due to the COVID-19 pandemic (OECD, 2022). Family migration was the largest category of immigrants and increased by 40 per cent in 2021, while labour migration increased by 45 per cent. As of mid-September 2022, almost 5 million refugees from Ukraine had arrived in OECD countries; overall permanent humanitarian migration rose slightly by four per cent in 2021. The number of new asylum applications to OECD countries rose to over 1 million in 2021, an increase of 28 per cent from the year before. The main origin countries were Nicaragua, Afghanistan and Syria (ibid).

2.3.2.3 Summary of data

Data on both migration inflows (those entering a country) and outflows (those leaving a country) are essential for understanding wider migration trends, the impacts of various factors and migration policies, and more. Nevertheless, data on migration flows are not available at the global level in the same way that data on stocks are.

Countries often use different techniques to estimate migration flows and base their statistics on a variety of data sources. Even more so than migrant stocks, the ways in which migration flows are defined and measured vary widely. For example, out of the 45 countries mentioned above, only 24 identify migrants as persons who plan to stay for at least one year, and for nine, a clear time criterion to classify migrants is not identifiable (UN DESA, 2015). Moreover, data sources used towards flow estimates vary nationally. Many countries use data from administrative sources, such as population registers, or from different types of residence permits (e.g. compiling data on temporary or permanent permits and/or by reason for entry) or border data. For example, while over half of the same 45 countries base their flow data on population registers, However, there is much variation in the remaining countries. In Portugal, data are derived from information on permits, in New Zealand from arrival and departure cards completed at the border, and in Ireland from a quarterly national household survey (ibid).

These common differences in concepts, definitions and methodologies to compile flow statistics make cross-country comparisons difficult. Further, there are specific challenges associated with the use of some data sources to understand flows. Administrative sources tend to record events and not actual migratory movements. While a residence permit may be issued, renewed or withdrawn, this may not necessarily reflect actual migration movements during that time; for instance, if a residence permit is not renewed but the person stays in the given country or it is renewed but the person in fact leaves the country (IOM, 2020a).

UNSD has a mandate to collate flow statistics from countries around the world through the Demographic Yearbook system. Based on this, it holds and shares statistics on international migration flows to and from selected countries since 2005, available by place of birth, citizenship or place of previous/next residence for both foreigners and nationals. Nevertheless, global data availability is still very low: as above, in 2015, data from only 45 countries were compiled, though this is an increase compared to 29 countries in 2008 (UN DESA, 2015).

Similarly to the process for migrant stocks, some regional bodies also compile and publish data on migration flows in countries. For example, the OECD's International Migration Database provides statistics on migrant flows in OECD countries, and Eurostat provides similar statistics on the EU-27 countries, Iceland, Liechtenstein, Norway and Switzerland.

Many countries collect data on or estimate migration flows in and out of their country using different methodologies and may publish these nationally; however, they may not share these data with UN organizations, OECD, Eurostat or other bodies. For example, in Jamaica, the population census is used to collect data on migration flows that adhere to international recommendations, though these estimates are not shared with UNSD (IOM, 2021c).

Given the lack of global flow data, some researchers and other actors have developed new estimation methodologies for migratory movements. Some of these are based on changes in migrant stocks over time (see, for example, Raymer et al., 2013). Others focus on bilateral migration flows, such as the DEMIG Country-to-Country database (DEMIG, 2015), or different ways to compile regional data, such as the Organization of American States' (OAS) Continuous Reporting System on International Migration in the Americas (SICREMI) project, which used administrative data from countries in the Americas (OAS, 2017). For further reading on measurement of migration flows, see UNSD (2017), Abel and Sander (2014), Lemaitre et al. (2008) and Nawrotzki and Jiang (2015).

2.3.3 Selected categories of migrants

While quality data on stocks and flows of international migrants are necessary to understand basic migration trends, there are many other topics on which migration policymakers need data. A few are summarized in Table 2.1, non-exhaustively, to give readers an idea of the extremely wide landscape of important migration aspects around which policies are designed, and therefore for which data are needed. These cover a few topics by reason for migration, and further considerations about migrants' characteristics, introducing key points and signposting to further resources.

Table 2.1 Selected categories of migrants: definitions, trends, summary of the data and key global actors

Topic	*Migrant workers*
Key definition(s)	The International Labour Organization (ILO) provides a definition of a migrant worker: "… all international migrants who are currently employed or unemployed and seeking employment in their present country of residence" (ILO, 2015). UNSD also provides a definition of a foreign migrant worker: Foreigners admitted by the receiving State for the specific purpose of exercising an economic activity remunerated from within the receiving country. Their length of stay is usually restricted as is the type of employment they can hold. Their dependents, if admitted, are also included in this category (UN SD, 2017).
Global trends	There were approximately 169 million international migrant workers in 2019, representing an increase of 5 million migrant workers (3.0 per cent) from 2017 (ILO, 2021). Around the world, migrant workers constitute 4.9 per cent of the labour force. Approximately 41.5 per cent are women and 58.5 per cent are men, with significant regional variation (ibid). 66.2 per cent of migrant workers work in services, 26.7 per cent in industry and 7.1 per cent in agriculture, again with significant regional variation. Overall, migrants tend to have higher labour force participation rates than non-migrants, meaning they are more likely to be working (ibid).
Summary of data	• Countries collect data on labour migration through censuses, household surveys (in particular, labour force surveys) or sometimes administrative sources (e.g. visas or work permits). • At regional level, various bodies compile and disseminate relevant data. • At the global level, the ILO maintains a database of labour statistics (named ILOSTAT) as well as a collection of labour force survey data. • Actors sometimes work together to improve data on labour migration; for example, the Joint Programme on Labour Migration Governance for Development and Integration in Africa (Joint Labour Migration Programme, or JLMP) is managed by the African Union Commission with IOM, the IO and United Nations Economic Commission for Africa (UNECA), supported by Statistics Sweden. The JLMP has published several editions of the *Report on Labour Migration Statistics in Africa*, compiling labour migration data from African countries, using population and housing censuses, as well as demographic projections and labour force surveys (ILO, IOM and UNECA, 2021).
Key global actors	ILO.

(*Continued*)

Table 2.1 (Continued)

Topic	International students
Key definition(s)	An international student is "an individual who has physically crossed an international border between two countries with the objective to participate in educational activities in a destination country, where the destination country is different from his or her country of origin" (UNESCO, 2015).
Global trends	Numbers of internationally mobile students are increasing. There were close to 6.3 million in 2020, up from 4.8 million in 2015 and 2 million in 2000 (UIS, 2022). The top destinations for international students were the United States, Australia, the United Kingdom, Germany, Canada, France and China. Key sending countries of international students are China, India, Germany, the Republic of Korea, Nigeria, France, Saudi Arabia and others (ibid.).
Summary of data	• Many countries that host large numbers of students, such as the United States, often collect and publish key data on these. • Regional bodies and other organizations, such as the OECD, also collect and/or compile relevant data in a region. • UNESCO's Institute for Statistics (UIS) provides the most comprehensive data on international student flows for more than 100 countries, compiled from data sent by countries on international students they host.
Key global actors	UNESCO, UNICEF.

Topic	Family migration
Key definition(s)	This type of migration can include reunification with a family member who migrated earlier; family accompanying a migrant; marriage between a citizen and immigrant, or someone living in, international adoptions and many other phenomena (IOM, 2023). Definitions used for different types of family migrants vary, as family reunification categorization or concepts often depend on national law. Meanwhile, the OECD defines accompanying family as "family members [who] are admitted together with the principal migrant" (OECD, 2017).
Global trends	Family migration to OECD countries increased by 40 per cent in 2021 and remained the largest category of inflows: more than four in ten new permanent migrants to the OECD were there for family-related reasons (OECD, 2022). However, overall in many OECD countries, family migration has declined due to more limited family reunification programmes, and more recently due to COVID-19 restrictions (ibid).
Summary of data	• At the country level, data on family migration are often based on administrative sources, including from dedicated family (re)unification programmes, population registers or survey data. • While there is no global comparable database on family migration, which covers all countries and areas of the world, some bodies, such as the OECD, consolidate data on family migration as above.
Key global actors	OECD.

(*Continued*)

Table 2.1 (Continued)

Topic	Forced migration or displaced populations
Key definition(s)	There are many types of forced migration and correspondingly, many different concepts and ways to define distinct categories of forcibly displaced migrants. There are diverse statistical and operational definitions in this space, including for those displaced for different reasons, within or across international borders, and more. For example, internally displaced persons (IDPs) are defined as persons or groups of persons who have been forced or obliged to flee or to leave their homes or places of habitual residence, in particular as a result of or in order to avoid the effects of armed conflict, situations of generalized violence, violations of human rights or natural or human-made disasters, and who have not crossed an internationally recognized State border (according to the Guiding Principles on Internal Displacement, UN, 1998). As above, refugees are persons who flee their country due to "well-founded fear" of persecution due to reasons of race, religion, nationality, membership of a particular social group or political opinion, and who are outside of their country of nationality or permanent residence and due to this fear are unable or unwilling to return to it, those in refugee-like situations, and others (according to the 1951 UN Convention relating to the Status of Refugees and 1967 Protocol, UNHCR, 2010).
Global trends	The number of persons displaced worldwide, including refugees, people in refugee-like situations, asylum seekers, IDPs, Venezuelans displaced abroad, and returned refugees and IDPs, reached 103 million in mid-2022 (UNHCR, n.d.). Now representing one per cent of the global population, this figure would be equivalent to the 14th most populous country in the world. At the end of 2021, there were 27.1 million refugees, 4.6 million asylum seekers, 4.4 million Venezuelans displaced abroad and 53.2 million IDPs (UNHCR, 2022). Over the last two decades, the forcibly displaced population has quintupled, driven by flows from Syria, Venezuela, Afghanistan, South Sudan, Myanmar and other countries. At the end of 2021, 59.1 million people were living in internal displacement as a result of conflict and violence as well as disasters (IDMC, 2022). Of these, 53.2 million were displaced by conflict and violence and at least 5.9 million by disasters. In 2021, 38.1 million new internal displacements across 141 countries and territories were recorded (ibid.), more than 62 per cent triggered by disasters. These figures will continue to increase, due to the climate emergency, and ongoing and new conflicts.
Summary of data	• Statistical definitions of displacement can be difficult to operationalize. • Some countries collect data on displaced populations, including through censuses, surveys, border data, administrative records and other data sources.

(Continued)

Table 2.1 (Continued)

Topic	Forced migration or displaced populations
	• Very often operational data or other data on forced migration collected by international actors are used towards statistics in this area. • Different regions face different issues with relevant statistics (for example, see, Singleton, 2016 on EU asylum data).
Key global actors	UNHCR, IDMC, IOM, others.

2.3.4 Characteristics of migrants

Knowing the reasons behind the migration of different migrant sub-groups in a country, and the size of each sub-group, is important from a programmatic and policy perspective. However, to understand their situations and craft policies that respond to these, further information is needed on the different characteristics of migrants within groups. Table 2.2 explains this further.

Table 2.2 Characteristics of migrants

Topic	Age	Sex and Gender
Key definition(s)	Various age classifications are used in data collection.	Various sex and gender classifications are used in data collection.
Global trends	Of the 281 million migrants in 2020, 35.5 million were under the age of 18 – the highest level ever recorded (UN DESA, 2020a). 31 million children live outside their country of birth, including 11 million child refugees and asylum seekers. Children are disproportionately represented in many forced migrant groups; nearly one in three children living outside their country of birth is a refugee; for adults, the proportion under UNHCR's mandate is less than 1 in 20 (UNICEF, 2016). Older migrants comprised an estimated 34.3 million or 12.2 per cent of the international migrant stock at mid-year 2020 (UN DESA, 2020a).	In 2020, 48 per cent (134.9 million) of all international migrants worldwide were women or girls (UN DESA, 2020a). While absolute numbers of female migrants have increased over the years, the share of female migrants has remained relatively stable, with some regional variation. The labour force participation rate of migrant women was higher than that of non-migrant women in 2017 – this was 63.5 per cent and 48.1 per cent respectively (ILO, 2018).

(Continued)

Table 2.2 (Continued)

Topic	Age	Sex and Gender
Summary of data	• Similar to gender, it is necessary to know the prevalence of different age groups among migrants to inform policy. Migrants at different ages find themselves in different situations and therefore have different needs; for example, child migrants need educational opportunities and some may be at higher risk of abuse, working age migrants are more likely to be seeking labour opportunities, and older migrants may face specific health-related challenges that require specialized assistance. • As for sex and gender, many key migration datasets are often disaggregated by age, meaning they are broken down by age or age group classifications. • Many phenomena specific to age and migration issues – for example, the topic of unaccompanied migrant children – lack solid data for policymakers to base interventions on.	• It is key to know the gender and/or sex of migrants in order to design responsive migration policies. Gender shapes the motives and consequences of migration for all individuals – it affects the experiences of men, women, boys, girls and persons identifying as lesbian, gay, bisexual, transgender and intersex (LGBTI) people, and others. • Many major data instruments that collect data on migration are sex-disaggregated, meaning they collect and present information showing the different sexes of respondents. • Similarly, at global level many migration-related datasets also give information by sex, and less commonly gender. • However, data can be patchy on specific topics related to migration and gender that may be of particular interest to policymakers – for example, migrant domestic work or gender-based discrimination among migrants.
Key global actors	UNICEF, UNFPA	UN Women, Data2X

2.3.5 *Data gaps and other topics*

The preceding section is only an introduction to the many different migration topics that exist on which data are needed. For each sub-topic where policies and programmes exist – be it labour market reintegration of returnees, tax returns of high-net-worth foreign-born individuals or benefit allowances for migrants with disabilities – quality, timely data are needed. More data are available on some topics – for example, on migrant stocks and remittances – compared to in others – such as migration flows and irregular migration.

A data gap does not necessarily mean that data on that area are not collected at all. It may also mean that data are incomplete, not easily accessible or not comparable across countries or other geographical units, or over time

(IOM, 2020b). Data quality can be poor; this often relates to completeness, timeliness, validity, accuracy and consistency (see ONS, 2021); often available migration data lack one or more of these characteristics. In particular, issues around timeliness of data have become more acute with the growing speed and complexity of some migration dynamics. This is especially critical when fast changes occur and urgent action is required, for example, in crisis situations. Data gaps can be related to geography; for example, more data are available on EU and OECD countries than countries in other parts of the world. How data gaps can be addressed will depend on the topic and context. For example, some aspects may require the development of new methodologies, while others may need initial awareness-raising across areas of government to build support to dedicate greater resources and time to improving data.

While data gaps will look different across countries and sectors, at global level relatively little data exist on environmental migration (see Chapter 6), return migration dynamics and irregular migration. Further, data on human trafficking, migrant smuggling, migrant deaths and disappearances, the impacts of migration policies and many topics within migration and health, and migration and development are patchy at best (see Chapters 5 and 7 for more). Further, aside from sex, gender and age, further migrant characteristics are often not visible or captured easily by data, such as disability (see Chapter 7). Finally, limited data are available on particular geographical regions and dynamics, such as the impacts of South-South migration. Many more urgent data gaps within migration are mentioned throughout this book (see also others' explorations of these, for example IOM, 2020b; Bircan et al., 2021).

This chapter has shown that when referring to the "migration evidence base", we are in fact talking about many different areas of information, with wildly different levels of quality and comprehensiveness. For some migration topics, there is a wealth of information, and for others, there is extremely little. The reasons behind this variability are very often linked to how migration data are collected and managed in countries; many key issues are related to limitations of common data sources, as well as to ways of working on data in government. The patchiness of migration data on specific topics (such as trafficking, gender or others) may have specific root causes, but very often gaps in wider migration statistics have identifiable shared reasons. In response to this, actors have worked on capacity development projects around the world addressing these. This is explored in the next chapter.

References

Abel, G.J. and Sander, N. (2014). Quantifying global international migration flows. *Science*, 343(6178), 1520–1522.

African Union Commission and JLMP partners (ILO, IOM, UNECA). (2021). *Report on Labour Migration Statistics in Africa*. 3rd ed. ISBN: 978–92–95119–63–5 (Print), 978-92-95119-64-2 (Web). Available at https://www.ilo.org/africa/information-resources/publications/WCMS_828865/lang--en/index.htm

Batalova, J. (2022). Top statistics on global migration and migrants. Migration Policy Institute (MPI). Available at https://www.migrationpolicy.org/article/top-statistics-global-migration-migrants

Betts, A. (2013). *Survival Migration: Failed Governance and the Crisis of Displacement.* Ithaca, NY: Cornell University Press. Available at https://www.cornellpress.cornell.edu/book/9780801479068/survival-migration/

Bilsborrow, R., Hugo, G., Oberai, A., and Zlotnik, H. (1997). *International Migration Statistics: Guidelines for Improving Data Collection Systems.* Geneva: International Labour Office.

Bircan, T., Ahmad Yar, A.W., Purkayastha, D., and Yilmaz, S. (2021). Find the Gap: Addressing the International Migration Data Gaps. Leuven: HumMingBird Project 870661 – H2020.

DEMIG. (2015). *DEMIG C2C, version 1.2,* Limited Online Edition. Oxford: International Migration Institute, University of Oxford. Available at www.migrationinstitute.org

European Commission, Eurostat, United Nations Organisation. (2020). *International Recommendations on Internally Displaced Persons Statistics (IRIS).* Luxembourg: Publications Office of the European Union.

Eurostat. (2023). Migrant stocks. Statistics Explained. Available at https://ec.europa.eu/eurostat/statistics-explained/index.php?title=Migration_and_migrant_population_statistics

Expert Group on Refugee and Internally Displaced Persons Statistics (EGRISS). (2018). *International Recommendations on Refugee Statistics (IRRS).* Luxembourg: Publications Office of the European Union. Available at https://ec.europa.eu/eurostat/documents/3859598/9315869/KS-GQ-18-004-EN-N.pdf/d331c9cc-1091-43c2-b589-2c250bccc281

Global Migration Group (GMG). (2017). *Handbook for Improving the Production and Use of Migration Data for Development.* Washington, DC: World Bank. Available at https://www.knomad.org/publication/handbook-improving-production-and-use-migration-data-development-0

Heleniak, T. (2002). *Migration Dilemmas Haunt Post-Soviet Russia.* Washington, DC: Migration Policy Institute. Available at https://www.migrationpolicy.org/article/migration-dilemmas-haunt-post-soviet-russia

Internal Displacement Monitoring Centre (IDMC). (2022). Global report on internal displacement 2022. Available at https://www.internal-displacement.org/global-report/grid2022/

International Labour Organization (ILO). (2015). *ILO Global Estimates on Migrant Workers: Results and Methodology.* Geneva: ILO. Available at https://www.ilo.org/wcmsp5/groups/public/---dgreports/---dcomm/documents/publication/wcms_436343.pdf

International Labour Organization (ILO). (2018). *Global Estimates on International Migrant Workers – Results and Methodology.* 2nd ed. Geneva: ILO.

International Labour Organization (ILO). (2021). *Global Estimates on International Migrant Workers – Results and Methodology.* 3rd ed. Geneva: International Labour Office – ILO.

International Organization for Migration (IOM). (2019). *Glossary on Migration.* IML Series No. 34.

International Organization for Migration (IOM). (2020a). *International migration flows. Migration Data Portal.* Berlin: IOM. Available at https://www.migrationdataportal.org/themes/international-migration-flows

International Organization for Migration (IOM). (2020b). *Migration data sources. Migration Data Portal.* Berlin: IOM. Available at https://www.migrationdataportal.org/themes/migration-data-sources

International Organization for Migration (IOM). (2021a). *IOM Migration Data Strategy: Informing Policy and Action on Migration, Mobility and Displacement 2020–2025.* Geneva: IOM. Available at https://publications.iom.int/books/iom-migration-data-strategy-brief-informing-policy-and-action-migration-mobility-and

International Organization for Migration (IOM). (2021b). *Global Migration Indicators. Global Migration Data Analysis Center (GMDAC).* Geneva: IOM. Available at https://publications.iom.int/books/global-migration-indicators-2021

International Organization for Migration (IOM). (2021c). *How Countries Manage Migration Data: Evidence from Six Countries.* Geneva: IOM. Available at https://publications.iom.int/books/how-countries-manage-migration-data-evidence-six-countries

International Organization for Migration (IOM). (2021d). *Migrant Stocks. Migration Data Portal.* Berlin: IOM. Available at https://www.migrationdataportal.org/themes/international-migrant-stocks

International Organization for Migration (IOM). (2022). *Mixed migration. Migration Data Portal.* Berlin: IOM. Available at https://www.migrationdataportal.org/themes/mixed-migration

International Organization for Migration (IOM). (2023). *Family Migration. Migration Data Portal.* Berlin: IOM. Available at https://www.migrationdataportal.org/themes/family-migration

IPUMS. (n.d.). Institute for Social Research and Data Innovation, University of Minnesota. IPUMS. Available at https://www.ipums.org/

Juran, S. and Snow, R. (2017). The potential of the 2010 population and housing census round for international migration analysis. *Migration Policy Practice*, 7(1), 6–8.

Lemaitre, G., Liebig, T., Thoreau, C., and Fron, P. (2008). *Standardised Statistics on Immigrant Inflows Results, Sources and Methods.* Paris: OECD. Available at https://www.oecd.org/els/mig/38832099.pdf

Nawrotzki, R.J. and Jiang, L. (2015). Indirectly estimating international net migration flows by age and gender: The Community Demographic Model International Migration (CDM-IM) dataset. *Hist Methods*, 48(3), 113–127. https://doi.org/10.1080/01615440.2014.999150. PMID: 26692590; PMCID: PMC4674838.

Office of the United Nations High Commissioner for Refugees (UNHCR). (2018). The global compact on refugees. Final draft. Available at www.unhcr.org/events/conferences/5b3295167/official-version-final-draft-global-compact-refugees.html

Organization of American States (OAS). (2017). International Migration in the Americas: Fourth Report of the Continuous Reporting System on International Migration in the Americas (SICREMI).

Organization of Economic Cooperation and Development (OECD). (2017). *Making Integration Work: Family Migrants.* Paris: OECD.

Organization of Economic Cooperation and Development (OECD). (2022). *International Migration Outlook 2022.* Paris: OECD.

Oxford Migration Observatory. (2011). *Top Ten Problems in the Evidence Base for Public Debate and Policy-Making on Immigration in the UK.* Oxford: Migration Observatory, COMPAS. Available at https://migrationobservatory.ox.ac.uk/resources/reports/top-ten-problems-in-the-evidence-base-for-public-debate-and-policy-making-on-immigration-in-the-uk/

Raymer, J., Wiśniowski, A., Forster, J.J., Smith, P.W.F., and Bijak, J. (2013). Integrated modeling of European migration. *Journal of the American Statistical Association*, 108(503), 801–819. https://doi.org/10.1080/01621459.2013.789435

Singleton, A. (2016). *Migration and Asylum Data for Policy-Making in the European Union – The Problem with Numbers.* Lib. Secur. Eur, CEPS, Brussels, Belgium, 89, 9.

UN Commission on Human Rights. (1998). Report of the Representative of the Secretary-General, Mr. Francis M. Deng, submitted pursuant to Commission resolution 1997/39. Addendum: Guiding Principles on Internal Displacement. Available at http://www.un-documents.net/gpid.htm

UN High Commissioner for Refugees (UNHCR). (2015). Policy on the protection of personal data of persons of concern to UNHCR, May 2015. Available at https://www.refworld.org/docid/55643c1d4.html

UNESCO. (2015). Facts and figures: Mobility in higher education. Available at https://en.unesco.org/node/252278

UNESCO Institute for Statistics (UIS) (2022). Global flow of tertiary-level students. Available at https://uis.unesco.org/en/uis-student-flow

UNHCR. (2001). Counting Forcibly Displaced Populations: Census and Registration Issues. Symposium on Global Review of 2000 Round of Population and Housing Censuses: Mid-Decade Assessment and Future Prospects. UNSD.

UNHCR. (2010). Convention and protocol relating to the status of refugees 1951; 1967 convention and protocol. Available at https://www.unhcr.org/sites/default/files/legacy-pdf/3b66c2aa10.pdf

UNHCR. (2022). *Global Trends Report 2021.* Geneva: UNHCR. Available at https://www.unhcr.org/global-trends

UNHCR. (n.d.). *Refugee Data Finder.* Geneva: UNHCR. Available at https://www.unhcr.org/refugee-statistics/

United Nations Children's Fund (UNICEF). (2016). Uprooted: The growing crisis for refugee and migrant children. UNICEF. Available at https://data.unicef.org/resources/uprooted-growing-crisis-refugee-migrant-children/

United Nations, Department of Economic and Social Affairs (UN DESA). (2015). International migration flows to and from selected countries: The 2015 revision (POP/DB/MIG/Flow/Rev.2015)

United Nations, Department of Economic and Social Affairs (UN DESA). (2017). International migration report 2017: Highlights. New York. Available at https://www.un.org/en/development/desa/population/migration/publications/migrationreport/docs/MigrationReport2017_Highlights.pdf

United Nations, Department of Economic and Social Affairs (UN DESA). (2020a). International migrant stock: The 2020 revision. (United Nations database, POP/DB/MIG/Stock/Rev.2020). New York. Available at https://www.un.org/development/desa/pd/content/international-migrant-stock

United Nations, Department of Economic and Social Affairs (UN DESA). (2020b). Methodology report international migrant stock 2020. Population Division Documentation POP/DB/MIG/Stock/Rev.2020 December 2020. Available at https://www.un.org/development/desa/pd/sites/www.un.org.development.desa.pd/files/undesa_pd_2020_international_migrant_stock_documentation.pdf

United Nations General Assembly. (2018). *Global Compact for Safe, Orderly and Regular Migration.* New York, NY: United Nations. Available at http://www.un.org/en/ga/search/view_doc.asp?symbol=A/RES/73/195

United Nations Statistical Commission (UNSC). (2021). 202c1 Migration statistics: Report of the Secretary-General. E/CN.3/2021/11. Statistical Commission, Fifty-second Session, 1–3 and 5 March. Available at https://unstats.un.org/unsd/statcom/52nd-session/documents/2021-11-MigrationStats-E.pdf

United Nations Statistics Division (UNSD). (1998). *Recommendations on Statistics of International Migration Revision 1*. New York, NY: United Nations. Available at https://unstats.un.org/unsd/publication/seriesm/seriesm_58rev1e.pdf

United Nations Statistics Division (UNSD). (2017). *Handbook on Measuring International Migration through Population Censuses*. New York, NY: United Nations. Available at https://unstats.un.org/unsd/statcom/48th-session/documents/BG-4a-Migration-Handbook-E.pdf

United Nations Statistics Division (UNSD). (2021a). Draft report on conceptual frameworks and concepts and definitions on international migration. In Revised overarching conceptual framework and concepts and definitions on international migration produced by the Expert Group on Migration Statistics. Prepared by UNSD for the United Nations Statistical Commission, Fifty-second Session, 1–3 and 5 March. Available at http://mdgs.un.org/unsd/statcom/52nd-session/documents/BG-3g-TF2-Conceptual_Framework-E.pdf

United Nations Statistics Division (UNSD). (2021b). Revised overarching conceptual framework and concepts and definitions on international migration produced by the Expert Group on Migration Statistics. Background document, Fifty-second session, 1–3 and 5 March. Statistical Commission. Available at https://unstats.un.org/unsd/statcom/52nd-session/documents/BG-3g-TF2-Conceptual_Framework-E.pdf

United Nations Statistics Division (UNSD). (2022). E/CN.3/2023/5. Social statistics Report of the Secretary-General. Statistical Commission Fifty-fourth session. Available at https://unstats.un.org/UNSDWebsite/statcom/session_54/documents/2023-5-SocialStats-E.pdf

United Nations Statistics Division (UNSD). (2023). Report of the UN Expert Group on Migration Statistics on Indicators for international migration and temporary mobility. Statistical Commission Fifty-fourth session. Available at https://unstats.un.org/UNSDWebsite/statcom/session_54/documents/BG-3b-EGMS-E.pdf

World Bank. (2023). *World Development Report 2023: Migrants, Refugees, and Societies*. Washington, DC: World Bank. https://doi.org/10.1596/978-1-4648-1941-4. License: Creative Commons Attribution CC BY 3.0 IGO.

3 How international migration data are managed

Challenges and solutions

3.1 How do migration data work? Migration data governance and sources

This chapter seeks to answer the following questions: How are migration data managed? What are common sources of migration data? What type of data is captured by each source, and who manages this? What are common challenges for countries in generating migration data?

The chapter explores how migration data are usually collected and managed. It examines typical migration data governance structures in countries, providing a high-level inventory of existing common migration data practices around the world, as well as explaining how regional and global actors also play a role. It introduces major sources of migration data, including statistical and administrative sources commonly found across countries. This outlines the availability of migration-relevant data from these sources, key strengths and weaknesses, and their usefulness for producing migration statistics.

Next, the chapter discusses key common obstacles to effectively collecting, managing and analysing migration data. A few methodological issues are discussed, including uneven adherence to official definitions related to migration data, and data fragmentation. Several practical challenges relating to migration data are outlined, such as poor coordination across government, and ethics and data protection issues.

Finally, the chapter discusses how migration data can be improved. It explores common approaches and activities towards this, by providing an overview of the data capacity development landscape. The chapter concludes by outlining key challenges associated with capacity development activities undertaken by international actors, and suggested approaches and practices to address these, along with concrete examples of innovative practices from around the world.

Data Governance – national, regional and global

To understand why the migration evidence base looks the way it does today, and why we know more about certain areas of migration than about others, it is important to know how migration data are governed in countries. While it

DOI: 10.4324/9781003266075-4

is also important to understand similar dynamics at regional and global levels, national-level dynamics are key to these. The majority of traditional migration data that exist around the world is generated by countries, meaning that what is collected and how, is in turn predominantly determined at national level. Who decides what data are collected in the first place? Who actually collects these? Where do these go? Who else is involved?

National

National migration data dynamics tend to reflect migration policy dynamics. Many actors are usually involved in any given country, and data governance is often highly fragmented. Why is this the case?

Several institutions and ministries are typically involved in managing migration. For example, different parts of government are responsible for setting strategies, laws and policies on general immigration policy, labour migration, family reunification, asylum and, particular migration topics such as human trafficking, diaspora engagement or irregular migration. Key aspects of a country's migration policy may be typically set by an interior ministry or a dedicated migration ministry, if one exists, while other migration-related elements may be governed by a labour ministry, dedicated human trafficking unit within another ministry, and a wide range of other government actors. Further, migration can be considered a cross-cutting policy issue, meaning that aside from migration-related legislation, policies and programmes, many other sectoral policies are also relevant to migration but that are designed by different ministries. For example, healthcare access for migrants is generally determined by a health ministry.

The way that migration policy is usually developed – i.e., by many different parts of government – dictates to a large extent how migration data are usually collected and managed. The National Statistical Office (NSO) in each country is usually the central authority that collects, harmonizes and disseminates national statistics, and this usually includes basic migration statistics, such as on stocks (IOM, 2021). However, beyond the NSO, migration data in a country are usually collected by many different institutions and actors. There are several common models of how data may be collected in countries. One particular institution may provide the most migration data, taking the lead on providing regular statistics on visas, permits, border crossings and more. Alternatively or in addition to this, in a more decentralised model many different national institutions collect and use different types of migration data according to their particular mandates – for example, collecting only data on human trafficking, or refugees. In order to coordinate migration data collection and use between these, many countries have established inter-ministerial committees or working groups.

How might this look in practice? One IOM study examined migration data governance structures in six countries – Canada, Djibouti, Jamaica, Moldova, Nigeria and Ireland. This found that in most countries, there was a single main institution leading national migration governance, which collected most migration data. However, this institution was different in each country; in Canada it was Immigration, Refugees and Citizenship Canada (IRCC), in Djibouti the Ministère de l'Intérieur (Interior Ministry, MOI), in Ireland the Immigration Service Delivery (ISD) under the Department of Justice (DOJ), in Jamaica the Passport, Immigration and Citizenship Agency (PICA) under the Ministry of National Security (MNS), in Nigeria the Nigeria Immigration Service (NIS) under the Federal Ministry of Interior (FMI) and in the Republic of Moldova the Ministry of Internal Affairs (MOIA) (IOM, 2021). This shows how varied national migration data practices can be across countries.

The study also found that many NSOs often had specialized units or teams dedicated to migration data (ibid). For example, the NSO in Djibouti (National Institute of Statistics of Djibouti, INSD) had established a Migration Study Unit. Further, other institutions in each country collect selected data as relevant to their specific roles; for example, ministries of foreign affairs often collected data on emigrants and diaspora populations. All countries had inter-ministerial structures dedicated to coordination migration and sometimes, migration data; for example, in Djibouti, the Technical Working Group on Migration Statistics (GTT) worked with the National Coordination Committee on Migration (CNCM), and in Jamaica, the National Working Group on International Migration and Development (NWGIMD) had a migration data subcommittee, the Data, Research and Information Systems Sub-Committee (DRISSC), chaired by the NSO. Sometimes, these coordination structures were not managed from within government. For example, the Economic and Social Research Institute (ESRI), an independent research institute in Ireland, established the Migrant Integration Strategy Data Group (MISDG) to improve collaboration on migration data among government agencies.

Regional and Global

While most migration data are generated nationally, several regional and global-level actors also have key roles and responsibilities related to migration data. As seen above, some bodies, such as UN DESA or the OECD, play an active, formalised role in collecting, compiling and/or disseminating data on stocks, flows and other topics. Further, many of these and other institutions also help develop or roll out standards and methodologies related to migration data. For example, UN DESA has published key guidance aimed at country stakeholders, such as its *Handbook on Measuring International Migration through Population Censuses*. Other such documents have been produced by IOM, ILO, UNECE, and many other bodies. Some have produced equivalent documents focused on specific regions (see Poulain et al., 2006). This forms part of a broader landscape of capacity development on migration data, described below, where different actors work together to help countries improve statistics.

Beyond work done by regional actors, individual UN agencies and other global entities also play a key role in migration data, such as the Expert Group on Migration Statistics, and the Expert Group on Refugee and Internally Displaced Persons Statistics (both mentioned in Chapter 2).

3.2 Data sources

Sources of migration data can be broadly grouped into three categories: statistical, administrative and novel or alternative (IOM, 2020). Each source has strengths and weaknesses, which are important to understand how to better leverage each to improve migration data.

Statistical data sources

Statistical data are "data that are collected and/or generated by statistics in process of statistical observations or statistical data processing" (EC, 2019). Statistical data sources include censuses and household surveys. These data are collated, cleaned, aggregated and used to produce official statistics. Statistical data tend to be collected, processed, disseminated, and preserved in accordance with legislation, guidelines and policies that are designed by relevant national bodies based on international standards and principles on privacy and data protection.

Population censuses are key statistical sources of migration data. Using census data on migration has key advantages. Censuses are universal, meaning they have full coverage of a population and are usually representative, and the data collected through them are often comparable across countries. However, censuses are very expensive to conduct, and countries implement them only every 10 years, meaning the data is easily outdated. Censuses can provide statistics on migrant stocks, some characteristics of migrants (including age, sex and often others, such as employment status and income), and in some countries, estimates of emigrants. To do this, UNSD recommends that census questionnaires include three core variables to identify international migrants: country of birth, country of citizenship, and year or period of arrival in the country for foreign-born persons. See what this means in practice in Box 3.1.

However, not all countries implement the above guidance on censuses. During the 2010 census round, more than 87 per cent of the 149 countries for which data are available had a census question about country of birth, but only 75 per cent asked about citizenship and just over half (50.3%) asked about the year or period of arrival (Juran and Snow, 2017). This varied across regions; for example, questions on year or period of arrival were much more common in censuses in North America and Europe than in Asia and Africa; see Figure 3.1.

Figure 3.1 Censuses and migration data.

Source: Based on data from UNFPA and UN DESA, IOM (2020).

Box 3.1   Core migration questions in data collection

Country of birth information is used to distinguish between the foreign-born and native-born populations. The following question is recommended for data collection instruments, accompanied by instructions to enter the name of the country:

Where was [name] born?
Where did _____'s mother reside when she gave birth to him/her?
This country, specify province and municipality:
○ Province: _____
○ Municipality: _____
Another country, specify country according to present borders:
○ Country: _____
○ Unknown
Country of birth unknown

Country of citizenship information is used to distinguish between foreigners and citizens. The country of citizenship is the country with which a person enjoys a particular legal bond, while a foreigner is a person who does not have citizenship in the country of enumeration (UN DESA, 2020c). The following questions are recommended for data collection instruments:

What is [person's] country of citizenship?
This country: _____
This country and another country, specify according to present borders:
○ The other country: _____
Another country, specify country according to present borders:
_____
☐ Unknown country
Country of citizenship unknown
No citizenship (stateless)

Information on **year/period of arrival** can help distinguish international migrants who have recently arrived from those who arrived many years ago. Questions on duration of stay serve the same purpose. Migrants who arrived more recently in a country often face more challenges related to, for example, communication and administrative barriers, requiring more government assistance compared to those who arrived many years ago. Such information can help policymakers across sectors understand differences in outcomes between those who entered the country at an early age and those who entered later, analyse migrant characteristics over time, and inform planning or evaluation of integration-related programming.

- For countries where immigrants have the right to free movement in and out of the country after having obtained relevant residence status, ask this of foreign-born individuals: In which year and month did [person] first arrive in [this country], and has [person] lived or does [person] intend to live in the country for at least one year?
  Year: _____ Month: _____ ☐ Unknown
- For countries where people migrate more than once, ask this of foreign-born individuals or return migrants: In which year and month did [person] last arrive in [this country], and has [person] lived or does [person] intend to live in the country for at least one year?
  Year: _____ Month: _____ ☐ Unknown

These three core questions are recommended by UNSD for inclusion in national censuses, and are encouraged to be included in many other large-scale national or official data collection instruments. Information on both country of birth and citizenship should be collected, if possible, as information on one of these alone may not necessarily reflect a person's migratory status or mean somebody is a migrant. For example, it is possible to be a foreign-born citizen or a native-born foreigner, as a person can be born abroad and be a citizen, or born in that country and be considered a foreigner, depending on national legislation. Country of birth may not reflect where a person spent most of their time living, and a person's country of citizenship can change over time, as those who are not citizens of a country by birth may acquire citizenship through naturalization, marriage or some other method. Further, dual citizens may or may not indicate their citizenship in the country of enumeration.

Adapted from Mosler Vidal, 2021, based on UNSD, 2017.

Household surveys, can also yield valuable information on migration, such as on the determinants of migration and certain migrant characteristics (see also Bilsborrow, 2018). Similar to censuses, many large-scale surveys collect data on participants' country of birth, and in this way provide information on migration. Migration data are available from Demographic and Health Surveys (DHS), Labour Force Surveys (LFS), and others. Often these data are comparable across countries and made available through microdata banks (see IPUMS, n.d. which provides data across topics from around the world). Unlike census data, household survey data are relatively timely, as many surveys are conducted annually. Further, they tend to be more flexible than censuses, and questions can often be added more easily. This means they can generate data on specific groups of interest or migration sub-topics. See Box 3.2 to learn more about different ways to generate migration data using surveys.

There are some challenges associated with using surveys to collect migration data. Some of these relate to how representative survey data are of migrants. The smaller a population sub-group is, the larger the sample size needs to be to generate statistically meaningful data on it. As most surveys were not designed to analyse specific sub-groups, like migrants, their sample sizes are often too small to identify them properly (see Mosler Vidal, 2021). Further, migrants are not usually equally distributed across a country's territory, but rather tend to be concentrated in certain areas, therefore sampling frames based on censuses (which are normally also used for surveys) are not enough to guarantee adequate coverage across all areas. As large sample sizes and/or revised sampling frames are needed to enable migrant representativeness, setting up new surveys can be difficult and expensive. It is also possible to adapt sampling strategies to increase representativeness of the migrant population (see OHCHR, 2018 and for specialised guidance on designing migration surveys, Hagen-Zanker et al., 2020).

Box 3.2   Examples of efforts on migration and surveys

Adding dedicated migration modules or specific migration questions to pre-existing household surveys can be a cost-effective way to collect key data on migration. For example:

- ILO developed a Labour Migration Module, consisting of a set of migration-related questions to be added to existing LFS. The module is designed as a cost-effective way for LFS to generate better statistics on labour migration, including by collecting data on characteristics of migrant workers such as their educational attainment and areas of training before departure, working conditions and more. The module has been implemented in Ukraine, Moldova, Zimbabwe and other countries (ILO, n.d.).
- The European Commission worked with eight Mediterranean countries, together with the World Bank, UNFPA, UNHCR, ILO, IOM and the League of Arab States to collect migration data through specialized surveys as part of the MED-HIMS (Households International Migration Surveys in the Mediterranean countries) project. This consisted of several survey modules collecting data on outmigration, return migration, forced migration, intention to migrate, circular migration, migration of highly skilled persons, irregular migration, type and use of remittances and attitudes and many other topics. Surveys have been carried out in Egypt, Jordan and Morocco (Eurostat, n.d.).

Administrative data sources

Administrative data are usually collected to support certain administrative processes in a country, rather than primarily to produce official statistics. In this sense, administrative data per se are not considered statistical data, although they maybe used towards the production of statistics. They can offer useful information on migration. Sources commonly include, for example, administrative registers, border data collection systems, databases on visas, residence and/or work permits, and consular records. Administrative data can cover a broad range of migration issues and be very detailed, and overall present a cost-effective way to better understand migration in a country without having to establish new data collection tools. Administrative sources can be used to produce statistics on the characteristics of migrants, migration flows (Box 3.3.) and other topics.

There are many challenges in using administrative sources to produce migration statistics (see IOM, 2020 for an overview). Comparability of this type of data can be limited even within countries, as each source may have its own methodology and/or use different coverage or definitions. Comparison across countries may also be difficult; for example, visa, residence and work permits use different definitions in each country. Often data are not consolidated effectively – in some cases they may not be digitized and exist only in the form of paper records – and data quality can be patchy. Each administrative source also has specific methodological issues. Commonly, administrative data usually record events and not necessarily actual movements; for example, registering with a local authority rather than moving across a border. This can affect the

---

Box 3.3   Administrative data and migration flows

In principle, administrative records such as those on border crossings, visa applications, residence and work permits issued, can be used to produce statistics on migration flows. This information is already collected on an ongoing basis in most countries – for example by landing cards or electronic passport readings – and, if adequately linked, could offer inexpensive and timely flow data. There has been considerable policy attention paid to this potential use of administrative data.

However, in practice it is challenging to do this. There are often key methodological issues: for example, entry and exit records collected at border crossings are very often not matched, making it difficult to understand individuals' duration of stay in or away from the country, and therefore to distinguish between migrants and travellers. Some countries do effectively link and use such data to estimate international migrants, for example the Republic of Moldova through cooperation between the General Inspectorate of Border Policy (GIBP) and the National Bureau of Statistics (NBS) (IOM, 2021).

data quality, for example resulting in double-counting of the same individual. Further, migration statistics from administrative records may be incomplete, for instance because a migrant may leave a country without de-registering, again highlighting the difference between collecting data on migrants, migration movements, and migration events. Further, border data collection systems only cover movements through official posts. Making use of administrative data usually entails sharing data across government areas; this can be difficult to set up (UNECE, 2016). While most countries collect migration data through statistical sources, there is huge potential to improve countries' use of their existing administrative data sources.

Alternative sources

As a result of rapid technological advancement, an unprecedented amount of migration-related information has become available in recent years. "Big data" are now generated through the use of digital devices, internet-based platforms, and online payment services (IOM, 2021), and efforts are ongoing to explore how these can help understand migration. While using such data could potentially help overcome some of the limitations of traditional sources, several issues, particularly around privacy and ethics, need to be addressed. Chapter 4 explores these in detail.

There are other potential alternative sources of migration data, including, for example, citizen-generated data (CGD). This is "data generated by people, for people," so that individuals are "directly involved in the design, collection, analysis, and use of data that describes them" (Jungcurt, 2022). Sometimes also called "community-driven" or "participatory data", these can take a number of different guises, and may include participation at a particular stage of the data life-cycle; one well-known example is that of open street mapping, where individuals can add information to maps. There are not yet many examples in the area of migration, but much potential for this, in particular for groups of migrants who are hard-to-reach, given the ability of citizen-generated data approaches to include perspectives not usually captured by official statistics. CGD offers creative ways to fill selected data gaps, and for governments to engage more directly with population sub-groups on policy topics (ibid).

Regional and international data sources

There are several key regional and international migration data sources, some of which are based on national statistics. Often specific UN agencies are responsible for compiling and disseminating migration statistics on particular topics from countries, and sometimes for directly collecting data themselves. For example, as mentioned above, UN DESA collects and disseminates various migration statistics, including on migrant stocks and flows. Several other UN agencies also collect, use and/or analyse migration data in specific areas, either through primary data collection or by using national data.

Through their programmes, such organisations collect operational data on various topics that could also be used towards statistics. However, sometimes this is not done as these data are not adequately processed, shared or analysed. For example, IOM collects and shares migration data across topics, including but not limited to human trafficking, resettlement, return and reintegration, migration governance, displacement (through its Displacement Tracking Matrix (DTM)), and missing migrants (through its Missing Migrants Project). Many other organizations collect operational data that relates to migration, and use this to various degrees towards analysis. For example, UNHCR collects and publishes data on refugees, asylum seekers, internally displaced persons (IDPs), returned refugees, returned IDPs, stateless persons and other population groups that often combines national statistics with UNHCR operational data. Further, the United Nations Office on Drugs and Crime (UNODC) collects and disseminates data on human trafficking and migrant smuggling, and the World Bank, including through its Global Knowledge Partnership on Migration and Development (KNOMAD) on migration topics such as volumes and costs of remittances.

3.3 What are the issues? Methodological, practical and other challenges

As seen in the preceding chapter, global migration data are patchy at best. Why is this? The previous chapter has outlined challenges related to specific data sources. Beyond these source-specific issues, several methodological, practical and other difficulties in measuring migration as a phenomenon affect both the quantity and quality of data, and in turn the overall evidence base. While countries around the world operate in very different contexts, their challenges related to migration are often similar. This chapter will provide more information on these, before discussing the landscape of capacity development for migration data.

Implementation of statistical definitions

While, as seen above, guidance and recommendations on statistical definitions of migrants do exist, these are not always fully implemented by countries. For instance, censuses and surveys do not always include the recommended questions on country of birth or citizenship, and in practice, many if not most states simply use information on country of birth or nationality to define a migrant – despite the existence of dedicated guidance on how to ask the right questions on both birth and citizenship countries in major national data collection tools (Box 3.1). Practices across countries differ. Not all countries use the recommended definition of a migrant, question formulations for country of birth, citizenship and year or period of arrival, or other relevant standards, and instead use different concepts and criteria to monitor international migration. Some of these variations correspond to the questions left open or harder to adhere to when using the 1998 definition of a migrant. For example, some countries use a different minimum duration of stay in the country to define migrants (ONS, 2020). As seen above not all countries collect data on the core census migration-related questions recommended by UNSD. For example, many OECD countries use instead definitions around those receiving long-term or permanent residence permits (see Lemaitre et al, 2008); out of 36 countries reporting international migration flow data to the OECD in 2018, only 11 did so based on a 12-month definition. Most either supplied data about temporary or permanent status grants, or entries onto the population register for an actual or intended duration of at least 3–6 months (OECD, 2018, p315, in Sumption, 2019). The six-country comparative study conducted by IOM (2021) similarly showed that many countries define and measure migration in different ways, and that questions included in censuses vary. Finally, as seen in the case of the World Bank above, not only do national actors often collect migration data using different definitions, but global-level actors may also conceptualise migrants differently and treat or analyse existing national data differently to fit their definition.

This patchy inclusion and harmonisation of migration terms in data collection tools damages the overall evidence base on migration. This is because it affects global comparability of data and means we cannot compile national migration data in a meaningful way. Comparing one country's statistics on IDPs with another's is not possible if the way IDPs are defined and measured in both is different. It is important that countries work to operationalise official guidance on migration data, so that at the global level, available data can be compiled, compared and meaningfully discussed.

In this context, the extent to which countries follow international guidance on migration statistics, understood by comparatively measuring which recommended questions are included in a country's most recent census, would be a useful measure of global migration data capacity and benchmark of progress towards this.

Fragmentation

In any given country, a considerable amount of migration data is already collected from across areas of government and through everyday civic and administrative life, and additionally through regular statistical exercises such as surveys and censuses. However, access to different types of migration data which are crucial for policymakers is often limited, because of how disparate the data often are. Poor intragovernmental coordination and systematic sharing of data collected by different parts of governments are common issues leading to a high degree of fragmentation in national migration data. Low coordination is especially relevant in the context of administrative data, and across sources fragmentation is often also linked to the lack of definition harmonisation. As the migration data that do exist reflect different harmonized definitions and conceptualizations, there cannot be interoperability of data collected by different national actors. Data comparability and interoperability challenges stand in the way of integrating data both at the global level – compiling data collected by states – and nationally – compiling data collected by diverse national stakeholders.

A lack of data integration inhibits effective use of existing migration data; each migration data source can only provide information about specific aspects of the phenomenon, and effective integration is necessary to obtain a comprehensive picture of migration trends, be it at the national, regional or global level. The fragmentation in migration data collection and management is at the root of much of the limited understanding of migration that we have today. Importantly, it is also linked to poor dissemination and communication of data on migration. Many government agencies may publish statistics based on the operational or statistical data they collect, however, integrated databases or publications featuring diverse data on migration are relatively rare. See Box 3.4 for examples of these.

Capacity and practical challenges

There are often more practical challenges limiting the overall evidence base on migration. Several of these relate to ways of working within, across and outside of government, and others to the capacities of personnel and institutions in the country to improve migration data. Many interact with the challenges mentioned above, supporting or entrenching uneven application of official definitions, and fragmentation of migration data. One common challenge is poor coordination among migration data stakeholders, most commonly, specifically between migration data producers (such as NSOs) and users (such as a health ministry). This means that relevant stakeholders with different roles and responsibilities may not discuss, plan or work together to address migration data needs that could be tackled together. As seen above, managing migration data is a complex task involving actors from a range of policy domains, and requires that data producers and users work together across siloes and at all levels of government. Low levels of coordination are often due to a lack of formalized migration data governance in a country. Without a dedicated structure, such as an inter-ministerial working group or other coordination mechanism, it is very difficult for the right stakeholders to convene and collaborate regularly to improve migration data.

Another challenge, related to and often underpinning all of the above, is limited capacity related to migration data. Multiplying demands for better migration data are a challenge for data producers and users, in particular many NSOs upon which the bulk of the burden is placed. NSOs are often underfunded and in many cases, lack capacity to generate basic migration statistics. National stakeholders such as NSOs may have limited skills or resources to take the necessary steps to improve migration data in that country.

> **Box 3.4 Data integration**
>
> To address the high degree of fragmentation in migration data, more data sharing and integration are needed among data producers. To this end, countries can work towards building integrated data systems (IOM, 2019) that could link data on individuals across datasets or compare different figures on various migration measures – such as flows – obtained through different data sources. Issues related to data protection, quality and harmonisation need to be addressed before data can be integrated.
>
> In some cases, such as where administrative data are not collected electronically, data will need to be digitized before they can be integrated with other information. Development of internal data sharing capacities, between line-ministries and NSOs, is also needed. International organizations may also provide direct technical assistance as part of capacity development efforts, which can take on many forms, such as providing software and technical capabilities or online databases; it can also include assistance in a data integration exercise. Below are examples of countries that used innovative methods to integrate and link different data relating to migration, to generate useful and more comprehensive migration statistics.
>
> - In Canada, the Longitudinal Immigration Database (IMDB), managed in collaboration with different ministries and authorities from across provinces, connects data on immigration and citizenship in Canada with existing longitudinal data on socioeconomic outcomes. It makes microdata files available to over 30 universities across the country, aiming to facilitate broad analysis and research (Canadian Research Data Centre Network, n.d.).
> - In the Republic of Georgia (Ministry of Justice, 2017), a Unified Migration Analytical System (UMAS) has been in development since 2014, to link migration-related administrative data collected by different state agencies involved in migration management, using advanced analytical software to provide a better understanding of migration flows to and from Georgia. This involves boosting coordination between relevant agencies, appropriate cleaning and preparation of the data, de-identifying and protecting the data and other steps.

This can look like anything from there not being advanced enough statistical analysis software available, to staff not having all the knowledge necessary to, for example, design and conduct a robust household survey or formulate migration questions that follow international standards, or knowing how to improve the country's migration data according to national priorities, but there not being enough money to launch new data collection, train enumerators, hire further staff, or take the necessary steps to do this. Limited capacity is not just about NSOs. For example, very often, relevant administrative data are collected in a country, but the relevant government agencies or ministries do not have the resources, technical capabilities or systems to harmonize, digitize, compile, share or analyse this information systematically. Further, limited resources for migration are not only an issue for lower-income countries; often it is a matter of national prioritization. Migration data may be given insufficient priority in national policy agendas, meaning that in turn, budget allocations for migration data are relatively low. As a consequence, in many cases, countries have concrete plans and the necessary know-how to improve migration data, but these are often held back by a lack of resources.

Insufficient attention to migration data in objective-setting exercises is common and can be linked to a limited awareness of its importance, or to heightened sensitivities around the topic. Awareness of the importance of migration data among government stakeholders at different levels may be low; migration may not seem relevant to national policy priorities at all, there may be a perception that basic figures on migrant stocks and flows are all that is needed, or there may be poor awareness of what migration data are, the issues with existing statistics, and how improved data can support better policy. Conversely in other cases, political sensitivities related to migration may loom large, and states or sub-national stakeholders may be reluctant to focus on it. Both limited awareness of the importance of migration data and the oft-sensitive politics of migration data both pose significant challenges to generating quality migration data. They both lead to reluctance to share migration data, make it more difficult to coordinate across government entities on data issues, and overall decrease government buy-in to improve migration data.

Generally, the uneven implementation of recommended terms, as well as high data fragmentation, often reflect the limited capacities of NSOs in countries and linked to this, the complexity involved in implementing these terms. There is a need, recognized but sometimes forgotten by the international statistical community, to look carefully at national experiences to examine why adherence to international standards is sometimes so low. While the ongoing development of definitions and standards is positive, attention must also be paid to ensuring standards are realistic for all countries to implement. In some countries, certain migration concepts will be more or less relevant and certain factors, such as for example the key migration data sources in that country, will shape what is desirable and possible in terms of migration statistics. In other cases, political interest and buy-in to improve migration data and invest in them may be, for different reasons, low.

Those developing international guidance on migration statistics have a responsibility to ensure that these are adopted and are in fact realistic for NSOs around the world, and to help generate a policy environment where the benefits of doing this are clear. To this end, stakeholders such as the Expert Group on Migration Statistics should, without sacrificing the detailed conceptual exchanges necessary to formulate sensitive and comprehensive migration data definitions, ensure wide representation of country stakeholders from countries with different profiles in relevant discussions. Stakeholders must increasingly focus on the practicalities of their rollout in different contexts, and consider the reasons behind the lack of harmonization and high fragmentation in migration statistics, for example by focusing on related capacity development activities. This is to an extent already underway with the Expert Group. Addressing the tension between theoretical and practical dimensions of migration data is necessary if real progress is to be made towards improving the international evidence base on migration.

Ethics and data protection

Another common set of challenges in improving migration data relate to issues of ethics and data protection. While better and more timely data are urgently needed to understand migration, collecting, sharing and processing data can pose significant risks to subjects – in this case, migrants – if appropriate safeguards are not in place. Data protection has become increasingly relevant in the context of migration (IOM, 2022) and beyond, at the same time as calls have increased to expand accessibility of migration data. For example, there are growing calls for more publicly available anonymized micro-data that can be used for analysis by researchers, and managing how to maintain the confidentiality requirements of such datasets can be complex. This means that a balance must be struck and practical solutions found to both make more migration data available, and strengthen ethics and data protection considerations.

Potential data theft, loss, and unauthorized or inappropriate use of data all raise serious concerns. Confidentiality is especially important when collecting data on people in vulnerable situations – such as refugees and IDPs, victims of human trafficking and many other migrant groups – and a lack of it can compromise a migrant's security. In some contexts, ethics and data protection considerations can be particularly challenging to implement, but all the more important – for example, in emergency contexts where data on displaced populations are needed very quickly in order to inform rapid response efforts. In these cases, gaining informed consent of participants can be a challenge (Trigwell and Hirani, 2022). Further, the growing field of big data and increasing use of other non-traditional data sources have highlighted the importance of these conversations (see Chapter 4 for more, including an example of data misuse). Personal data on migrants must be prevented from reaching others not involved in the data collection exercise, and data collection and management must not only not create any new risks for migrants and follow the "do no harm" principle, but should ideally also help meet the needs of migrants.

Further, migration data should only be used for information purposes and to support policy, and not, for example, to support law enforcement, or any legal proceedings.

Data protection is approached differently by countries, though it is increasingly regulated. 137 out of 194 countries have some legislation on data protection and privacy in place (UNCTAD, 2021). There are also international instruments on data protection and the right to privacy, such as Article 12 of the Universal Declaration of Human Rights, which is about the right to privacy, and the UN Principles on Personal Data Protection and Privacy of 2018. International organizations have also sought to develop and implement their own policies or frameworks on data protection; for example, IOM developed its Data Protection Manual (IOM, 2015) and the United Nations High Commissioner for Refugees its Policy on the Protection of Personal Data of Persons of Concern to UNHCR (UNCHR, 2015). Further, there is discussion around developing a global data governance mechanism across the UN, to help promote appropriate ethical and quality standards and address the complexity of these issues (MacFeely et al. 2021). Strong data governance is needed a local, national, regional and global levels, to enable migration data to be effectively used to inform policy, while safeguarding against misuse. This can be challenging in many countries; many do not have a strong data governance framework designed to do this. Components of strong data governance may include data infrastructure policies, policies, laws, and regulations, data governance institutions and more (World Bank, 2021, p10). Ideally, migration data governance would fit into this larger existing framework, but this is not always the case.

Data protection and privacy safeguards for any migration data exercise should adhere to relevant international, national and other laws. They need to be designed and implemented along the entire lifecycle of migration data – across collection, storage, processing, sharing and dissemination. This should be done both in accordance with national legislation and relevant international guidance, for example ensuring that individual data collected by statistical agencies are kept strictly confidential and used exclusively for statistical purposes. In practice, building in data protection and privacy safeguards usually entails steps such as removing data that could identify individuals, ensuring encryption of storage of relevant data, organising security clearance of staff processing data, and many others, depending on the type of data collected and other contextual factors. Ideally migrants and any other relevant affected communities are actively engaged in the design and implementation of the process.

3.4 Migration statistics and capacity development: How can data be improved?

Each country's migration data collection and use take place in a different context, which means that ways to improve migration will look different in each, and plans should be tailor-made. Yet, as there are several common national challenges on migration, some potential ways to address these are similar and can be useful across contexts.

Statistical capacity development

Capacity development is a core concept in international development. Overall, it "aims to develop and strengthen the organizational performance of institutions and human resources" (UNCEPA, 2006 in IOM, 2019). This tends to be a long-term process, in which many different stakeholders participate, including ministries, local authorities, NGOs, and others, and where local actors are encouraged to get involved (UNDP, 2016). The terms "capacity-building," and "capacity-development" describe similar processes and are often used interchangeably. The former arguably refers to a more linear and set conception of progress, and the latter emphasizes a dynamic process which builds on pre-existing skills and relies on collaboration with local actors (EPRS, 2017 in IOM, 2019).

The need to develop capacities on migration statistics is recognised in the GCM and the SDGs (UN 2015; UN, 2018; see aso Kraly and Hovy, 2020). Such a need relates to both national migration data that responds to specific country concerns or policy issues, and to information on migration topics relevant to international frameworks such as the SDGs and the GCM. In recent years, many initiatives by international organizations, regional bodies and other actors have focused on improving migration data through capacity development. Capacity development efforts to sustainably improve migration data could include improving its availability, quality, use, understanding, access, timeliness and many other aspects. Efforts have included but not been limited to training individuals with relevant skills and knowledge, and changing institutional, regulatory or legal frameworks. Below are some common activities and steps in capacity development on migration data.

Given that often, enough migration data are collected in a country but just not made available, one key cost-effective way to begin any capacity development exercise is to assess what information is already collected. This involves conducting an assessment of migration data, mapping out existing data sources on migration in a city, country or region, and listing exactly what migration data are collected in each. This can help determine to what extent data collection instruments adhere to international standards, and evaluate the overall effectiveness of how data are collected, stored, processed, used, shared and disseminated. This comprehensive exercise explores any data held by a wide range of stakeholders – from key national stakeholders, such as NSOs and other government ministries, to NGOs that may be key operational actors in the country and collect their own data on beneficiaries. As part of this exercise, a needs assessment can be conducted in close collaboration with national stakeholders, discussing what migration data needs are to support relevant migration policies and strategies, and identifying which steps need to be taken to meet these, based on the data assessment. In this way, such an assessment can form the basis of a migration data plan or help stakeholders design a programme addressing specific needs – for example, to collect new data on certain migrant groups, add migration-related questions to a household survey or make better use of administrative data (IOM, 2019).

There are some examples of in-depth assessments and discussions of national data, for example, in the UK (ONS, 2019); further, some global-level tools have been designed to comprehensively assess data, for example, the *Guidance for the Integrated Data Ecosystem Assessment and Strengthening (IDEAS) Tool* (UNICEF, 2018). Further, there are some regional assessments of migration data; for example, a report assessing all migration-related information available in household surveys and censuses in Latin America and how representative this is (Rico and Camilo, 2019).

A very common activity of capacity development projects is to conduct training for government agencies, NSOs and other relevant entities. International organizations often hold training workshops, which usually bring in migration data experts to share knowledge on and exchange with participants from relevant government agencies involved in migration data. Workshops may be online or in person, tend to be highly interactive and could be general or on one or many specific data areas, depending on participant needs. Some workshops, known as "Training of Trainers" (ToT), are designed to train other people to become trainers. Here, an expert trains a group on how to best train others, who in turn train groups of participants in their own countries. This acts as a cost-effective way to share knowledge with more people and generate greater national ownership of the process. Several training centres around the world pool expertise and conduct training activities across a region, working closely on migration data issues with national and regional stakeholders in one area.

For example, IOM has worked on migration data capacity development since 2015, providing guidance and training on data collection, analysis and governance to governments and regional bodies around the world including in Ghana, Namibia, Egypt, Azerbaijan, Zambia and many other places. Capacity-development activities commonly include holding a number of training workshops on different topics depending on needs; for example, zooming in to provide a week-long workshop on migration and development, or a day workshop on a specific stage of the data lifecycle, such as migration data collection and how to adhere to recommended guidance.

Another common component of capacity development is producing written technical guidance and other material on migration data, in the form of guidelines, handbooks or written reports (IOM, 2019). International organizations have produced several such documents in recent years, addressing specific aspects of migration statistics and/or aimed at different stakeholders.

These may, for example, translate international data recommendations into simple step-by-step instructions that practitioners can implement easily.

UN agencies have published several such documents. For example, UN DESA has developed many (2022; UNSD 2017a; 2017b, see also UN DESA, 2018). IOM similarly developed many guidance documents, including regional guidelines on migration statistics in ECOWAS (IOM, 2018). ILO developed guidelines concerning statistics on international labour migration (ILO, 2018), and the United Nations Economic Commission for Europe (UNECE) has produced several handbooks on migration data (2016). Beyond individual organizations, the Expert Group on Migration Statistics has, as seen above, been involved in the production of guidance materials, and the Expert Group on Refugee and Internally Displaced Persons Statistics produced the *International Recommendations on Refugee Statistics* (European Union and the United Nations, 2018) and the *International Recommendations on Internally Displaced Persons Statistics (IRIS)* (European Union and the United Nations, 2020).

One focus of capacity development activities is often to boost coordination between migration data users and producers in a city, country or region. As seen above, strengthening cooperation and coordination between NSOs, ministries and others is key. This can be done by ensuring capacity development activities, such as workshops and other events, that include a wide range of stakeholders who produce or use migration data. Participation can be tailored to the overall objective of the capacity development programme, to include new actors in coordination efforts. For example, initiatives to boost administrative data use could involve a representative of region- or city-level staff working on immigration or border control if relevant, who may be tasked with such data collection. These efforts can also be regional, aiming to establish or support regional networks, cooperation and data exchange. Coordination challenges also exist at the global level; some countries face a confusing plethora of UN-driven capacity development efforts with duplicating or overlapping aims and activities. In response, there has been an increased awareness among international statistical programmes of the need to better coordinate efforts at national, regional and international levels. Staff or learning visits or exchanges between stakeholders from a mix of countries help these to not only learn from and work with relevant organizations but also boost regional or international coordination on migration data.

For example, at national level, IOM has helped governments set up interministerial working groups on migration data in many countries. At regional level, the Africa Migration Data Network (AMDN) established in 2021 aims to promote continental exchange of practices on migration data, facilitate coordination and collaboration in the implementation of migration data-related initiatives, and more. This is a key effort to better coordinate migration data across Africa, so that stakeholders can coordinate and collaborate on capacity development activities, promote data sharing and set up joint efforts to harmonize regional data (IOM, n.d.). At global level, there are efforts to address a lack of UN coordination on migration data and capacity development. Launched in 2020, the International Data Alliance for Children on the Move (IDAC) is a global coalition of governments, international and regional organizations, NGOs, think tanks, academics and civil society actors. Its main objective is to improve data on migrant and forcibly displaced children and it does this partially by combatting the fragmentation of relevant data by bringing together many stakeholders (see more in Chapter 8).

Some initiatives focus on developing solutions to specific issues, such as limited accessibility of migration data. These focus on how to better disseminate and communicate migration data and facilitate access to migration statistics for a wide range of data users. Before migration data can be disseminated in a timely and user-friendly format, for example to the public, they must undergo a process to evaluate and address their quality (IOM, 2019) and several data protection concerns. Many data dissemination efforts take care to provide methodological information on how the data were collected and more detail on what this includes, in the form of metadata. Others make download or analysis of the data easier through customizable tabulations, or accompanying explainer blogs or social media posts. For example, IPUMS offers free-of-charge services to share census and survey data from different countries, allowing users to conduct comparative research across time and places, merge information across data types and much more. Many of the datasets include variables on country of birth and/or citizenship, providing a key resource for migration researchers. However, in relative terms, there are fewer capacity development projects related to these stages of the data life cycle, and that involve government stakeholders beyond NSOs. For example, a World Bank evaluation of their capacity development projects related to statistics suggested that few initiatives focused on building the capacities of data users or policymakers and on data sharing (World Bank, 2018a).

We have seen that the migration data landscape can be highly politicized, that the migration evidence base is patchy and that even when data are available, they can be highly fragmented and/or use different definitions and concepts. Taken together, these factors mean that there is a need to communicate migration data effectively and clearly, so that migration data users – whether they are researchers, policymakers or the general public – understand exactly what these mean and how to use them. The Global Migration Data Portal launched in 2017 by IOM with the cooperation of several organizations aims to serve as a "single access point" to quality migration data globally. This website offers and visualizes migration data from many different sources in a user-friendly format, explains the strengths and weaknesses of data on different migration subtopics and much more. Improving communication of migration data can also look like explaining different concepts, definitions and data sources relevant to a particular city or country. For example, the Migration Observatory at the University of Oxford published a briefing on the different ways that migrants are defined in the UK (Anderson and Blinder, 2019), and a guide to local data in the UK designed to help people understand key questions about migration in their local area (Kierans, 2022).

Some capacity development initiatives focus on knowledge sharing on migration data at national, regional or international level. Knowledge-sharing events, such as conferences, often bring together experts and practitioners from around the world from different sectors including the private sector and academia (IOM, 2019). These enable exchange of information on migration data and interactive sharing and discussion of real-life experiences on migration data challenges and solutions.

For example, the International Forum on Migration Statistics (IFMS), organized jointly by the OECD, IOM and UN DESA, has had three iterations. The forum provides a space to discuss how to improve migration data worldwide and mobilizes academic expertise from a range of disciplines, practitioners in different sectors, and national-level producers and users of migration statistics. The latest iteration was in Chile in January 2023, where dozens of sessions and side events covered a range of topics related to migration data, from how to better measure human trafficking to strengthening use of administrative data to measure migration flows, understanding the education of people on the move, the impact of COVID-19 on migration statistics and global standards related to labour migration (UN DESA, n.d.).

Challenges to capacity-building and tips for success

Data capacity-building activities often face common challenges. Some are linked to the fragmentation that these activities are often trying to combat; it can be difficult to target all relevant stakeholders and establish effective coordination among them to smoothly conduct planned activities. It is not easy to kickstart coordination between stakeholders who do not usually work together, and if communication and workflow between data producers and users remains a challenge, this can impact the success of activities. For example, relevant representatives may not be present at training workshops, or efforts to co-produce or sign off documents such as a migration data strategy may be slow, or at times even blocked.

Linked to this, it can sometimes be difficult to gain effective buy-in from different government stakeholders on improving migration data in the first place or to sustain this over time. Political will to improve migration data and support from high-level officials are key, as these can authorize decisions and resources needed to help make capacity development sustainable in the long run (see IOM, 2019). Without this, the scope, efficacy and sustainability of capacity development activities will be limited.

Sustainability of capacity development activities can be another common challenge. For example, high turnover or regular rotation of ministry staff is common. This can be challenging for capacity development at all levels; for example, buy-in for longer term programmes will be in danger if senior officials are regularly replaced. In training workshops aimed at working-level staff, the same material may need to be used repeatedly with the same agencies but with different individuals, limiting potential for overall advancement of that institution. Finally, it is difficult to monitor the success and sustainability of capacity development activities on migration data. For example, it is a challenge to effectively measure the impact of a training session, especially from a long-term perspective (IOM, 2019).

For these kinds of projects to succeed, the specific context should be kept in mind and activities should be tailor-made, based on a real understanding of local socio-political systems, culture and more. Keeping in mind the overall need to be context-specific, and demand-driven, Box 3.5 shows selected practices that can help improve the success and sustainability of migration data capacity-building efforts.

Box 3.5   Practices to boost capacity development success

- Work with governments to link migration data efforts to policy objectives. Identifying and improving migration data that would support existing goals can help generate political will for capacity development and ensure this is useful to national stakeholders.
- Engage with a wide range of local stakeholders early and often in the process, seek continuous feedback and enable their direct participation throughout the programme.
- Set up nationally owned inter-ministerial frameworks to oversee capacity development activities and coordination. As far as possible, build on existing structures, mechanisms or processes such as technical working group set up for a Migration Profile exercise.
- Partner with local actors and institutions, such as researchers or research institutes, to strengthen local capacity and links to the international community. This could be done by twinning local researchers with international experts.
- Mitigate loss of training knowledge through high government staff turnover by making training workshop documentation available to others who did not attend.
- Encourage regional-level approaches so that migration data systems and practices can be harmonized between countries from the same region to enable comparability of data, and so stakeholders can share experiences. Training can be held to bring together countries in a region or countries that share migration corridors.
- Build in some way to measure progress, by formulating measurable outcomes of success of capacity development activities. Ways to do

this will differ depending on the activity or intervention. If a migration data strategy is in place, a periodic review could state how far objectives have been met, migration data availability or timeliness could be regularly monitored, the ability to report on selected migration indicators could be tracked, or a migration data assessment could be periodically repeated or refreshed to evaluate progress (see the case of Armenia in Manke, 2011 and Mosler Vidal, 2019).
- Develop a national or regional **migration data strategy**, bringing together collectively agreed objectives and a plan of action to meet these. While most capacity development activities are done on an ad hoc basis without a migration data strategy, tying these to a strategy would support more sustainable progress (IOM, 2019). Such a strategy could include a set of actions, key performance indicators and more.

Attention to and visibility of statistical capacity development writ large have been growing in recent years, including for migration data. This has been demonstrated, for example, by high-level commitments to improve this such as the GCM, dedicated migration data institutions being established, such as the UNHCR–World Bank Joint Data Centre on Forced Displacement in 2019, and various migration observatories in Africa. However, this has not necessarily been met with a sustained increase in funding allocated to statistical capacity-building, which has remained around 0.33 per cent of total Overseas Development Assistance (ODA) around the world (Calleja and Rogerson, 2019). It is difficult to calculate how much ODA or other funding for statistical capacity-building is allocated specifically to migration data (see Jenkins and Mosler Vidal, 2021). How much is needed? This is difficult to say. Gender statistics have been a major recent focus for donors. In 2015–2018, financing for gender data – which cuts across many sectors – was estimated to be between USD 217 and USD 272 million per year on average (ibid; ODW and Data2X, 2021). Nevertheless, this is not enough; the shortfall for gender data has been calculated to be USD 2.7 billion, or about USD 448 million a year (ODW and Data2X, 2021). No such funding gap has been calculated for migration statistics. In these and other ways, such as communication of data, the migration data world could learn from the gender data world.

Further, the capacity development landscape suffers from a lack of coordination itself. To date investments are often "disjointed, duplicative, and concentrated in one-off initiatives" (Global Partnership for Sustainable Development Data and United Nations, 2022), which undermine efforts' impact and sustainability. In order to be more effective, capacity development activities need greater and more coordinated investment. Providing tailored, comprehensive and sustainable support requires a more coherent funding approach than that in place now; see Box 3.6 for one attempt to do this through pooled funding instruments and improved mechanisms for tracking data investments.

66 *The state of migration data*

> **Box 3.6   The UN Complex Risk Analytics Fund**
>
> The UN Complex Risk Analytics Fund (CRAF'd) and World Bank Global Data Facility (GDF) are pooled funds that aim to raise and deploy over USD 500 million for data and data ecosystems. CRAF'd will coordinate investments in risk data and analytics to enable faster, more efficient and effective programs in fragile and crisis-affected settings, while GDF is designed to catalyse long-term support for integrated national data ecosystems in LICs and MICs. As pooled funds, CRAF'd and GDF help contributors maximize the impact of their resources, by facilitating efficiencies (e.g. by cutting transaction costs) and access to advocacy, financial know-how and stakeholder networks to design investments that can catalyse additional funding (Global Partnership for Sustainable Development Data and United Nations, 2022).

Many actors are thinking more critically about statistical capacity development and calling for new paradigms and ways of working. For example, the *World Development Report 2021* details how data can increase accountability for governments and improve policymaking and service delivery, calling for

> *a new social contract for data—one that enables the use and reuse of data to create economic and social value, promotes equitable opportunities to benefit from data, and fosters citizens' trust that they will not be harmed by misuse of the data they provide.*
>
> (World Bank, 2021)

PARIS21 carries out ongoing work to redefine statistical capacity development, and published its *Guidelines for Developing Statistical Capacity* pooling expertise to advise NSOs and development agencies on how to engage in country-led, sustainable and participatory statistical capacity development (PARIS21, 2020). Migration data must not be left behind. Conversations on capacity development for migration statistics need to be included in dialogue and planning around development data, and in turn migration data actors must stay abreast of wider capacity-building developments.

Broader conceptions of and new approaches to migration data capacity development are needed. For example, most initiatives focus on data producers and not enough on building capacities of data users, to help policymakers and practitioners interpret and use migration data (World Bank, 2018a). Further, the capacity development landscape moving forward will need to regularly start building in evaluations of the effectiveness of activities. There are some existing measures of overall statistical capacity: for example, the World Bank's Statistical Capacity Indicator (SCI) assigns a composite score to a country's statistical system based on methodology, data sources, periodicity and timeliness of statistics (World Bank, 2018b; in IOM, 2019). An equivalent metric could be developed to measure progress on migration data.

References

Anderson, B. and Blinder, S. (2019). Who counts as a migrant? Definitions and their consequences. Migration Observatory briefing, COMPAS, University of Oxford, UK. Available at https://migrationobservatory.ox.ac.uk/resources/briefings/who-counts-as-a-migrant-definitions-and-their-consequences/

Bilsborrow, R. (2018). The global need for better data on international migration and the special potential of household surveys. Improving Data on International Migration Towards, 20. Available at https://www.un.org/en/development/desa/population/publications/technical/improving-data-on-international-migration-towards-agenda-2030-report-of-the-secretary-general-with-annex_2018.shtml

Calleja, R. and Rogerson, A. (2019). Financing challenges for developing statistical systems: A review of financing options. PARIS21 Discussion Paper, No. 14. Available at https://www.paris21.org/sites/default/files/2019-01/Financing%20challenges%20for%20developing%20statistical%20systems%20%28DP14%29.pdf

Canadian Research Data Centre Network. (n.d.). Longitudinal immigration database: 1980–2021. CRDCN. Available at https://crdcn.ca/data/longitudinal-immigration-database/

European Commission (EC). (2019). Statistical data. Portal on Collaboration in Research and Methodology for Official Statistics. Available at https://cros-legacy.ec.europa.eu/content/statistical-data_en#:~:text=DEFINITION%3A,observations%20or%20statistical%20data%20processing

European Parliamentary Research Service, Ionel Zamfir. (2017). *Understanding Capacity-Building/Capacity Development: A Core Concept of Development Policy*. Brussels: European Union. Available at https://www.europarl.europa.eu/RegData/etudes/BRIE/2017/599411/EPRS_BRI(2017)599411_EN.pdf

European Union and the United Nations. (2020). *International Recommendations on Internally Displaced Persons Statistics (IRIS)*. Luxembourg: Publications Office of the European Union.

Eurostat. (n.d.). Households international migration surveys in the Mediterranean countries (MED-HIMS). European Neighbourhood Policy. Eurostat. Available at https://ec.europa.eu/eurostat/web/european-neighbourhood-policy/enp-south/med-hims

Global Partnership for Sustainable Development Data and United Nations. (2022). Investment case: Multiplying progress through data ecosystems. Global Partnership for Sustainable Development Data. Available at https://www.data4sdgs.org/sites/default/files/file_uploads/Investment%2Bcase_Multiplying%2Bprogress%2Bthrough%2Bdata%2Becosystems_vFINAL.pdf

Hagen-Zanker, J., Hennessey, G., Carling, J., and Memon, R. (2020). *Survey Data Collection. MIGNEX Handbook Chapter 7 (v1)*. Peace Research Institute Oslo. www.mignex.org/d031

International Labour Organization (ILO). (2018). Guidelines concerning statistics of international labour migration. 20th International Conference of Labour Statisticians. Geneva. Available at https://www.ilo.org/wcmsp5/groups/public/---dgreports/---stat/documents/meetingdocument/wcms_648922.pdf

International Labour Organization (ILO). (n.d.). ILO labour migration module. Available at https://www.ilo.org/dyn/migpractice/migmain.showPractice?p_lang=en&p_practice_id=42

International Organization for Migration (IOM). (2015). *IOM Data Protection Manual.* Geneva: International Organization for Migration. Available at https://publications.iom.int/books/iom-data-protection-manual

International Organization for Migration (IOM). (2018). *Guidelines for the Harmonization of Migration Data Management in the ECOWAS Region.* Abuja, Nigeria: IOM. Available at https://publications.iom.int/books/guidelines-harmonization-migration-data-management-ecowas-region

International Organization for Migration (IOM). (2019). Building migration data capacity: Examples of good practices for the African region. In *Central Mediterranean Route Thematic Report Series.* Geneva: International Organization for Migration.

International Organization for Migration. (2020). Migration data sources. Migration Data Portal. Available at https://www.migrationdataportal.org/themes/migration-data-sources

International Organization for Migration. (2021a). Big data, migration and human mobility. Migration Data Portal. Available at https://www.migrationdataportal.org/themes/big-data-migration-and-human-mobility

International Organization for Migration (IOM). (2021b). *How Countries Manage Migration Data: Evidence from Six Countries.* Geneva. Available at https://publications.iom.int/books/how-countries-manage-migration-data-evidence-six-countries

International Organization for Migration. (2022). Migration and data protection. Migration Data Portal. Available at https://www.migrationdataportal.org/themes/migration-and-data-protection

International Organization for Migration (IOM). (n.d.). African Migration Data Network (AMDN). Available at https://gmdac.iom.int/africa-migration-data-network-amdn

Jenkins, J. and Mosler Vidal, E. (2021). Goal 17: Migration data capacity-building. In Elisa Mosler Vidal and Frank Laczko (Eds.), *International Organization for Migration.* Migration and SDGs: Measuring Progress. Available at https://publications.iom.int/books/migration-and-sdgs-measuring-progress-edited-volume

Jungcurt, S. 2022. *Citizen-Generated Data: Data by People, for People.* IISD. Available at https://www.iisd.org/articles/insight/citizen-generated-data-people#:~:text=What%20is%20citizen%2Dgenerated%20data,of%20data%20that%20describes%20them.

Juran, S. and Snow, R. (2017). The potential of the 2010 population and housing census round for international migration analysis. *Migration Policy Practice,* 7(1), 6–8.

Khoury, R. (2020). Hard-to-survey populations and respondent-driven sampling: Expanding the political science toolbox. *Perspectives on Politics,* 18(2), 509–526.

Kierans, D. (2022). *Local Data on Migrants in the UK.* The Migration Observatory, at the University of Oxford, COMPAS (Centre on Migration, Policy and Society), University of Oxford. Available at https://migrationobservatory.ox.ac.uk/projects/local-data-guide/

Kraly, E.P. and Hovy, B. (2020). Data and research to inform global policy: The global compact for safe, orderly and regular migration. *Comparative Migration Studies,* 8(11). https://comparativemigrationstudies.springeropen.com/articles/10.1186/s40878-019-0166-y

Lemaitre, G., Liebig, T., Thoreau, C., and Fron, P. (2008). *Standardised Statistics on Immigrant Inflows Results, Sources and Methods.* Paris: OECD. Available at https://www.oecd.org/els/mig/38832099.pdf

MacFeely, S., Me, A., and Fu, H. (2022). A brief glimpse into the fascinating world of international statistics. *Statistical Journal of the IAOS*, 38(3), 683–685. https://content.iospress.com/articles/statistical-journal-of-the-iaos/sji220073?utm_source=TrendMD&utm_medium=cpc&utm_campaign=Statistical_Journal_of_the_IAOS_TrendMD_0

Manke, M. (2011). *Enhancing Migration Data Collection, Processing and Sharing in the Republic of Armenia*. Geneva: International Organization for Migration. Available at https://armstat.am/file/article/part1_eng.pdf

Ministry of Justice of Georgia, Nino Ghvinadze. (2017). Synthesis of Administrative Data and Big Data Technologies for Improved Migration Data. Geneva: UNECE Work Session on Migration Statistics. Available at https://www.unece.org/fileadmin/DAM/stats/documents/ece/ces/ge.10/2017/mtg1/2017_UNECE_Migration_WP_03_Georgia_Ghvinadze_ENG.pdf

Mosler Vidal, E. (2019). *Migration Data in the Context of the 2030 Agenda: Measuring Migration and Development in Armenia*. Armenia: IOM. Available at https://armenia.un.org/sites/default/files/2021-07/Migration%20data%20in%20the%20context%20of%20the%202030%20agenda_ENG.pdf

Mosler Vidal, E. (2021). *Leave No Migrant Behind: The 2030 Agenda and Data Disaggregation*. Geneva: International Organization for Migration (IOM).

OECD. (2018). *International Migration Outlook 2018*. Paris: OECD. Available online.

Office for National Statistics (ONS). (2019). *Understanding Different Migration Data Sources: August 2019 Progress Report*. ONS. Available at https://www.ons.gov.uk/peoplepopulationandcommunity/populationandmigration/internationalmigration/articles/understandingdifferentmigrationdatasources/augustprogressreport

Office for National Statistics (ONS). (2020). *Defining and Measuring International Migration*. ONS. Available at https://www.ons.gov.uk/peoplepopulationandcommunity/populationandmigration/internationalmigration/articles/definingandmeasuringinternationalmigration/2020-02-14

Office for National Statistics (ONS). (2021). *Meet the Data Quality Dimensions*. Government Data Quality HUB, ONS. Available at https://www.gov.uk/government/news/meet-the-data-quality-dimensions

Office of the United Nations High Commissioner for Human Rights (OHCHR). (2018). *A Human Rights–Based Approach to Data: Leaving No One Behind in the 2030 Agenda for Sustainable Development*. Geneva. Available at https://www.ohchr.org/en/documents/tools-and-resources/human-rights-based-approach-data-leaving-no-one-behind-2030-agenda

Open Data Watch (ODW) and Data2X. (2021). State of gender data financing 2021. Available at https://data2x.org/resource-center/state-of-gender-data-financing-2021/

Partnership in Statistics for Development in the 21st Century (PARIS21). (2020). The Partner Report on Support to Statistics (PRESS) 2020. Available at https://paris21.org/sites/default/files/inline-files/PRESS2020%20Final.pdf.

Poulain, M., Perrin, N., Singleton, A., and THESIM Project. (2006). *THESIM: Towards Harmonised European Statistics on International Migration*. Hors collection; Louvain-la-Neuve, Belgium: Presses universitaires de Louvain.

Rico, G. and Camilo, C. (2019). Making migrants visible: A review of information on migrants in censuses and household surveys in Latin America and the Caribbean. Available at https://policycommons.net/artifacts/2680637/making-migrants-visible/3704064/

Sumption, M. (2019). *What Migration Statistics are needed for Public and Policy Debates about Migration?* Migration Observatory, COMPAS, Oxford. Available at https://migrationobservatory.ox.ac.uk/resources/commentaries/what-migration-statistics-are-needed-for-public-and-policy-debates-about-migration/

Trigwell, R. and Hirani, P. (2022). Connecting the dots: Why ethical standards in humanitarian data more important than ever. IOM Medium. Available at https://medium.com/@Unmigration/connecting-the-dots-why-ethical-standards-in-humanitarian-data-more-important-than-ever-bba561d20b21

United Nations Committee of Experts on Public Administration (UNCEPA). (2006). Definition of basic concepts and terminologies in governance and public administration. United Nations Economic and Social Council, E/C.16/2006/4. New York. Available at https://digitallibrary.un.org/record/566603?ln=en

UNCTAD. (2021). Data protection and privacy legislation worldwide. Available at https://unctad.org/page/data-protection-and-privacy-legislation-worldwide

UN High Commissioner for Refugees (UNHCR). (2015). Policy on the protection of personal data of persons of concern to UNHCR, May 2015. Available at https://www.refworld.org/docid/55643c1d4.html

UNICEF. (2018). Guidance for the Integrated Data Ecosystem Assessment and Strengthening (IDEAS) tool. Available at https://www.unicef.org/media/67506/file/IDEAS-guidance%20document%20%20FINAL%20.pdf

United Nations. (2015). Transforming our world: The 2030 Agenda for Sustainable Development. Resolution adopted by the General Assembly on 25 September 2015. Available at https://documents-dds-ny.un.org/doc/UNDOC/GEN/N15/291/89/PDF/N1529189.pdf?OpenElement

United Nations Department of Economic and Social Affairs (DESA). (2018). Standard questions on international migration: Guidance note for the use in population censuses and household surveys. Available at https://migrationnetwork.un.org/resources/standard-questions-international-migration

United Nations Department of Economic and Social Affairs (UN DESA). (2022). *Handbook on Measuring International Migration through Population Censuses.* New York: UN DESA.

United Nations Department of Economic and Social Affairs (UN DESA). (n.d.). The 3rd International Forum on Migration Statistics (IFMS 2023). Available at https://unstats.un.org/unsd/demographic-social/migrationstat-forum-2023/

United Nations Development Program (UNDP). (2015). Capacity development: A UNDP primer. New York. Available at https://www.undp.org/publications/capacity-development-undp-primer

United Nations Economic Commission for Europe (UNECE). (2016). Handbook on the use of administrative sources and sample surveys to measure international migration in CIS countries. UNECE. Available at https://unece.org/info/Statistics/pub/21846

United Nations General Assembly. (2018). *Global Compact for Safe, Orderly and Regular Migration.* New York, NY: United Nations. Available at http://www.un.org/en/ga/search/view_doc.asp?symbol=A/RES/73/195

United Nations, Statistical Division (UNSD). (2017a). Principles and recommendations for population and housing censuses, revision 3, ST/ESA/STAT/SER.M/67/Rev.3.

United Nations Statistics Division (UNSD). (2017b). *Handbook on Measuring International Migration through Population Censuses.* New York, NY: United Nations.

Available at https://unstats.un.org/unsd/statcom/48th-session/documents/BG-4a-Migration-Handbook-E.pdf

World Bank. (2018). *Data for Development An Evaluation of World Bank Support for Data and Statistical Capacity.* Independent Evaluation Group, Washington, DC: World Bank

World Bank. (2018). Data of statistical capacity. Bulletin board on statistical capacity. Available at http://bbsc.worldbank.org

World Bank. (2021). *World Development Report 2021: Data for Better Lives.* Washington, DC: World Bank. https://doi.org/10.1596/978-1-4648-1600-0. License: Creative Commons Attribution CC BY 3.0 IGO.

4 Big data
How much can they tell us about migrants and migration policy?

This chapter takes stock of existing uses of big data in the field of migration and human mobility. It begins by defining what is meant by big data and providing a simple categorization of big data sources, based on some of their main applications to analyse aspects related to migration and human mobility. It then describes some of the key challenges associated with these and outlines a series of recent initiatives that have been undertaken by various actors to address these and enable more systematic and responsible use of private datasets for migration and human mobility analysis and policy. The chapter concludes by providing recommendations to enhance responsible and ethical big data use to further evidence on migration around the world.

4.1 What is meant by big data, new data sources, data innovation and why do these matter?

First off, what is meant by big data? Experts have advanced various definitions of this term, each highlighting the unique characteristics of these data compared to other, traditional data. In its initial conception (Laney, 2001), big data were defined as data characterized not only by huge Volume, as suggested by the term, but also unprecedented Velocity – i.e. being generated in real time – and great Variety, or complexity, involving structured and unstructured kinds of data. These were the so-called "Three Vs" of big data, to which two were subsequently added – for Veracity (quality of the data) and the Value that could be generated through their use. Big data refer to the translation of human actions and interactions with digital platforms that has accompanied the digital age (Latour, 2007) and data from sensors such as satellites.

The terms "non-traditional data", "novel data sources" and "digital trace data" are often used interchangeably, although they focus on different aspects of the data – their being innovative, or the modality through which they are generated (the use of digital devices). Some scholars have differentiated between data that are digitally *captured*, such as data from mobile phones and online transactions, that are *mediated*, such as social media or online data, and that are *observed*, such as satellite data, all of these using new instruments that are often in the hands of private entities (Bosco et al., 2022). "Data

DOI: 10.4324/9781003266075-5

innovation" would normally also be an umbrella term, including data that are *inferred* using innovative analytical methods, such as machine learning and artificial intelligence, and the use of a combination of traditional and non-traditional data sources (ibid and IOM, 2023). All these terms hint at the storage and analytical capacities as well as computing power needed to process and make sense of vast amounts of complex and varied data (Mayer Schonberger and Cukier, 2013), all of which are fast-evolving.

More specifically, what are the different kinds of new data sources we will be referring to in this chapter? This does not aim to be an exhaustive taxonomy, but rather highlight some of the key non-traditional data sources that have been used so far to tackle migration and human mobility questions and that seem to hold the greatest potential for migration studies and policy to date. These can be broadly classified under three main categories (Global Migration Group, 2017):

a   Mobile phone-based, such as call detail records (CDRs) and mobile positioning data (MPD).
b   Internet-based, such as social media or Google search data.
c   Sensor-based, such as earth observation data from satellites.

This chapter will focus on these non-traditional data, describing their characteristics and their potential as it relates to the study of migration.

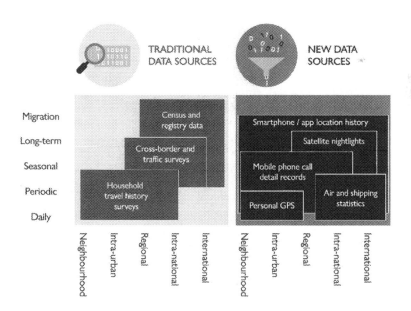

Figure 4.1 Sources of data for measuring migration and human mobility.
Source: Tatem et al., in IOM (2023).

As part of the Big Data for Migration Alliance,[1] IOM has compiled information about more than 60 projects using new data sources and methods to analyse migration and human mobility topics in a Data Innovation Directory.[2] This can also be a useful tool to compare different uses and partners involved, as well as the relevance of each project to objectives of the Global Compact for Safe, Orderly and Regular Migration, or specific targets in the 2030 Agenda for Sustainable Development. Some of these examples are referenced below, though providing a fully comprehensive and exhaustive account of big data uses in migration and human mobility is beyond the scope of this chapter.

Despite the progress made in recent years to enhance migration statistics and the promising innovations described in previous chapters, our collective understanding of migration and human mobility phenomena, particularly in some regions of the world, is still fairly limited. Anyone who has worked on migration and mobility knows how uniquely complex existing data are and how difficult they are to make sense of and handle. As seen in Chapters 2, and 3 this is true at the national level, because of the various ways in which migration statistics are compiled and migration data are collected, with different data sources describing distinct aspects of the phenomenon, and is even more valid at the international level, with statistics of varied nature being produced by various entities, based on different definitions and data collection or estimation methods.

Making sense of migration data is challenging, not only due to the inherent difficulties of measuring international migration and mobility as phenomena, starting with definitional issues of who should be counted as a migrant and why, but also because the tools that governments and international organizations have to measure these phenomena cannot describe them fully. These gaps hinder the ability of policymakers and practitioners to (a) understand past and current migration trends (descriptive analysis); (b) identify the drivers of shifts in migration and mobility patterns as well as their impact on individuals and communities at large (causal analysis); (c) make predictions about how these patterns will evolve in the short or long term, or anticipate future shifts (predictive analysis) and (d) assess the impact of policy and programmatic measures on migration and related areas, as well as monitor the effectiveness of specific policy interventions over time (impact analysis).

Meanwhile, an abundance of data relevant to understanding migration and human mobility exists but is currently not fully harnessed for migration research and policy. Enormous quantities of data are generated and stored in real time through the use of mobile phones, social media and other internet-based platforms or digital devices as well as satellites and other sensors. These data are primarily owned by private sector entities and collected for commercial purposes but – if managed ethically and responsibly – can offer insights on aspects of migration and human mobility that are currently hard to capture through traditional data, holding the potential to complement traditional statistics. The value of these data sources has become more and more apparent thanks to a fast-growing number of applications, particularly in the academic sphere. Interdisciplinary collaborations between demographers, data and computer scientists and social scientists have given way to a growing migration-related literature using digital methods. In parallel, several initiatives at the global level have focused on how to use new data sources and analytical methods effectively for official statistics, sustainable development more broadly, and migration and human mobility (Box 4.1).

> **Box 4.1   UN and regional initiatives to harness the potential of big data**
>
> Calls for a Development "Data Revolution" following the adoption of the 2030 Agenda for Sustainable Development gave impetus to data innovation and use of new technologies to fill data gaps, leading to a rapid evolution in this field and a much greater acceptance of the need to look beyond traditional means of evidence production on several topics, including migration. The ambitious framework for global development meant greater demand for data from national statistical offices and data-producing bodies around the world. The Global Compact for Safe, Orderly and Regular Migration also highlights the need to invest much more in increasing countries' capacities to produce better statistics, including by levering big data and new technologies.
>
> Several initiatives were launched at the global and UN level to promote data innovation for policy more broadly. The UN Secretary General's "Data Strategy for Action by Everyone, Everywhere" for 2020–2022, which sets out the Secretary's General vision for a "data-driven transformation" of the UN, mentions big data among the fundamental sources of data to be exploited to improve outcomes for people everywhere and for the planet, for instance, by informing and monitoring climate action.[3] The International Organization for Migration's IOM Data Strategy[4] features data innovation as one of the organization's cross-cutting priorities, highlighting specific actions such as "investigating new data sources and technologies, such as big data, and pioneer novel methods of data analysis, including methodologies for integrating new data solutions with complementary data sources for quality analysis and dissemination and communication of findings". The need to apply data protection and ethical standards and safeguards when using these kinds of data features prominently in both the UN and IOM's Data Strategy. While these aspects are critical with any kind of data, be they traditional or new, the risks of misuse of big data can be far greater, primarily because of the way these are generated – often without the users' full awareness, even in the presence of consent – and because these data are collected by private actors, operating under different incentive structures and outside legal mandates for statistical production. Machine learning and AI methods

can also exacerbate risks by perpetuating biases that already exist in the data they are trained on. These challenges are further discussed below.

The establishment by the UN Statistical Commission of a Global Working Group on Big Data for Official Statistics in 2014 – recently renamed UN Committee of Experts on Big Data and Data Science for Official Statistics (UN-CEBD)[5] – marked the official recognition by the global statistical community of the potential of big data for official statistics, in which a significant deal of scepticism had until then prevailed. The group is composed of 31 UN Member States and 16 International Organizations and its mandate is, among other aspects, to "provide a strategic vision, direction and coordination for a global programme on big data for official statistics" and to "promote practical use of big data sources", as well as to "build public trust in the use of big data for official statistics". Already back in 2009, the UN Global Pulse was created as the "Innovation Lab" of the UN Secretary-General, aiming to draw on big data and artificial intelligence to anticipate and respond to global challenges. More recently, in 2020, the UN Department for Political and Peacebuilding Affairs launched the Innovation Cell to design, experiment and prototype new methods and digital applications, including the use of big data, with a focus on prevention, peace-making and peacebuilding.[6]

In 2018, the UN Secretary General also convened a High-Level Panel on Digital Cooperation "to advance proposals to strengthen cooperation in the digital space" among a variety of actors, including governments, private entities and civil society. The work of the panel resulted in a set of recommendations issued by the UN SG to enhance global digital cooperation in a number of areas, including digital inclusion, human rights protection and trustworthy data innovation.

Finally, in 2019, a UN Interagency Working Group on AI (IAWG-AI) was established to "Identify practical applications of AI, scale solutions for global impact and accelerate progress towards the SDGs".[7] The group is co-led by UNESCO and the International Telecommunications Unit and includes 40 UN agencies and bodies sharing experiences and practices involving use of AI for different purposes from across the UN system.

Aside from UN-led initiatives, several regional initiatives were also launched, such as the Expert Group on facilitating the use of new data sources for official statistics, set up by Eurostat, the statistical office of the European Union, in 2021. Gathering a group of independent domain experts, this initiative aimed to "discuss the framework that would ensure effective and sustainable data access to data collected and held in the private sector for producing official statistics", and resulted in the publication of a report proposing a European approach to the re-use of privately held data for official statistics.[8]

Recent years have also seen greater investments on big data and re-use of private datasets for public good by private actors themselves, particularly after the beginning of the COVID-19 pandemic. In 2017, Meta launched its Data for Good initiative "to empower partners with privacy- preserving tools that strengthen communities and make progress on social issues". The Meta's Data for Good began by sharing maps to assist in humanitarian response in the aftermath of disasters and evolved into a programme providing access to anonymized Meta datasets to academics and practitioners, either as open datasets or upon subscription of a data licensing agreement, for instance, on human mobility, poverty and people's perceptions on a variety of issues. Under the umbrella of its Corporate Social Responsibility, in 2020, Microsoft launched the *Open Data Campaign* to "close the data divide", and build tools, frameworks and templates to facilitate sharing of data to address societal issues at large.[9] Microsoft also launched an AI for Good initiative, whereby it provides technology and resources to support organizations working to address a variety of global challenges.[10]

The COVID-19 pandemic marked a defining moment in the debate on the use of non-traditional data sources, ethics and data responsibility. Amid a rapidly unfolding situation and in the absence of timely and detailed traditional statistics, decision-makers all around the world started turning to new data sources, including big data, to understand and mitigate the impact of the pandemic. During public health crises, such as global pandemics, the capacities of governments to collect data from traditional sources can be severely reduced but the need for accurate and timely data is greatest. Examples from the COVID-19 pandemic response show how non-traditional data were used to understand people's mobility and help anticipate or "nowcast" the spread of the pandemic, as well as to assess the effectiveness of policy measures such as mobility restrictions and stay-at-home regulations.[11] Uses of non-traditional data sources were also seen in other areas, such as understanding public health, impact on the economy or people's perceptions of the pandemic and vaccination campaigns (Tjaden, 2021). However, as documented (Chafetz et al., 2022), even during COVID-19 most of the efforts and partnerships aimed at using non-traditional data for pandemic response were largely fragmented, uncoordinated and often could not be sustained beyond the initial project phase and scaled up. Also, many of these initiatives led to concerns about ethical risks due to insufficiently developed regulatory and ethical frameworks for non-traditional data use.

In sum, there are clear signs of the significant progress made in the conversation about big data and new data sources in public policy. From a prevalent initial scepticism around new data sources, over the past ten years decision-makers and practitioners have increasingly realized the importance of looking beyond traditional statistical systems, at data that are already available but not effectively and systematically harnessed, either due to limited capacities, or inaccessibility, costs, and an underdeveloped regulatory environment. However, despite the rapid proliferation of studies and emerging computational social sciences approaches – see, for instance, Salah et al. (2022), Bosco et al. (2022) and IOM (2023) – the relevance or applicability of big data and re-use of private datasets for decisions related to migration and human mobility is still under scrutiny. To date, the public value of private datasets remains largely hidden due to a series of issues, ranging from ethical aspects and legal uncertainty to access to the data, data quality and empirical challenges, as well as issues of limited and unequally distributed capacities.

4.1.1 Mobile phone-based data

Mobile phone data are collected by mobile network operators (MNOs) in real time whenever users make phone calls, send text messages, turn the phone on or connect to the internet. These signals or digital traces can be very relevant for the analysis of migration and human mobility, particularly the so-called "mobile positioning data" (MPD), which contain information about the locations of mobile phone network subscribers. Among the most common types of MPD are CDRs and signalling data. CDRs are anonymized digital records collected by MNO in real time for every call made, text message sent and every bit of network data used by subscribers. These records include the location of the cell tower to which the SIM (Subscriber Identity Module) card in the sender's phone is connecting, as well as the location of the cell tower nearest the receiving end (IOM, 2021). Signalling data are passive records collected at very high frequency when a mobile phone is on and in a signal coverage area. Both CRD and signalling data can also contain sociodemographic characteristics about the mobile phone subscribers within a country, such as age, sex and preferred language.

These records are most helpful for the analysis of migration and mobility within a country, as people may change SIM cards, but to a certain extent they can also be used for the analysis of international mobility, e.g., when roaming data services are used or to analyse cross-border seasonal mobility or commuting patterns, as well as transnationalism, which are notoriously difficult to analyse using traditional data sources due to their temporary and relatively high-frequency nature (Box 4.2).

The potential of these data sources lies primarily in the timeliness and the high frequency at which information can be updated. MPD usually also have very wide coverage, as they are aggregate records of all SIM card users in a country. Considering that the vast majority of the population globally uses a mobile phone – 5.31 billion people in 2022 were unique mobile phone users, equal to 67 per cent of the global population (We Are Social and Hootsuite, 2023) the potential of these data is quite unique, also in terms of the level of detail about users' sociodemographic characteristics of the subscribers. However, some variations exist by gender and income groups, particularly in low-income countries, and there may be issues of reliability of this information, as the data would reflect the profiles of individuals signing the contract with an MNO, who may not necessarily correspond to the SIM card users.

Box 4.2 Examples of mobile phone data uses

In Namibia, Lai et al. (2019) showed how CDR obtained from the main mobile phone network operator in the country could help model yearly internal migration at the subnational level, with high levels of accuracies if compared with estimates derived from census migration statistics. CDR data have also been employed to analyse displacement in the aftermath of disasters. In some of the pioneering applications of CDR data in these contexts, Lu et al. (2016) used data from 1.9 million mobile phone users in Haiti before and after the disastrous earthquake that hit the country in 2010 to understand patterns of displacement, by comparing data before and after the event. Similarly, in Nepal, CDR data proved to be helpful in estimating patterns of displacement, by comparing changes in movements from the "home location" – the location corresponding to the highest levels of mobile phone activity on any given day – before and after the earthquake (Wilson et al., 2016). In this case, the analysis also included the length of time spent away from the "home location" registered before the event, which can be helpful to understand patterns of return after displacement. Mobile phone data can also be used in conjunction with weather data to model migration due to environmental factors. For instance, Isaacman et al. (2018) used CDR and weather data to model people's displacement during a severe drought in Colombia in 2014. This type of analysis can be crucial to inform appropriate and timely responses in the absence of traditional data, as the incidence of climate-related events increases globally.

Mobile phone data have also been employed in the analysis of refugee integration aspects, for instance of Syrian refugees in Turkey (Salah et al., 2019). In this case, an anonymized dataset including mobile phone records from one million users in Turkey, collected over a period of one year, was made available for research purposes through the Data for Refugees (D4R) Challenge – a non-for-profit initiative co-organized by the main telecom operator in Turkey, Turk Telekom, together with several international and civil society organizations, to better understand and enhance living conditions of Syrian refugees in Turkey.[12] The CDR dataset was unique as it allowed to differentiate the refugee from the non-refugee population with high probability, based on a number of variables provided by the telecom operator. This allowed the researchers to analyse aspects of social integration, proxied by calls made by refugees to nationals, relative to the total number of calls made; it also allowed to study aspects of spatial integration, based on differential patterns of use of urban spaces between the refugee and non-refugee population, as well as economic integration, through the identification of home and work locations and commuting patterns of refugees versus non-refugees. This sort of applications comes with important challenges, including access to the data, lack of coverage of children and, depending on the context, women, and clearly ethical risks that need to be fully assessed and mitigated for in advance.

> Indonesia has been successful at leveraging MPD in a variety of policy areas, including migration and tourism statistics. It has been able to do so thanks to a continued partnership between the country's national statistical office and the main mobile phone network operator in the country (CEBD Handbook).

4.1.2 Internet-based data: social media

Social media data refer to data generated through users' activity on social networking sites, such as Facebook, Twitter, LinkedIn and others. Certain anonymized, aggregated social media data can be publicly and freely available, for instance, through Application Public Interfaces (APIs) offered by these platforms, or can be purchased for a price, or obtained through licensing or data and analytics sharing agreements of various kinds. (Verhulst et al., 2018). Geolocated social media data can be particularly helpful in the analysis of migration and human mobility, as they contain information about active users, be it self-reported information on geotagged posts or automatic geolocation via GPS/log-in activity (Box 4.3). Data from social media platforms, in the form of unstructured text content from users' activity and their interactions with their online networks can provide insights into public opinion or the prevalent sentiment on a variety of topics, through the use of advanced analytical natural language processing techniques.

Clearly, several issues need to be considered: first, the reliability of these data, particularly if they are derived from self-reported information by users of the platform. The number of fake or double accounts can be estimated but cannot be fully determined. Second, there are also challenges in terms definitions used: for one, it is unclear what the definition used by Facebook is, how Facebook classifies 'those who have changed country of residence' – this is based not only on self-reported information but also on geo-referenced activity and network of friends (Spyratos et al., 2019). Definitions are based on proprietary algorithms that are not disclosed by social media platforms, which is one of the key challenges in using these figures for migration research and analysis. Also, the length of time spent by users who have changed their country in the new country of residence – another key variable in traditional migration statistics – cannot be obtained through the advertising platform, meaning these data cannot be compared with traditional statistics based on the UN-recommended definition of an international migrant.[14]

Challenges also relate to the inherent bias of social media platforms: these networking sites are not equally popular across countries or geographies, and even within the same country, use of these platforms varies based on sociodemographic and economic characteristics, as well as cultural norms. Penetration rates, i.e. the number of users relative to the total population in a country, and biases fluctuate, as the popularity of these platforms shifts in time in ways that are hard to predict. There have been attempts to quantify the bias of Facebook data, which would be the first step towards being able to correct it and reduce the noise in these datasets. For instance, Spyratos et al.

Box 4.3 Examples of social media data uses

Estimating numbers of migrants in real time using the Facebook advertising platform

With over 2.98 billion monthly active users by the first quarter of 2023[13], Facebook remains one of the most popular social networking sites globally. Various studies have demonstrated how data from its advertising platform can be used to estimate number of migrants from country *a* in country *b* at any point in time, or movements (changes in prevalent geolocated activity) over a period of time, with relative levels of accuracy when compared to official statistics (Zagheni et al., 2017; Spyratos et al., 2019; Kim et al. in IOM, 2023). The Facebook Network API allows advertisers to select a desired target audience based on a number of characteristics – country of residence/birth, age, sex, education, interests, etc. For a specific selection, the social media application will provide an estimate of the size of the audience (daily or monthly active users), if the group is larger than 1,000 people, for privacy safeguards. Estimates are anonymized and publicly available.

One of the variables offered by the Facebook advertising platform relates to users who 'used to live in country X', or 'live abroad' and 'recently moved', all of which are relevant from a migration perspective, as change in country of residence is one of the key variables to identify the migrant population in a country. Since these data can be extracted in close-to-real time, some scholars have referred to the Facebook Network estimates as a sort of 'real-time census', as the API allows to estimate the number of people who have changed their country in close-to-real time.

The value of these data has also been demonstrated in contexts of displacement due to conflict or disasters, where traditional data are harder to collect. Estimates derived from Facebook of Venezuelan migrants and refugees across 17 destination countries were found to be highly correlated with official statistics in the same countries (Palotti et al., 2020). In the case of Ukraine, Facebook advertising data also proved quite helpful in understanding almost in real time movements from Ukraine to EU countries in the aftermath of the Russian invasion, which can be critical to inform reception and integration policies in destination countries, as well as to inform prompt and targeted humanitarian assistance to people in need (Minora et al., 2022). Leasure et al. (2023) leveraged similar kinds of data from Facebook, together with population data from before the conflict, to nowcast – i.e. estimate in close-to-real time – daily population displacement in the country. This information is extremely difficult to collect via traditional data sources, especially during conflict, but is crucial for humanitarian response to people in need.

(2019) account for differences in penetration rates by age and sex in both country of current and previous residence.

In some cases, the discrepancy between official statistics and Facebook estimates could be a useful indication of emerging trends that have not yet been recorded in official statistics: for instance, Spyratos et al. (ibid.) showed how data from the Facebook advertising platform successfully picked up an increase in Venezuelan migrants and refugees in Colombia and Spain – a trend that was later verified through official statistics for the two destination countries.

These studies show how the potential of social media data lies mostly in nowcasting or describing a phenomenon as it is occurring. This kind of timeliness cannot be achieved through official statistics. The usefulness is not in forecasting or predicting the actual absolute number of migrants in one country at one point in time, but in signalling changing trends that may deserve policy attention as they are happening. These data are also useful in that they may offer a finer description of the characteristics of the migrant population than traditional data. For instance, the Facebook advertising platform also provides information about other variables of interest of the user base, such as self-reported level of education, field of study, personal interests and behaviours, such as 'frequent traveller'. Finally, these data are also amenable to capturing forms of migration that may not appear in official statistics and that fall under the umbrella term of human mobility, rather than migration *strictu sensu*, such as temporary or seasonal movements.

However, official statistics are and will be needed to verify the validity of results from non-traditional data, calibrate models and gradually and iteratively improve the use of non-traditional data. In other words, how do estimates or predictions based on big data fare relative to models based on "ground-truth" (traditional data) in specific contexts and at different aggregation levels (municipalities, regions, countries)? Can any regularities in those discrepancies be identified and eventually used to adjust big data estimates and models, so that these can provide a more accurate depiction of reality? Researchers and practitioners will have to grapple with these questions to demonstrate that certain big data streams can effectively be used to understand migration patterns and behaviours. However, and somewhat paradoxically, this also means that the more systematic use of novel data sources in the future will largely depend on the availability and quality of traditional data, too.

For instance, when it comes to migration forecasting, some studies have demonstrated the potential of using data on Google searches to anticipate movements (see the next section). This is based on the key insight that people interested in migrating to another country might search for information on travels, visas, work permits and routes, whether ahead of or during their journeys. Publicly available tools like Google Trends Index (GTI) show the relative popularity of terms searched on Google, potentially providing insights into people's migration plans. This data source has been explored in several studies. For instance, the Pew Research Centre looked at Arabic-language Google searches of countries such as "Greece" during 2015 and 2016, a period of increased movements of asylum seekers to Europe, particularly from Syria and Iraq. Results showed a correlation between online searches and subsequent arrivals into Greece, as well as with asylum applications in EU countries by Syrians and Iraqi nationals. Similar research was conducted on migration flows from Latin America to Spain, resulting in an apparent correlation between online searches and subsequent migration flows, and to improvements of models aimed at predicting international migration (Wladyka, 2013).

However, no serious migration policymaker or practitioner would trust Google Trends data on their own. These insights would be of little value if not compared with "ground truth" data from traditional sources, which would allow to assess the relative reliability and significance of a particular novel data source in studying migration within a certain locality or on a specific route. Similarly, in studies using Facebook to estimate the numbers of international migrants in different countries, it would be difficult to evaluate the reliability of Facebook as a source without comparing its estimates with data from traditional sources, such as national population censuses (Spyratos et al., 2019). By applying the same kind of validation, time and time again, and noticing how correlation patterns differ over time for the same country or region, it should be possible to estimate an average margin of error and account for it when using estimates derived from Facebook or other social media platforms.

The key to improving evidence on migration and human mobility may hinge on the ability of governments and other entities to use these disparate data sources – both 'big' and 'small' – in combination.

Box 4.4 Social media data to understand people's opinion and sentiment about migration

Publicly available data from social media platforms, such as Twitter, and innovative analytical methods, such as natural language processing, can also be used to understand people's opinion about a variety of topics, such as migration. Although users of social media platforms are a self-selected sample of the entire population, and despite opinions on social media often appearing more polarized than they are in reality, signalling potential shifts in narratives around certain topics, particularly at the local level, and understanding how to break cycles of inaccurate, false or misleading information from spreading further are critical from a policy and programmatic perspective.

Traditionally, data on public opinion are collected through surveys, interviews or ethnographies, all of which have their inherent issues: these are costly exercises and are usually conducted infrequently, meaning they cannot provide timely information about shifts in sentiment or public opinion. They are also usually based on small samples of the national population, so cannot provide detailed information on local-level changes. Most public opinion surveys also contain only a limited number of questions about migration, which can be subject to various interpretations and are therefore not immune from respondent bias. Data from social media platforms offer possibilities to tackle some of these limitations, particularly given their timeliness and spatial granularity, as shown by several studies (McCormick et al., 2017; Freire-Vidal and Graells-Garrido, 2019, Rowe et al., 2021). Opinions about politically controversial topics such as migration can shift quickly in conjunction with specific events, such as a global pandemic, calling for new, innovative ways of analysing the phenomenon in close-to-real time. For instance, Rowe et al. (2021) were able to document increased negative sentiment towards migrants and migration in the early stages of the COVID-19 pandemic in five countries, when concerns about episodes of discrimination of individuals of Asian descent grew in some of these countries; however, the analysis also showed a parallel and contrasting increase of positive sentiment, reflecting the key role many migrant workers employed in essential sectors played during the pandemic.

Once again, the challenges of this kind of analysis cannot be understated. First, the methodological challenges: the search terms and the nuances associated with these terms in various languages significantly affect the interpretation of results. For instance, the term "illegal alien" commonly used in the US policy context to refer to an undocumented migrant would have a very negative connotation in a different context. Further, natural language processing methods, used to assess whether people feel positively, negatively or neutral about certain topics, are still affected by challenges such as attribution of positive/negative sentiment. For instance, the wording of sentence may be negative but overall sentiment expressed towards a certain subject might still be positive; e.g., in the case of sarcastic or rhetorical statements. There are also language translation issues when algorithms are mostly trained in English. Second, there are issues related to access to the data – the platform dictates the conditions and access modalities, which also affects the potential continuity of these data streams for purposes of public policy and raises questions about unforeseen changes to these policies when sudden shifts in ownership and leadership of these platforms occur.[15] Lastly but fundamentally, there are ethical challenges associated with analysis of these data which falls outside the terms and conditions users sign up to when subscribing to these platforms. The possibilities of identification of single users or group of users are real and should be addressed through new regulatory frameworks and guidance on ethical and responsible data. These frameworks should aim at not only protecting users from misuse but also allowing for uses of these data that would benefit society at large, as explained later in the chapter.

Aside from public opinion and sentiment, social media data can also offer insights into migrant inclusion and integration, or "acculturation" – i.e. the level of attachment of individuals to their country of origin and country of current residence, depending on the prevalence of certain topics in their online interactions that are specific to each of those countries (Kim et al. in IOM, 2023).

Social media platforms can also be used to recruit respondents for sample surveys relatively cheaply (via targeted ads) and – depending on the country – effectively, as demonstrated by Potschke in IOM (2023), Perrotta et al. (2021) and Whitaker et al. (2017). Among the main advantages of these methods, aside from the affordability, is the possibility of including hard-to-reach populations in the sample, provided they have internet access. For instance, undocumented migrants may not be included in national household surveys but may still be users of social media platforms. Although these would not be classified strictly as analysis of big/non-traditional data, the possibilities offered by technologies and digital methods to advance migration research should be noted (cfr. Potzschke and Rinken, 2022).

4.1.3 Internet-based data: online search data

Online search platforms constitute another promising source of information on migration and human mobility. Google for instance has over a billion users worldwide and is the most widely used search engine globally (87 per cent of the market), reflecting what people are interested in or curious about (Tjaden et al., 2021). GTI is a publicly accessible tool for search data which shows the relative popularity of certain search terms over time and across locations, in a normalized index (for confidentiality reasons), where 100 is the maximum search interest and 0 is the minimum.

Because individuals may use the internet to prepare for a migratory journey, or at any point during the journey, GTI has been used to anticipate migration patterns worldwide. As mentioned above, several studies show that Google Trends can generate insights on migration plans and patterns, particularly through the comparison between GTI data and subsequent traditional data on migratory movements to a certain country. For instance, these data have been used to predict asylum-related migration to Europe (Connor, 2017), or study migration intentions and predict emigration more generally (Boehme et al., 2020). Aside from anticipating future migration, GTI data also offer opportunities to map diasporas; e.g., to identify localities with high concentration of certain nationalities, as well as their characteristics (age group and sex) and interests. For instance, Newson and Sievers in IOM (2023) estimated the size of the Moldovan diaspora across Italian cities, based on searches on main Moldovan media websites. This kind of analysis can be used for outreach to and targeting of diaspora engagement for specific development programmes that may be in line with their interests (IOM, 2023).

4.1.4 Sensor-based data: satellite imagery

Remote-sensing data, for instance, satellite imagery, offer possibilities to estimate patterns of human movements in specific settings, often in the absence of, or else in combination with, other data sources. For instance, satellite images indicating the presence of lights and lighting of fires in low-income settings have helped understand timings and volume of seasonal movements in West Africa (Bharti et al., 2016). Satellite data also allow to track changes in human settlements, refugee camps, etc., which can also offer information into human mobility patterns, as well as population needs in humanitarian contexts (see for instance the HOT project in the African Great Lakes region[16] and Quinn et al., 2018).

Satellite imagery combined with traditional displacement data allowed to estimate population in highly unstable and resource-poor contexts such as South Sudan, at a level of spatial detail that would not be attainable without using these sources (Tatem et al., in IOM, 2023). These examples in particular highlight the value of the integration of different data sources, novel and traditional, provided that ethical risks are properly assessed and accounted for, given that linkages of different (particularly geospatial) datasets can lead to re-identification, despite the anonymization of individual records. Remote sensing data can also be helpful in estimating future climate-related migration (Sirbu et al., 2021). For instance, individual-level information from longitudinal survey data in Pakistan was linked to measures of climate variability derived from satellites to understand factors driving long-term migration within the country (Mueller et al., 2014). These applications clearly also pose serious ethical challenges, particularly in situations of conflict, political instability, fragility and poor data protection standards, as explained in more detail in the next section.

The rest of the chapter dives deeper into the main challenges related to use of novel data sources for migration and human mobility analysis, outlining steps forward to maximize benefits and minimize risks inherent in the use of non-traditional data.

4.2 What are the obstacles to using big data for migration?

The potential of using new data sources and methods in terms of availability of data and analytical capacities are matched by a series of challenges and open questions.

First, there are issues related to the actual availability of data. This includes concrete access to datasets that may not be publicly available, such as mobile phone network operator data. It also concerns questions of continuity of data streams, consistency, and ultimately autonomy and independence of the data, when datasets from commercial enterprises are re-purposed to address public policy matters. Sharing of data between private owners and public entities not only requires investment and resources – financial, technical and human – but also implies risks that are difficult for private entities to anticipate in what is still an underdeveloped regulatory environment. Despite the multiple examples of such "data collaboratives" – new forms of partnerships between private and public entities around data sharing and use – practitioners would agree that most of these are difficult to sustain beyond the pilot phase, including in cases of clear public needs, such as the COVID-19 pandemic (Chafetz et al., 2022).

Even when data are made available to the research community or public entities to address public policy questions, ranging from how to monitor compliance with mobility restrictions during a pandemic, to understanding gender gaps in access to public transport in certain localities, or how climate change is impacting land and resource use (GovLab, 2023), there is no guarantee that conditions for accessing the data or available variables, definitions or algorithms underpinning the data will not change. For instance, in the case of data from the Facebook advertising platform, very little to no information is provided by the company into how the figures on "migrants" or "expats" are produced. Any changes in aggregate figures overtime might be attributed to changes in the methodology used to estimate audience size, rather than actual changes in the population of active users of Facebook itself.

As noted throughout the chapter, there are quality and interpretation issues with re-purposing private datasets for the analysis of migration. First of all, data from social media platforms or mobile phones are characterized by an inherent bias, insofar as the (even very large) population of users of these devices and platforms is not representative of the general population, and tend to over-represent or underrepresent specific categories of people, depending on their age, sex, socioeconomic background, place of residence and prevailing cultural norms (Cukier and Mayer-Schoenberger, 2013). Even within the same country or people of similar demographics, the popularity of social media platforms changes over time, so the bias is not a static one. Methodologies to quantify this bias and adjust for it exist, but of course a margin of error will remain. The incidence of fake or double accounts or bots may further undermine the quality of the information that can be extracted from social media platforms.

Since most people in the world today use a mobile phone, the issue of representativity may not be as prominent with MPD, but it still exists, as older people tend to use mobile devices to a lesser extent than people in younger cohorts, or as SIM card subscribers may not necessarily correspond to the actual mobile phone user. Also, people may use multiple SIM cards and change SIM card when travelling abroad, which may make it harder to use these data to study international migration or mobility.

Importantly, serious ethical, fundamental human rights and data responsibility issues arise in conjunction with the re-use of private datasets and innovative technologies. The challenges are even more pronounced when data concern individuals in vulnerable situations, such as those facing displacement during conflicts or disasters, or who might not have legal status in a country, and in contexts where migration is highly politicized. There are questions about the effectiveness of existing normative instruments and mechanisms in protecting individual fundamental rights and liberties amidst a context of rapid technological change, and particularly about the use of AI and new technologies in migration policy (e.g., for border management) (Beduschi, 2021; Bircan and Korkmaz, 2021). Openly available location data from social media could be used to track movements of vulnerable groups or to monitor behaviours in ways that could possibly infringe on their civil liberties.

First, the use of novel data sources and technologies have implications for fundamental human rights – including data protection and privacy, equality and non-discrimination, and access to justice (Reichel and Molnar in IOM, 2023). The right to privacy and the protection of personal information is a fundamental human right, regulated by a number of global and regional instruments (UN Development Group, 2017). In the big data age, the risks to privacy arise not only when datasets contain personally identifiable information, such as individuals' names, address or social security number, but also when these identifiers are removed, but datasets are used in conjunction with other information, or contain unique characteristics that may make individuals vulnerable to identification. Indeed, the level of detail of some novel datasets might easily lead to identification of individuals or may contain sensitive information, such as people's ethnicity or gender identity. The question of individual consent also arise with the re-use of private datasets, as the point of re-using existing datasets runs counter to the common data protection principle of "specific and explicit" purpose for data collection (the point is exactly to re-use the data for other, often unanticipated purposes), and of "data minimization", or to collect and store the minimum amount of personal data that is relevant and necessary to a specific purpose; new data sources are instead characterized by an "oversupply" of information (ICRC, 2020). Data protection issues are often also due to limited awareness on the part of users of what data social media companies collect, process and share with third parties (ibid.).

Challenges of equality and non-discrimination arise when use of data and new technologies may exacerbate existing social inequalities and lead to discrimination of certain population groups, on the basis of their personal attributes. This happens because data are rarely neutral, as they are themselves the result of existing societal structures and historical patterns of discrimination against, or outright exclusion of, certain population groups. This is particularly problematic in certain applications of artificial intelligence, where biased data may lead to biased algorithms and therefore biased decisions. Also, when data and new technologies are used to make decisions that impact individuals, people should be able to challenge such decisions and seek redress. In practice, access to judicial remedy becomes much more complicated when decisions are based on data from private actors, collected according to unknown algorithms or methods, or on artificial intelligence tools.

Risks related to breaches of data protection, human security and fundamental rights can be particularly serious for people who are displaced by conflict or violence, or in otherwise vulnerable situations and in need of humanitarian assistance (Sievers et al., 2022). Data handled irresponsibly or unethically can lead to political persecution (See Box 4.6 and UNHCR, 2021), expose individuals to false information (Gibney, 2018), and contribute to surveillance of people, racial profiling and discrimination against people of colour, religious and ethnic minorities, particularly those with an irregular migrant status (PICUM, 2019). The same information that can be used to inform targeted medical assistance in an emergency, for instance, the location of health facilities, can be very sensitive when these populations are the target of violent action by state or non-state actors (DSEG, 2020). Analyses of future movements of asylum seekers can be used by potential destination countries to better prepare and allocate resources or to inform border closure and undermine the right to seek asylum (DSEG, 2020). While these risks are also present in the case of traditional data, to the extent that personal data are collected and individuals and their locations can be identified, the risks with big data and privately held data are heightened because of their volume, their speed and the fact that these data are often collected by private entities, who operate based on different incentive structures (Leslie, 2019; OCHA, 2020).

Several efforts have been made, particularly at the EU level, where a strong and well-developed legal framework exists to protect fundamental human rights, and proposals have been advanced to ensure AI applications are trustworthy and human-centred. Still these risks are to date not adequately covered by existing normative and non-normative standards (Sievers et al., 2022). Further, the regulatory environment around data and new technologies is still nascent in many countries around the world, posing serious risks related to the use of non-traditional data sources and methods in such contexts. The "digital divide" globally not only is visible in disparities in access to and use of digital technologies but also translates into large differentials of capacities to ensure secure sharing of data and prevent breaches that may harm individuals and overall trust in innovation for social good (OCHA, 2020).

In contexts of acute humanitarian crisis or vulnerable situations, the ability of actors to respond effectively, and therefore the well-being of individuals, depends to a large extent on the availability of reliable and timely data (Box 4.5). However, inappropriate or unethical management of data can also harm the same populations. Policy and regulatory efforts should therefore focus on striking a balance between the need for critical information and the implementation of appropriate safeguards to fundamental rights. The key question is how to regulate the re-use of private data for policy in ways that not only respect individuals' privacy but that do not – advertently or inadvertently – harm the individuals that governments and other actors are supposed to serve.

On a more theoretical level, another challenge posed by novel data sources is the risk of a growing disconnect between theory and evidence: when using big data or new methods there may be a tendency to let the data or sophisticated AI and ML technologies 'speak for themselves', without due consideration of the

> **Box 4.5 When big data "goes right": big data and efforts to counter trafficking in persons**
>
> An example of successful and responsible use of big data in migration-related topics concerns data on trafficking in persons. Through its National Human Trafficking Hotline and BeFree Textline, Polaris maintains a large dataset on victims of trafficking in person in the United States. The dataset includes aggregated information based on phone calls, texts and online exchanges received by the Trafficking Hotline related to human trafficking cases in the country. Each request is then assessed for evidence of potential human trafficking, according to detailed protocols. In 2021 alone, the Hotline received 51,073 "signals", (phone calls, texts, online chats, online tip reports or emails) related to human trafficking, of which 13,277 were from victims or survivors of human trafficking. Of these, a total of 10,360 unique incidents of potential human trafficking were identified, upon further evaluation. The statistics are also available by country of origin and broad demographics of the potential victim(s) and type of human trafficking (e.g. sex or labour).
>
> Leveraging intelligence analytics on the Hotline database, Polaris is able to project the potential geographic locations of calls and, through a partnership with PayPal, interrupt cash flows related to trafficking in persons, among other crimes. While data from Polaris only reflect (directly or indirectly) reported cases of trafficking in persons, they can help to identify patterns and, coupled with other sources, be used to dismantle trafficking networks. Polaris is also a founding partner and data contributor to the Counter-Trafficking Data Collaborative,[17] the first global hub on human trafficking, providing access to harmonized data from counter-trafficking organizations around the world and facilitating sharing of information to inform appropriate responses to the phenomenon.

context and of the theoretical evidence underpinning the topic. Just as data scientists and experts place importance on the robustness of the methodological approach, innovation in research methods should be anchored in solid theoretical frameworks and an understanding of the context and the phenomenon. Interdisciplinary approaches will be more and more important to help in correctly interpreting findings, placing them in context and promoting their usability for decision-making.

Policymakers and practitioners aiming to use these data sources for policy or programming purposes should be fully aware of these issues and not expect big data to provide definitive answers. However, rather than a reason to overlook these data, the challenges reinforce the need to combine and integrate these data streams with additional data sources, particularly "ground truth" or traditional datasets as a way to verify the validity of the information

Big data 91

Box 4.6 When big data goes wrong: the case of Rohingya refugees in Bangladesh

The risks of irresponsible data management are not unique to big data or novel data sources. The collection, processing and sharing of personally identifiable information poses risks to individuals, particularly when they are in vulnerable situations. Data protection legislation and non-normative frameworks exist to ensure that the fundamental right to the protection of personal information is safeguarded and to avoid that personally identifiable and sensitive information fall in the wrong hands and be used to harm people. Data on individual displaced by conflict and violence or human rights abuses in their own countries are needed to inform assistance and protection responses by international organizations and non-governmental actors, to understand the scale of the phenomenon and to hold governments to account. However, irresponsible management of such data can heighten the risk of these individuals being identified, located and rounded up by state or non-state actors perpetrating the same abuses, further undermining people's safety and security. A case in point is the biometric registration data collected by UNHCR on over 800,000 Rohingya refugees in Cox's Bazar, which was then shared with Myanmar to assess the feasibility of refugees' repatriation to the country, at times without their full consent, according to a Human Rights Watch report.[18] In 2022, the personal information of over 6,000 asylum seekers in the US was mistakenly posted on the website of the Immigration and Customs Enforcement (ICE) Agency for several hours before being taken down. Such breaches could lead to asylum seekers' family members in home countries facing retribution. Collecting information on victims of human trafficking and modern slavery is equally important to inform policy and programmatic interventions; but insecure data storing or sharing can put people in harm's way by allowing traffickers to identify and locate them.

---

obtained. In practice, it might not always be easy to guarantee some level of "interoperability", or possibility to use traditional and novel datasets in combination, given the complexity and diversity of novel datasets, but this chapter includes a few successful examples to build upon.

Indeed, the value of big data sources as complementary pieces of the puzzle becomes evident in several applications. For instance, and as noted in Tatem et al. in IOM (2023), geographical information is one feature that datasets collected independently and from different sources usually have in common. Datasets relevant to migration and human mobility may be available at different administrative levels in a country or can provide precise GPS location (e.g., in the case of geotagged big data from social media). This offers an opportunity to "link" datasets together, or "overlay" them, allowing to compare them and analyse them in conjunction. Examples of such efforts include linking migration data from censuses with mobile phone data (Wesolowski et al., 2013), smartphone location history and surveys on individual travel histories (Ruktanonchai et al., 2018), surveys on population displacement with census and satellite data to estimate population distribution at fine geographic scales (WorldPop, 2020), and airline passenger data with survey data to measure the impact of disaster on internal migration (Schachter et al., in IOM, 2023). How to successfully integrate different kinds of datasets will be one of the key questions for researchers and data professionals in the years to come, and it will not only require technical skills, but importantly, contextual knowledge and expertise.

There may be possibilities of negotiating agreements with social media companies that provide actors with more control over how the data are being produced and pre-processed and more guarantees of the continuity of the data. Successful initiatives such as the World Bank Development Data Partnership (World Bank, 2023) exist and programmes such as these contribute to clarifying the conditions for success for this kind of partnerships. Innovation in regulatory frameworks, involving all relevant stakeholders, is also needed to address challenges of access in a way that can also drive private entity engagement.

4.3 How can the uses of this type of data be improved?

So how can some of these issues be addressed and what does the future hold when it comes to the use of big data and new technologies in the migration and human mobility sphere? The potential new data sources seems clear, but the value of these insights and actual usability of these methods for policy decisions remains less so. Most of the innovation so far has happened in the academic realm, with strong pushes from UN-led initiatives, and the uptake in terms of policy is not immediately evident, except in humanitarian contexts or during the COVID-19 pandemic. For innovations to be effective and worthwhile, and for their potential adverse consequences and risks to be fully understood and addressed, they should respond to a specific purpose or need. This final section will outline existing initiatives aimed at enhancing the responsible and ethical use of non-traditional methods. These efforts can be classified under four main domains: ethics and data responsibility; cross-sectoral partnerships and access to data and/or technologies; strengthening of capacities to use big data and novel methods; and financing investments in new applications.

4.3.1 *Legislation, ethics and data responsibility: building new regulatory frameworks for using big data and new technologies for migration*

Despite the existence of relevant legislation, particularly at the EU level, technological developments have far outpaced progress in terms of normative frameworks regulating the use of big data and new technologies for policy.

The global context is highly diverse: in certain countries, existing legislation does not allow for the use of novel data sources, while in others, provisions exist for national statistical offices to use non-traditional data given the high cost of traditional data collection systems (UNESCAP, 2021). Relevant frameworks exist, but effective regulation around use of big data and new technologies in the migration realm is insufficient (Bircan and Korkmaz, 2021). Scholars have suggested that from a human rights law perspective, companies or data owners are less well regulated than states and international organizations. International treaties such as the International Covenant on Civil and Political Rights or the European Convention on Human Rights are binding on states but not on private companies, that are simply encouraged to safeguard these rights (Beduschi, 2021). Other non-normative instruments and guiding principles cover collaborations with private entities, such as the UN Guiding Principles on Business and Human Rights, the OCHA Guidance note on partnerships between public humanitarian organizations and the private sector (2020), and the UNSDG (2017) guidance note on data protection principles for big data analytics in the development sector.

A recent trend towards the development and adoption of normative instruments and regulations around the use of big data and new technologies is taking place and is particularly prominent in Europe. The EU General Data Protection Regulation (GDPR), considered as the 'gold standard' in terms of data privacy and security legislation, provides a reference framework for how to protect fundamental human rights in the digital age. Other initiatives at the EU level aim at providing principles and guidance for sharing private sector data, such as the proposed Data Act (or "Proposed Regulation on harmonized rules and fair access to and use of data"),[19] which aims at setting the rules governing the use of data and consistency in rights to access business data from either consumers, other businesses or government entities. Some of the measures will include "means for public sector bodies to access and use data held by the private sector that is necessary for specific public interest purpose", such as responding promptly to a public emergency. These initiatives are promising as they are bound to eliminate the legal uncertainty surrounding the use of big data for public policy purposes, furthering trust in these collaborations.

Still, significant efforts will be required to strengthen normative frameworks and develop new legislation in other parts of the world. This is all the more important, as countries with more limited traditional data collection capabilities are the ones that potentially stand to benefit the most from the responsible and ethical re-use of private datasets. International dialogue and cooperation across a variety of sectors will be necessary, given the need for guidance in the area of data protection and ethical data responsibility principles, and for translation of existing provisions and guidance across different country contexts. In humanitarian situations, for instance, the concepts developed by the Humanitarian Data Science and Ethics Group (DSEG) and contained in *A Framework for the Ethical Use of Advanced Data Science Methods in the Humanitarian Sector* (DSEG, 2020) provides accessible, step-by-step guidance to ensure responsible, purpose-driven and methodologically robust data science applications.

4.3.2 Capacity-strengthening: enhancing capacities to use big data for migration and human mobility

Given the disparities in access to digital technologies and financing for big data and methodological innovation around the world, progress in the use of big data and new technologies for social purposes will largely depend on investments by national, regional and global actors in strengthening human and technical capacities in countries around the world. As mentioned earlier, the value of new data sources can be particularly significant in countries with limited resources for traditional statistical activities, especially in emergency situations. However, the limited capacities to use big data and new technologies effectively are not related to financial resources only, and do not exclusively concern low-income countries.

Even in countries with more advanced statistical systems, there is often a lack of qualified teams within public administrations or in international organizations, individuals who are able to make sense of large and novel datasets and who can extract meaningful and actionable insights from the data (Alemany Oliver and Vayre, 2015). Many organizations face skill and capacity gaps in terms of data science or AI experts that hinder sustainable data collaborations. Clearly, this is exacerbated in countries that have significant traditional data skills gaps. The "data innovation revolution" could be instrumental in closing the digital divide; however, it also risks widening it if adequate investments in responsible data use do not materialize. Without the right skills and capacities, all the data in the world would not be put to effective use.

Investments from the international community should be directed towards several fronts simultaneously – legislative capacities, with new data protection legislation and data responsibility frameworks, and technical, to build the necessary infrastructure for secure data sharing, and human, to guarantee sustainable, effective and purpose-driven big data uses. As seen at the beginning of the chapter, many companies have created specific functions devoted to data for social good and partnerships with the public sector or "data stewards" (Verhulst, 2021). However, several experts have argued that the financial sustainability of the model for private sector actors sharing data and technologies is essential to make the project move beyond the pilot phase and ensure continuity, which again underlines the importance of adequate financing for these initiatives (ibid.).

4.3.3 Partnerships and data access: promoting dialogue between the private and public sector around "data collaboratives"

Since large amounts of data relevant to migration and human mobility are owned by private entities, partnerships between private and public actors working across different domains will be necessary to leverage novel datasets. The term "data collaborative" is often used to describe this kind of partnerships, that centre around access to private datasets for re-use in public policy or social good initiatives, including on migration and human mobility. The GovLab at

New York University has compiled different kinds of data collaboratives in various policy domains around the world, identifying six core models for such collaborations (Verhulst and Young., 2019). These range from companies providing access to specific datasets via public interfaces – for example, Application Programming Interfaces, as in the Facebook example in the chapter, or data platforms – to trusted third-party intermediaries acting as brokers between data holders and users, to prizes and challenges, whereby data holders make datasets available to selected participants in a competition aimed to address specific policy questions (e.g. the examples of CDR data for the Syrian refugees in Turkey).

While successful examples exist, as documented in this chapter, much remains to be done to promote more systematic data collaboratives in the migration field. Verlhust and Young in IOM (2023) suggested four practical steps to ensure the transition from ad-hoc pilot projects to more sustainable collaborative efforts: the first step is to ensure that data collaboratives are purpose-driven, i.e. they respond to a clearly articulated need for information that is currently not answered through existing data. Articulating the demand for new data sources and information is easier said than done but should be the basis of the data innovation application, as this would also help better understand the ethical and risk implications of using novel data sources and have appropriate mitigation and accountability measures in place. The second step is to identify and empower a new profile within each of the parties to a data collaborative or "data stewards" – individuals or teams responsible for determining modalities and conditions for data sharing and promoting such partnerships (Verhulst, 2021). The third step would be to design context-specific models for data collaboratives, responding to the specific questions identified and adapting to the local reality. For instance, within the framework of the Big Data for Migration Alliance (BD4M) – a joint initiative of IOM, the GovLab and the European Commission Joint Research Centre – a "studio" methodology was developed to prototype data collaboratives around key questions, helping to identify enabling conditions, obstacles and incentives for data collaboratives to occur. The fourth and final step is to develop frameworks to enable the responsible and systematic sharing of data.

Building systematic data collaboratives for migration and human mobility will also require bringing together existing knowledge about what innovations are more or less likely to work in different contexts, facilitating exchange of good practices and replication, and sharing this knowledge effectively, through platforms and tools such as the Data Innovation Directory of the BD4M.[20]

4.3.4 Communication and trust: raising awareness and promoting transparency and accountability

Lastly, communicating the value of data and big data uses for social good will be critical to build the public trust required for these innovations to be implemented more systematically, successfully and sustainably. The often-implicit assumption in the "evidence-based" policy mantra is that the availability of reliable and timely data automatically translates into actual use of data for decision-making. In reality, the relationship is not as straightforward, particularly in politically contentious topics such as migration, and especially in an age when basic facts and scientific evidence about any topic are put into question, and traded for ideological positions. Better use of data, be it from traditional or novel sources, requires a societal shift, the promotion of a culture of data on the side of data users – decision-makers – as much as that of the public, the individuals providing the data through their engagement in real and digital life, who will ultimately be affected by those decisions, and who should therefore keep decision-makers to account.

Attempts at participatory data approaches, promoting better inclusion of the "data subjects" and empowerment of individuals so that they can participate in decisions made about their own data have been growing in recent years. For instance, the Humanitarian Open Street Map Team (HOT) works through a network of volunteers and local communities to provide open map data and inform response during disasters. Inclusive approaches of this kind require having appropriate data governance structures that allow for the data subject perspectives to be included, all the while not placing the burden on individuals that may already be in vulnerable situations. It also requires being able to explain to the individuals providing data how the data are being used and what insights derive from them that may help decision-making, in other words greater transparency through communication. Ultimately, understanding the needs of the various groups of individuals who are the target of certain policy or programmatic decisions leads to greater trust and better outcomes for all.

In the era of big data, between risks of misuse of data and risks of "missed use" or the cost opportunity of not using available datasets, traditional data protection principles such as the need for individuals' "informed consent" may not suffice to guarantee public agency and scrutiny over how personal data are used. Concepts such as "digital self-determination" have been advanced as a way to promote autonomy and agency of individuals in the digital age. Although it may seem like quite an abstract concept, digital self-determination is ultimately about power asymmetries and imbalances between organizations collecting the data and individuals providing their own data, either directly or indirectly through the use of digital technologies. Ensuring greater autonomy and inclusion of migrants and mobile populations in decisions about their own data is essential to realize the vision of human-centric innovation and requires innovation in policy, processes and technologies across the data lifecycle (Kalkar, 2022).

In sum, the promises of new data sources and technologies are already clear, but much more experimentation and innovation, particularly in terms of regulation and ethical frameworks for re-use of private data, capacity-building, communication and trust as well as sustainable partnership models between the private and the public sector will be needed for big data to be used effectively for the benefit of migrants and communities at large.

Notes

1. See https://data4migration.org/ (last accessed on 20 May 2023).
2. See https://www.migrationdataportal.org/data-innovation (last accessed on 20 May 2023).
3. See https://www.un.org/en/content/datastrategy/images/pdf/UN_SG_Data-Strategy.pdf
4. See https://publications.iom.int/books/iom-migration-data-strategy-informing-policy-and-action-migration-mobility-and-displacement#:~:text=The%20Migration%20Data%20Strategy%20maps%20out%20a%20path,of%20migration%20data%20for%20sound%20policy%20and%20decision-making.
5. See https://unstats.un.org/bigdata/about/mandate.cshtml
6. See https://dppa.un.org/sites/default/files/innovation_cell_vision_deck_-_042020.pdf
7. See https://aiforgood.itu.int/about-ai-for-good/
8. See https://cros-legacy.ec.europa.eu/content/expert-group-facilitating-use-new-data-sources-official-statistics_en#:~:text=Eurostat%2C%20the%20statistical%20office%20of%20the%20European%20Union,statistical%20offices%20in%20the%20data-driven%20society%20and%20economy
9. See https://www.microsoft.com/en-us/corporate-responsibility/open-data?activetab=pivot1:primaryr6
10. See https://www.microsoft.com/en-us/ai/ai-for-good
11. See https://thelivinglib.org/the-covid-19-review-assessing-the-use-of-non-traditional-data-during-a-pandemic-crisis/ for a review of the use of non-traditional data during the COVID-19 pandemic.
12. For more information, see https://datapopalliance.org/d4r/ (last accessed on 20 May 2023)
13. https://www.statista.com/statistics/264810/number-of-monthly-active-facebook-users-worldwide/ (last accessed on 20 May 2023).
14. In this sense, the inclusion of forms of human mobility in the revised conceptual framework for migration endorsed by the international statistical community, seen in Chapter 2, might facilitate the use of social media or other sources for migration analysis.
15. See for instance https://www.vox.com/recode/2022/10/27/23427106/elon-musk-twitter-privacy-settings-data-direct-messages.
16. See https://www.hotosm.org/updates/scaling-missing-maps-in-africas-great-lakes-region-project-kisoro-district-uganda/ (last accessed on 20 May 2023).
17. See https://www.ctdatacollaborative.org/page/about
18. See https://www.hrw.org/news/2021/06/15/un-shared-rohingya-data-without-informed-consent (last accessed on 25 May 2023).
19. See https://digital-strategy.ec.europa.eu/en/policies/data-act (last accessed on 19 November 2022).
20. See https://www.migrationdataportal.org/data-innovation (last accessed on 23 May 2023).

References

Alemany Oliver, M. and Vayre, J. (2015). Big data and the future of knowledge production in marketing research: Ethics, digital traces, and abductive reasoning. *Journal of Marketing Analytics*, 3, 5–13. https://doi.org/10.1057/jma.2015.1

Beduschi, A. (2021, September) International migration management in the age of artificial intelligence. *Migration Studies*, 9(3), 576–596. https://doi.org/10.1093/migration/mnaa003

Bharti, N., Djibo, A., and Tatem, A. et al. (2016). Measuring populations to improve vaccination coverage. *Scientific Reports*, 6, 34541. https://doi.org/10.1038/srep34541

Bircan, T. and Korkmaz, E.E. (2021). Big data for whose sake? Governing migration through artificial intelligence. *Nature – Humanities and Social Sciences Communications*, 241. https://doi.org/10.1057/s41599-021-00910-x

Boehme, M.H., Groeger, A., and Stoehr, T. (2020). Searching for a better life: Predicting international migration with online search keywords. *Journal of Development Economics*, 142, 102347. https://doi.org/10.1016/j.jdeveco.2019.04.002

Boehme, M.H., Groeger, A., and Stohr, T. (2020). Searching for a better life: Predicting international migration with online search keywords. *Journal of Development Economics*, 142(C). https://doi.org/10.1016/j.jdeveco.2019.04.002

Bosco, C., Grubanov-Boskovic, S., Iacus, S., Minora, U., Sermi, F., and Spyratos, S. (2022). *Data Innovation in Demography, Migration and Human Mobility*. EUR 30907 EN, Luxembourg: Publications Office of the European Union. ISBN 978-92-76-46702-1, https://doi.org/10.2760/958409, JRC127369.

Chafetz, H., Zahuranec, A.J., Marcucci S., Dabletov, B., and Verhulst, S. (2022). The #Data4COVID19 review. Assessing the use of non-traditional data during a pandemic crisis. The GovLab and the Knight Foundation. Available at https://review.data4covid19.org/

Connor, P. (2017). The digital footprint of Europe's refugees. Available at https://www.pewresearch.org/global/2017/06/08/digital-footprint-of-europes-refugees/

Cukier, K. and Mayer-Schonberger, V. (2013). *Big Data: A Revolution That Will Transform How We Live, Work, and Think*. London: John Murray.

Data Science and Ethics Group (DSEG) (2020). A framework for the ethical use of advanced data science methods in the humanitarian sector. Available at www.humdseg.org/sites/default/files/2020-10/Framework%20for%20the%20ethical%20use.pdf

Freire-Vidal, Y. and Graells-Garrido, E. (2019). Characterization of local attitudes toward immigration using social media. Companion Proceedings of the 2019 World Wide Web Conference, May 2019. Pages 783–790. https://doi.org/10.1145/3308560.3316455

Gibney, E. (2018). The scant science behind the Cambridge Analytica's controversial marketing techniques. Available at www.nature.com/articles/d41586-018-03880-4

Global Migration Group (GMG). (2017). *Handbook for Improving the Production and Use of Migration Data for Development*. Global Knowledge Partnership for Migration and Development (KNOMAD), Washington, DC: World Bank. Available at www.knomad.org/publication/handbook-improving-production-and-use-migration-data-development-0.

GovLab. (2023). Data collaboratives explorer. Available at https://datacollaboratives.org/explorer.html

International Confederation of the Red Cross. (2020). Handbook on data protection in humanitarian action. Available at https://www.icrc.org/en/data-protection-humanitarian-action-handbook

International Organization for Migration (IOM). (2021). Assessing the use of Call Detail Records (CDR) for monitoring mobility and displacement. Available at https://www.migrationdataportal.org/resource/assessing-use-call-detail-records-cdr-monitoring-mobility-and-displacement

International Organization for Migration (IOM). (2023). Harnessing data innovation for migration policy. Geneva. Available at https://publications.iom.int/books/harnessing-data-innovation-migration-policy-handbook-practitioners
Isaacman, S., Frias-Martinez, V., and Frais-Martinez, E. (2018). Modeling human migration patterns during drought conditions in La Guajira, Colombia. COMPASS '18: Proceedings of the 1st ACM SIGCAS Conference on Computing and Sustainable Societies. Article n. 31, pp. 1–9. https://doi.org/10.1145/3209811.3209861
Kalkar, U. (2022). Digital self-determination as a tool for migrant empowerment. Available at https://medium.com/data-stewards-network/digital-self-determination-as-a-tool-for-migrant-empowerment-f0dc386c8a41
Lai, S., Erbach-Schoenberg, E.z., Pezzulo, C., Ruktanonchai N.W., Sorichetta, A., Steele, J., Li, T., Dooley, C.A., and Tatem, A. (2019) Exploring the use of mobile phone data for national migration statistics. *Palgrave Communications*, 5, 34. https://doi.org/10.1057/s41599-019-0242-9.
Laney, D. (2001). Three Vs of big data (Volume, Variety and Velocity). *Application Delivery Strategies*, 1–4, META Group Inc.
Latour, B. (2007). *Reassembling the Social: An Introduction to Actor-Networktheory*. Oxford: Oxford University Press
Leasure, D.R., Kashyap, R., Rampazzo, F., Dooley, C.A., Elbers, B., Bondarenko, M., Verhagen, M., Frey, A., Yan, J., Akimova, E.T., Fatehkia, M., Trigwell, R., Tatem, A.J., Weber, I., and Mills, M. (2023). Nowcasting daily population displacement in Ukraine through social media advertising data. *Population and Development Review*, 49(2), 231–254. https://doi.org/10.1111/padr.12558.
Leslie, D. (2019). Understanding artificial intelligence and safety: A guide for the responsible design and implementation of AI systems in the public sector. The Alan Turing Institute. https://www.turing.ac.uk/news/publications/understanding-artificial-intelligence-ethics-and-safety
Lu, X., Wrathall, D.J., Sundsøy, P.R., Nadiruzzaman, Md., Wetter, E., Iqbal, A., Qureshi, T., Tatem, A., Canright, G., Engø-Monsen, K., and Bengtsson, L. (2016). Unveiling hidden migration and mobility patterns in climate stressed regions: A longitudinal study of six million anonymous mobile phone users in Bangladesh. *Global Environmental Change*, 38, 1–7, ISSN 0959-3780, https://doi.org/10.1016/j.gloenvcha.2016.02.002
McCormick, T.H., Lee, H., Cesare, N., Shojaie, A., and Spiro, E.S. (2017). Using Twitter for demographic and social science research: Tools for data collection and processing. *Sociological Methods & Research*, 46(3), 390–421.
Minora, U., Bosco, C., Iacus, S.M., Grubanov-Boskovic, S., Sermi, F., and Spyratos, S. (2022). The potential of Facebook advertising data for understanding flows of people from Ukraine to the European Union. arXiv:2206.12352v2 [stat.AP], 5 July 2022.
Mueller, V., Gray, C., and Kosec, K. (2014). Heat stress increases long-term human migration in rural Pakistan. *Nature Climate Change*, 4, 182–185. https://doi.org/10.1038/nclimate2103
National Human Trafficking Hotline. (2021). National human trafficking hotline data report. Available at https://humantraffickinghotline.org/en/statistics
Palotti, J., Adler, N., Morales-Guzman, A., Villaveces, J., Sekara, V., Garcia Herranz, M., Al-Asad, M., and Weber, I. (2020). Monitoring of the Venezuelan exodus through Facebook's advertising platform. *PLoS ONE*, 15(2), e0229155. https://doi.org/10.1371/journal.pone.0229175.

Perrotta, D., Rampazzo, F., Cimentada, J., Del Fava, E., Gil-Clavel, B., Zagheni, E. (2021). Behaviours and attitudes in response to the COVID-19 pandemic: Insights from a cross-national Facebook survey. *EPJ Data Science*, 10, 17, 1–13. https://doi.org/10.1140/epjds/s13688-021-00270-1.

Platform for International Cooperation on Undocumented Migrants (PICUM). (2019). Data protection, immigration enforcement and fundamental rights: What the EU's regulation on interoperability mean for people with irregular status. Available at https://picum.org/wp-content/uploads/2019/11/Data-Protection-Immigration-Enforcement-and-Fundamental-Rights-Full-Report-EN.pdf

Potzschke, S., and Rinken, S. (2022). Migration research in a digitized world – Using innovative technology to tackle methodological challenges. Available at https://link.springer.com/book/10.1007/978-3-031-01319-5#toc

Quinn, J.A., Nyhan, M.M., Navarro, C., Coluccia, D., Bromley, L., and Luengo-Oroz, M. (2018). Humanitarian applications of machine learning with remote sensing data: Review and case study in refugee settlement mapping. The Royal Society Publishing. https://doi.org/10.1098/rsta.2017.0363

Rowe, F., Mahony, M., Graells-Garrido, E., Rango, M., and Sievers, N. (2021). Using Twitter to track immigration sentiment during early stages of the COVID-19 pandemic. *Data & Policy*, 3, e36.

Ruktanonchai, N.W., Ruktanonchai, C. W., Rhona Floyd, J., and Tatem, A. (2018). Using Google Location Histody Data to quantify fine-scale human mobility. *International Journal of Health Geographics*, 17, 28. https://doi.org/10.1186/s12942-018-0150-z.

Salah, A.A., Pentland, A., Lepri, B., Letouze, E., de Montoye, Y., Dong, X., Dagdelen, O., and Vinck, P. (2019). Introduction to the data for refugees challenge on mobility of Syrian refugees in Turkey. *Data for Refugees Challenge*, 3–27. Available at https://dblp.org/rec/books/sp/19/SalahPLLMDDV19.html

Salah, A.A., Korkmaz, E.E., and Bircan, T. (2022). *Data Science for Migration and Mobility*. Oxford University Press.

Sievers, N., Griesmer, L., Rango, M., Trigwell, R., and Jusselme, D. (2022). Ethical considerations in re-using private sector data for migration-related policy: A practitioners' perspective. Available at https://gmdac.iom.int/sites/g/files/tmzbdl1416/files/documents/Ethic_05_RA.pdf

Sirbu, A., Andrienko, G., Andrienko, N., Boldrini, C., Conti, M., Giannotti, F., Guidotti, R., Bertoli, S., Kim, J., Ioana Muntean, C., Pappalardo, L., Passarella, A., Pedreschi, D., Pollacci, L., Pratesi, F., and Sharma, R. (2021). Human migration: The big data perspective. *International Journal of Data Science and Analytics*, 11, 341–360. https://doi.org/10.1007/s41060-020-00213-5

Spyratos, S., Vespe, M., Natale, F., Weber, I., Zagheni, E., and Rango, M. (2019). Quantifying international human mobility patterns using Facebook Network data. *PLoS ONE*, 14(10), e0224134. https://doi.org/10.1371/journal.pone.0224134. Kim et al., in IOM, 2023.

Tjaden, J. (2021). Measuring migration 2.0: A review of digital data sources. *Comparative Migration Studies*, 9, 59. https://doi.org/10.1186/s40878-021-00273-x

Tjaden, J., Arau, A., Nuermaimaiti, M., Cetin, I., Acostamadiedo, E., and Rango, M. (2021). Using "Big Data" to forecast migration. Available at https://medium.com/@UNmigration/using-big-data-to-forecast-migration-8c8e64703559.

UN Conference of the Parties to the UN Convention against Transnational Organized Crime. (2021). Successful strategies for addressing the use of technology to facilitate trafficking in persons and to prevent and investigate trafficking in persons. Available at https://www.unodc.org/documents/treaties/WG_TiP_2021/CTOC_COP_WG.4_2021_2/ctoc_cop_wg.4_2021_2_E.pdf

UN Development Group. (2017). Data privacy, ethics and protection: Guidance note on big data for achievement of the 2030 agenda. Available at https://unsdg.un.org/sites/default/files/UNDG_BigData_final_web.pdf

UNESCAP (2021). Big data for Population and Social Statistics. Issue no. 29, April 2021. Available at https://www.unescap.org/kp/2021/big-data-population-and-social-statistics.

UN High Commissioner for Refugees. (2021). Statement on refugee registration and data collection in Bangladesh. Available at www.unhcr.org/news/press/2021/6/60c85a7b4/news-comment-statement-refugee-registration-data-collectionbangladesh.html

UN Office for the Coordination of Humanitarian Affairs (OCHA) (2020). Note #3: Data responsibility in public-private partnerships. https://centre.humdata.org/guidance-note-data-responsibility-in-public-private-partnerships/

Verhulst, S. G. and Young, A. (2019). The potential and practice of data collaboratives for migration. In Salah, A., Pentland, A., Lepri, B., & Letouzé, E. (Eds.), *Guide to Mobile Data Analytics in Refugee Scenarios*. Cham: Springer. https://doi.org/10.1007/978-3-030-12554-7_24.

Verhulst, S. G. (2021). Reimagining data responsibility: 10 new approaches toward a culture of trust in re-using data to address critical public needs. *Data & Policy*, 3, E6. https://doi.org/10.1017/dap.2021.4

Verhulst, S., Young, A., and Srinivasan, P. (2018). An introduction to data collaboratives. Creating public value by exchanging data. Available at https://datacollaboratives.org/static/files/data-collaboratives-intro.pdf

We Are Social and Hootsuite. (2023). Digital 2022 global overview report. Available at https://datareportal.com/reports/digital-2022-global-overview-report

Wesolowski, A., Buckee, C.O., Pindolia, D.K., Eagle, N., Smith, D.L., Garcia, A.J., and Tatem, A.J. The Use of Census Migration Data to Approximate Human Movement Patterns across Temporal Scales. PLoS ONE 8(1): e52971. https://doi.org/10.1371/journal.pone.0052971

Whitaker, C., Stevelink, S., and Fear, N. (2017). The use of Facebook in recruiting participants for health research purposes: A systematic review. *Journal of Medical Internet Research*, 19(8), e290. https://doi.org/10.2196/jmir.7071

Wilson, R., Erbach-Schoenberg, E., Albert, M., Power, D., Tudge, S., Gonzalez, M., Guthrie, S., Chamberlain, H., Brooks, C., Hughes, C., Pitonakova, L., Buckee, C., Lu, X., Wetter, E., Tatem, A., and Bengtsson, L. (2016). Rapid and near real-time assessments of population displacement using mobile phone data following disasters: The 2015 Nepal earthquake. Available at https://doi.org/10.1371/currents.dis.d073fbece328e4c39087bc086d694b5c.

Wladyka, D. (2013). The queries to Google Search as predictors of migration flows from Latin America to Spain. Available at https://core.ac.uk/download/pdf/294832951.pdf.

World Bank. (2023). Development data partnership. Available at https://datapartnership.org/.

WorldPop. (2020). South Sudan 2019 gridded population estimates from census projections adjusted for displacement, version 2.0. Available at https://data.worldpop.org/repo/docs/dooley2021description/South_Sudan_population_estimates_with_displacement.pdf

Zagheni, E., Weber, I., and Gummadi, K. (2017). Leveraging Facebook's advertising platform to monitor stocks of migrants. Available at https://onlinelibrary.wiley.com/doi/abs/10.1111/padr.12102

Part II

Data availability on key migration topics

5 Migration and sustainable development

Measuring progress

5.1 The migration-development nexus: what is it and why is it important?

Often emigration has been seen as a problem resulting from poor development, and immigration as a challenge to a country's economy and society. Over the last 20 years these perspectives have started shifting, as, for example, there has been a growing recognition that migration decisions are more complex than previously thought, and that if managed effectively, migration has the potential to bring development benefits to origin and destination communities. The "migration–development nexus" has become a topic of great focus in the past decades. The linkages between migration and development have become important for policymakers, academia, the international community and civil society alike, who have tried to understand both the effects of migration on development and vice versa.

The nexus has been defined as "the totality of mechanisms through which migration and development dynamics affect each other" (Carling, 2017). Migration can affect development and development can affect migration, and both relationships can have negative, positive, neutral or mixed impacts. These impacts differ at the individual, community, national or other levels, and for all those involved; for example, for migrants themselves, those in the community they grew up in or live in today. They may be normatively or otherwise defined. This all can be conceptually complex; what is meant by development varies and this is itself a moving conceptual target as theoretical and policy debates evolve.

How might this look on the ground? Major migration and development questions on which there has been sustained global policy attention include how far economic remittances boost development in origin countries, and what the effects of health workers emigrating are on origin countries. However, all of the following questions are also related to migration and development: How many people tried and did not manage to leave Bangladesh last year? How many entrepreneurs in Silicon Valley are migrants, and are they more likely to set up businesses immediately or after a few years of living there (Mosler Vidal, 2021)? How can water pumps in rural Ecuador be financed if government resources are limited? What happens to Bostonians' wages when

DOI: 10.4324/9781003266075-7

Dominican migrants arrive in town to work? Where are Italians working in Lugano every day legally insured? Do children in China with emigrant parents get good grades? How many nurses in an average Canadian emergency ward are migrants? These are all about migration and development, showing the range of policy questions that countries have an interest in answering. These also show how the development implications of migration are highly heterogenous (de Haas, 2010) and can be linked to poverty, education, climate change or any other number of topics, on different levels and in different places.

There has been increasing interest in how to leverage the benefits of migration for development in policy and academic debates. However, right now, there are simply not enough quality data on migration and development to know how to do this effectively. This has long been recognized at global level. The Declaration of the 2013 High-Level Dialogue on International Migration and Development emphasized "the need for reliable statistical data on international migration, including when possible on the contributions of migrants to development in both origin and destination countries;" the Global Forum on Migration and Development (GFMD) since 2007 has emphasized the need for accurate, policy-relevant and timely data on migration and its impacts on economic, social and sustainable development in countries of origin, destination and transit (GFMD, 2008; UN, 2016). Other resolutions, statements and declarations have also highlighted the need to improve migration and development data (UN, 2015).

But what is meant by data on migration and development? One probably thinks of information on remittances or maybe diaspora contributions. However, it is much more than this, and relevant research has recently grown and diversified accordingly (Clemens et al., 2014). All of the following data points are relevant to migration and development: school enrolment rates in a city by migratory status, number of labour rights violations of migrant domestic workers in a continent and number of new businesses set up by return migrants in a neighbourhood. Data relating to migration and development are broad and complex, and scholarship in this area is very active. Meanwhile, many exciting initiatives exist to improve data on migration and development on the ground, led by different actors.

The relevance of this topic cannot be overstated. While migration dynamics continue to evolve, the world today faces serious development challenges. It will be necessary for policymakers in the next decades to understand more about the links between migration and development; put simply, they cannot afford not to. There is a huge opportunity for migration and development experts in countries, international organizations, academia and elsewhere to combine their expertise and collaborate to achieve better outcomes for all and the planet. The contributions of migration to development can be strengthened while its negative effects limited, and policies in the realms of migration and development can complement, rather than detract from each other's effectiveness. Having better information to feed into this dialogue is crucial and with better data, much can be achieved.

5.1.1 Context of migration and development debates

Before discussing the key types of data on migration and development that may be needed at global level to inform policy, it is necessary to understand the broader context of these debates. Academic debates on migration and development are lively; several theoretical frameworks have shaped thought on migration and development and are helpful to contextualize the ensuing discussion on data (for more comprehensive review and analysis, see de Haas, 2010).

The new economics of labour migration (NELM) dominant in the 1980s and 1990s saw migration essentially as a way for households to maximize income, where individuals migrated to diversify household risk and support the family through remittances (Stark and Bloom, 1985; Taylor, 1999). Emerging livelihood perspectives saw migration as a deliberate strategy to overall improve livelihoods, defined much more widely than just through income (McDowell and de Haan, 1997; de Haan et al., 2000). Meanwhile, transnationalism perspectives recognized that migrants have transnational identities and that the migration process and its impacts are understood only when considering together the different places it links (see Glick Schiller et al., 1992; Levitt and Glick Schiller, 2004; Castles et al., 2014). The emerging capabilities approach to human development, emphasizing that development is "a process of enlarging people's choices" and that welfare is multi-dimensional (UNDP, 1997), inspired a new migration theoretical framework, which saw the ability to migrate as a specific capability that reflects social processes and development outcomes (Carling, 2019; de Haas, 2021). Many scholars use hybrid frameworks today.

Data relevant to each debate vary. For example, in the context of livelihood approaches, information on migrants' and non-migrants' livelihoods and on structural factors affecting local contexts and opportunities is needed. Scholarship using these various frameworks has produced its own analysis, and the evolving theoretical context and methodologies used have led to many empirical findings across migration and development topics, often conflicting. Did the arrival of Cuban workers in Miami have no effect on native workers' wages? Or did wages actually go down for some native workers (see Clemens and Hunt, 2019)? Indeed, navigating the evidence base on migration and development can be confusing, as data presented are often based on different sources, methods and assumptions. Further, it can be difficult to separate findings from their context of charged and often-changing public and policy opinion – described by de Haas (2010) as the "migration and development pendulum" swinging between optimism and pessimism on the topic – and know how to interpret the data. Ultimately, while research findings can be highly contextual and difficult to extrapolate to other settings, countries around the world would benefit from improved methodologies and data availability on key migration and development topics at global level, as well as ongoing dialogue on how to generate better data on this nationally. Important questions for countries remain:

108 *Data availability on key migration topics*

How is this relevant to our specific national context? What data can we try to generate that would be useful?

This chapter takes a broad view of migration and development data, to mean information about any linkage between migration and development. Like the rest of this book, it will have a special focus on data that can be regularly produced or collected by countries, that is as comparable and representative as possible, and that may be most useful to policymakers.

5.2   What is meant by data on migration and development?

This section first discusses data on three selected topics that have been classically considered central to migration and development, outlining typical data sources, existing datasets and selected issues related to production of statistics. It goes on to discuss other key areas of data on migration and development. This is not comprehensive and instead introduces the reader to the wider topic and signposts to a few areas of interest.

5.2.1   Key migration and development data topics

5.2.1.1   Economic remittances

Remittances, usually understood as "the money or goods that migrants send back to families and friends in origin countries" (IOM, 2023), are commonly the most well-known link between migration and development. These are one way in which migrants can affect development in the communities or countries they come from and are often of much interest to countries of origin. Statistics on the value of remittances received and the costs of sending these are available for most countries around the world. The World Bank provides annual estimates of global remittance flows based on national balance of payment statistics, and of the cost of sending remittances, in the Remittance Prices Worldwide database. Though useful, these estimates are far from accurate due to several well-documented methodological challenges (Clemens and McKenzie, 2014; Alvarez et al., 2015; Plaza and Ratha, 2017). For example, remittance flow statistics often overestimate amounts of money sent back by migrants, as they include embassy, UN and foreign companies' staff salaries. Beyond this, other key areas of relevant information include remittance use at household or community level, for example exploring how far these are used for healthcare, education and other types of expenditures. Few comparable data on this exist that are nationally produced.

Overall, current availability of remittance data is linked to concerted efforts by the World Bank and IMF, with national governments and central banks, to improve reporting. What is counted counts: if a word association game were played in policy circles, "remittances" would likely be revealed as the primary term linked to "migration and development". Remittances and their punchy accompanying annually record-breaking figures captured much policy attention. Indeed, remittances support millions of households worldwide, have exciting poverty-reduction potential and consumption-smoothing properties, and dwarf official development assistance globally (Ratha, 2007). However, these properties have been contextualized, often found to vary considerably across contexts, and additionally, some negative effects of remittances on individuals, households and countries have been found alongside their benefits (see Amuedo-Dorantes, 2014). While economic remittances are an important piece of the puzzle on migration and development and data on this are certainly relevant, scholarship has broadened to focus on other ways migration may support development (Clemens et al., 2014). Today we know that economic remittances reflect just one of the many links between migration and development. In some ways, remittance statistics for migration and development are similar to what GDP figures are for a country's development – though a significant area of data and relevant to policy, one with limits.

5.2.2 Diaspora contributions

Diasporas, sometimes referred to as expatriates or transnational communities, can play an important role in migration and development (see Newland and Plaza, 2013). Today diaspora engagement is of much policy interest, particularly to countries of origin looking to leverage this for national development – for example, through programmes to facilitate transfer of knowledge and skills or to encourage return migration – and many relevant initiatives have been established (see de Haas, 2006). Accurate data are needed for a range of policy objectives, at the most basic level to reach diaspora members. Nevertheless, quality data on numbers and profiles of diaspora members around the world are scarce. The concept of diaspora itself is hard to define and measure. There is no single statistical definition of diaspora (IOM, 2020), and operational definitions differ among governments and organizations, often making reference to intangible phenomena that are impossible to reliably quantify. While no official, comparable statistics exist on global diaspora populations, there are useful proxies, such as emigrant stocks, or the number of a country's citizens or native-born population residing abroad. Some countries include questions on emigration in their censuses or use other mechanisms to try to estimate how many of their nationals live abroad. Others, such as Nigeria, manage diaspora population databases based on voluntary online registrations (NIDO, n.d.). Though such initiatives are useful, they often have imperfect coverage, giving an incomplete picture of diaspora populations, and cannot be compared across countries as they may use different definitions. Further, in some countries, several projects with similar aims exist but are not integrated (see the case of Jamaica in IOM, 2021). Some relevant data on diasporas are available from international organizations. For example, IOM has conducted over 150 surveys on diaspora communities and works to standardize methodologies to do this and to better understand and quantify diasporas' diverse contributions to development (IOM, 2022). There are also regional-level studies or summaries of evidence (see African Union, 2020).

Diasporas do not only send economic remittances. Social remittances, a growing area of focus, are "the ideas, behaviours, identities and social capital that flow from receiving- to sending-country communities" (Levitt, 1998, p. 927). Migrants may share innovative new ideas acquired as part of the migration process, from health-related knowledge to political values or new technological skills, with their networks back home or elsewhere (Levitt and Lamba-Nieves, 2011). Though social remittances are more complex to quantify than economic remittances, research has explored how these can influence gender roles, health, population growth, democracy diffusion and many other topics in both origin and destination communities (see Vari-Lavoisier, 2020 for an overview).

Diaspora populations may engage in investment, philanthropy, tourism and other activities that could affect development in origin countries (see Mendoza and Newland, 2012, for more). Overall, limited comparable data exist on the broad topic of diaspora engagement, and it is therefore hard to understand the impacts of diaspora groups on different types of development. More systematic ways to measure specific kinds of diaspora contributions and impact are needed, especially given their rising prominence in migration policy frameworks, and countries' interest in creating policy on this. Some areas of diaspora engagement are easier to quantify than others – for example, diaspora investment funds, transnational loans or diaspora bonds are relatively easier to measure than social remittances. Given it is a broad area, efforts could be made to prioritize which types of engagement to monitor and to conceptualize innovative standardised ways to do this across countries.

5.2.3 Migrant rights

Migrants often face different types of vulnerabilities or risks to their rights at various stages in the migration process, including before, during and after migration. Several international human rights treaties and protocols grant rights to migrants by virtue of their humanity, such as the 1948 Universal Declaration of Human Rights (UN, 1948). Other key treaties from international public law also convey migrants' rights, such as the 1951 Convention relating to the Status of Refugees (UNGA, 1950). There is a continued need for more information to protect migrants' rights throughout the migration process. Migrant rights issues and data are highly relevant for policymaking, particularly in the context of rights-based approaches to development.

Migrant rights may be monitored by measuring rights granted in principle or in practice (IOM, 2022). The former is relatively straightforward and involves examining relevant treaty ratifications, national laws and other legal documents. There are several data sources that measure migrant rights in principle, including various managed by the UN Office of the High Commissioner for Human Rights (OHCHR, n.d.). Generating data on migrant rights in practice and examining whether migrants' rights are upheld in reality is much more challenging, and official statistics on this are generally not available. Some initiatives attempt to do this through proposed indicator frameworks, such as by the Global Knowledge Partnership on Migration and Development (KNOMAD), which includes indicators on the rights to non-discrimination, education, health and decent work (Cernadas et al., 2015; Hernandez, 2017). Other relevant types of data include events-based data, which track specific violations of migrant rights (e.g., press releases and media, government or NGO reports) and data based on expert judgements (e.g., reports from advocacy groups and academia). Some relevant data may be collected on an ad hoc basis, often through surveys (e.g. the Regional Mixed Migration Secretariat's Mixed Migration Monitoring Mechanism Initiative). Data on migrant rights have distinct strengths and limitations. For example, they tend to include necessary contextual information to understand the situation of migrants in a given country, and considering that coverage varies widely, these data are generally not comparable across countries.

5.2.4 Other areas

Other topics central to migration and development debates include labour migration and related issues (see GMG, 2017). Often countries are interested in more information on this in the context of labour migrants' contributions or impacts on employment or output in different labour markets. Within this broad field, different data areas exist with varying levels of availability, such as recruitment costs and skill profiles of different migrant groups (including potential migrants or return migrants). This is an area of data where some international data standards are available, including on statistical definitions of migrant workers. Sometimes different datasets in a country are managed under a national Labour Market Information System (LMIS). Labour migration is also an active area in academia, with emerging research on targeted questions such as how a worker's location impacts their productivity, all with a view to better understand the bidirectional links between labour migration and development.

Taking a sectoral lens – in other words examining the relationship between a particular sector (such as education) and migration – myriad other topics bring alive the migration and development nexus. For example, migration has potential to impact health, and is considered a social determinant of health. Migration can increase vulnerability to ill health through anything from exposure to harmful chemicals during migrant workers' shifts or through decreased access to health services, or conversely, migration can improve migrants' health or that of others in their networks through increased resources to spend on healthcare, or access to healthcare with better trained medical personnel. Not only is protecting migrants' health important to safeguard their wellbeing, but it is a prerequisite for migrants to work and contribute to the social and economic development of communities of origin and destination. Relevant data may include profiles on migrants' health status and their disease burden, details on migrants' access to health services or share of medical professionals in a country who are migrants. Depending on the sub-topic of interest, relevant data can be found in a country's civil registration system, population censuses, household surveys, such as Demographic and Health Surveys (DHS) or in administrative sources; for example, hospital records. Data on migration and health form a complex and sometimes fragmented landscape, emblematic of many other sectors' links to migration, which policymakers have to navigate if they wish to create informed policy on anything from COVID-19 vaccines for migrants to recognition of nurses' qualifications across countries. See Box 5.1 for an example of how to improve data on this, and Chapter 7 for more information.

The points above mainly focus on how migration affects development. This is where countries and international organizations have typically invested their data efforts, and as a result more comparable cross-country data on this are available. Meanwhile, scholarship has increasingly focused on how different development dynamics affect migration. For example, there have been efforts to define concepts further linked to capabilities approaches, such as migration aspirations, migrant decision-making and involuntary immobility (see Andersson and Siegel, 2019), though these have generally not yet had as significant impact on countries' own regular data collection.

Box 5.1   Migration and health: diverse initiatives

There is much active research and analysis on the links between migration and health; see a selection of initiatiaves below.

- **Evaluating migrants' health.** The Government of Sri Lanka, in co-ordination with IOM, published a compendium of migration health research, including key data on the health of different types of migrants and their disease burdens (IOM, 2017). This led to the formulation of a National Migration Health Policy and Action plan for Sri Lanka.
- **Assessing migration and health policy.** The Migration Integration Policy Index (MIPEX) health strand uses 38 indicators, refined by over 100 experts, to measure how equitable a country's policies are for migrants. This assessment has been carried out in 56 countries (MIPEX, n.d.). This is discussed in more detail in Chapter 7.
- **Improving data accessibility and partnering for knowledge production.** With various academic institutions and researchers, IOM's Migration Health Division (MHD) developed the online Migration Health Research Portal as a repository of relevant IOM data and helped set up the Migration Health and Development Research Initiative (MHADRI), a network of migration health academics, civil society, and others researching the relationship between migration and health.

There are too many topics related to migration and development to list here, and they vary in priority across contexts; relevant data could refer to information on migration and almost any sector. For example, data on migration and climate change and the environment (see Chapter 6), gender (Hennebry et al., 2021), trade (Genc, 2014; IOM 2021), urban planning (IOM, n.d.), the effects of migrant return and re-integration programmes, integration and public perceptions of migrants in developing countries, and many others. These all have differing levels of data availability and their own set of challenges and opportunities.

A few other limitations and gaps on the overall state of the migration and development evidence base are important to note. The tendency has been to study the causes and impacts of migration separately (de Haas, 2010). This means that data on migration and development are often not only seen thematically (as per the list of topics above) but also in terms of direction of impact, so that evidence tends to be either about how migration affects development or how development affects migration, but usually not both. To date, data collection and analysis on migration and development have focused disproportionally on migration from low- to high-income countries. As in fact migration flows between low- and middle-income countries, or "South-South migration" are comparatively larger, this means we may not fully understand how these migration and development phenomena may look in other contexts. Often evidence on migration and development focuses on the country level or other relatively large unit of analysis so that data focusing on the individual level is lacking, and evidence is often not migrant-centric. Further, there is a lack of data on the effects of migration and development programmes and policies implemented by national authorities and international organizations (Ardittis and Laczko, 2008).

5.3 What are the obstacles? Common challenges

Many common challenges identified in preceding chapters in this book also apply; for example, fragmentation of migration data governance, limited resources and different statistical definitions. In turn, challenges to generating the migration and development data that are needed in a particular policy context will be specific to the context and topic at hand. This section discusses selected challenges in producing statistics on migration and development, focusing on common obstacles impeding national-level data collection and use.

Every data challenge is different. For example, data on the number of migrants contributing to the garment or IT sector may be unavailable because relevant labour market data do not include information on how many workers are migrants and non-migrants in each sector. Information on tuberculosis rates for migrants may not be available in a city because only paper notification records are used, and these can get damaged or lost. However, there are some challenges common to the national production of official statistics on migration and development. Here are four, non-exhaustive challenges:

constrained statistical capacity, nature of hard-to-reach populations, inadequate coordination and limited political will.

As seen in the preceding chapters, the overall state of the global evidence base on migration is patchy. We have seen how many countries struggle to generate "basic" data – for example on migration flows. Therefore, it is hardly a surprise that countries are often unable to generate data on migration sub-topics, including its relationship to development which is complex and often requires sophisticated design and analysis to make meaningful conclusions. How can a country that does not know how many migrants live inside it know how those migrants may affect national healthcare service provision? Data will be constrained by different capacity limitations. Even if necessary expertise is available in the country, limited resources may force those in National Statistical Offices (NSOs) to prioritize certain migration data over others – for example, to produce estimates of diaspora populations every year but not to embark on new targeted data collection on how exactly they support their families. Often migration and development data are simply not prioritized enough; for example, some international donors tend to fund more projects around border controls and countering human trafficking and fewer on diaspora benefits (Chappell and Laczko, 2011).

Some migrant groups are part of hard-to-reach populations that are not easily counted by traditional data collection systems. For example, migrant domestic workers or homeless migrants, who may be at particular risk of rights violations or poor wellbeing, do not always appear in official statistics. Other examples include migrants while they are travelling, unaccompanied minors, many IDPs, undocumented migrants, seasonal workers who may not change their primary place of residence, migrants living in group quarters, migrants at risk or facing multiple and intersecting forms of discrimination (such as LGBTIQA+ individuals), and others, all of whom may have urgent health, educational, economic and other needs. Certain sub-groups may be physically or otherwise difficult to reach. Often, as in the case for undocumented migrants, they are not included in official sampling frames of household surveys or censuses or are by definition excluded from administrative records, such as population registers and residence permits (UNECE, 2012; UN DESA, 2017). Some may be purposefully elusive – for example, unwilling to be included in data collection exercises, for fear of possible detection or deportation by law enforcement. While several indirect methods exist to estimate hard-to-reach populations, it often remains difficult for policies and programmes to reach the most vulnerable, simply because data on them are insufficient. See Box 5.2 for some examples of how to address these issues.

Poor or non-existent coordination across relevant government and other actors, a common issue for many types of migration statistics, can be a special challenge for data on migration and development, as this can require high levels of inter-ministerial coordination, given that relevant data are often collected by different ministries. Often data producers and users from different areas of government and different levels must work together – for example, an

Box 5.2 Data collection and research on hard-to-reach migrant groups

The Joint Data Center on Forced Displacement (JDC) helps include some migrants who may be hard to reach in data collection, to better understand their needs. For example, they extend survey sampling frames to include those affected by forced displacement. The World Bank and the Office of the United Nations High Commissioner for Refugees (UNHCR) carried out the Kalobeyei Socioeconomic Profiling Survey in Kenya, a survey that included refugees and aligned its questions with socioeconomic indicators from various existing Kenyan household surveys. This generated quality, comparable, representative information on refugees' poverty status and other topics (UNHCR and World Bank, 2020).

The HelpAge International and UNHCR report *A Claim to Dignity: Ageing on the Move* evaluated the situation of older persons on the move in El Salvador, Honduras, Colombia, Ecuador and Peru, including those with disabilities (UNHCR and HelpAge International, 2021). This shed light on an under-studied migrant sub-group and the intersectionality between ageing and being a migrant. The results showed this sub-group was often more vulnerable – 48 per cent of those with disabilities interviewed reported being abused, in contrast to 29 per cent of those without disabilities.

NSO, a health ministry at the central level, a local healthcare service provider and migration policymakers. Some ministries or offices may be unaccustomed to making conceptual or working links to the migration world. To this end, producing statistics on migration and development in a country often necessitates strengthening cooperation and coordination between NSOs, ministries and actors outside of government, and usually requires raising awareness about the importance of this early on.

Limited political will to explore a particular policy issue can be a challenge to improving migration and development data. The political economy of migration and development policy can dictate where data collection is focused. For example, a country may choose to invest in counting how many of their diaspora members are doctors, but not how a changing climate is affecting farmers in that country, leading them to move. This in turn can negatively impact statistical capacity in a country to understand the migration and development nexus in that context. As there is sometimes a lack of awareness of the importance of generating data about migrants in a particular sector, this is given insufficient priority in policy agendas and related budget allocations.

In addition, important methodological challenges remain in understanding the links between migration and development. Though these are particularly relevant for academia or others designing studies on migration and development, they are relevant for all actors. Regardless of the theoretical framework used, researchers face numerous methodological challenges when assessing the causal impacts of migration on development (Andersson and Siegel, 2019). This has often meant that studies use different approaches and look at different units of analysis and outcome areas, making it difficult to draw overarching conclusions. The effects of migration on development or vice versa may differ or only show over time; it is very difficult to account for temporality in studies. Qualitative data can help elucidate some migration and development sub-topics further; for example, data gathered through interviews can complement quantitative data by documenting in more detail the experiences of certain migrant sub-groups, information that cannot easily be captured by quantitative tools. However, it can be difficult to collect reliable qualitative data at scale and to combine this in a standardized way with quantitative data. These and many other methodological challenges are more extensively explained in the migration and development literature (see, for instance, Andersson and Siegel, 2019 for a clear set of challenges in establishing a causal link between migration and development).

5.4 How to improve data on migration and development?

This section dives into solutions to improve the evidence base on migration and development. Firstly, it explores one opportunity – the 2030 Agenda for Sustainable Development (2030 Agenda) as a key global policy process that can help influence this. Secondly, it presents several examples of innovative approaches and initiatives to improve migration and development data.

5.4.1 The 2030 Agenda for Sustainable Development

The 2030 Agenda for Sustainable Development was adopted by United Nations Member States in 2015. This blueprint for global development is broad in its definition of sustainable development and scope, and commits to attaining 17 Sustainable Development Goals (SDGs) and 169 targets by 2030, spanning many topics. The 2030 Agenda explicitly recognizes migration as relevant to development – a first in such a high-level framework – and that migration can both contribute to development and expose migrants to new risks. Migration is woven into many of the SDG targets (see ODI, 2018; IOM, 2018), for example on reducing remittance transaction costs and ending human trafficking, and in target 10.7, which calls upon countries to "facilitate orderly, safe, regular and responsible migration and mobility of people, including through the implementation of planned and well-managed migration policies" (UN, 2015). The 2030 Agenda has a multi-layered mechanism to review progress, including a system where over 230 indicators are to be monitored across countries every year. While the responsibility of SDG reporting lies with national governments, each indicator has "custodian agencies", usually international organizations or other bodies who compile and submit national statistics to the United Nations Statistics Division (UNSD) on countries' behalf. Each indicator is given a 'Tier' to categorize the robustness of its methodology.[1] Because many of these indicators refer explicitly to migration – see Table 5.1 – this was considered a significant opportunity to improve data on migration

Table 5.1 Sustainable development indicators directly referencing migration

SDG indicator	Custodian(s)	Partner(s)	Tier
3.c.1 Health worker density and distribution	World Health Organization	World Health Organization	I
4.b.1 Volume of official development assistance flows for scholarships by sector and type of study	Organization for Economic Co-operation and Development (OECD)	United Nations Educational, Scientific and Cultural Organization (UNESCO) Institute for Statistics	I
8.8.1 Fatal and non-fatal occupational injuries per 100,000 workers, by sex and migrant status	International Labour Organization		II
8.8.2 Level of national compliance with labour rights (freedom of association and collective bargaining) based on ILO textual sources and national legislation, by sex and migrant status	ILO		II
10.7.1 Recruitment cost borne by employees as a proportion of yearly income earned in country of destination	ILO, World Bank		II
10.7.2 Number of countries with migration policies to facilitate orderly, safe, regular and responsible migration and mobility of people	United Nations Department of Economic and Social Affairs (DESA), IOM, OECD	World Bank, Global Migration Group, Office of the United Nations High Commissioner for Refugee (UNHCR), United Nations Office for Drug and Crime (UNODC), OECD	II
10.7.3 Number of people who died or disappeared in the process of migration towards an international destination	IOM		I

(*Continued*)

118 *Data availability on key migration topics*

Table 5.1 (Continued)

SDG indicator	Custodian(s)	Partner(s)	Tier
10.7.4 Proportion of the population who are refugees, by country of origin	UNHCR		I
10.c.1 Remittance costs as a proportion of the amount remitted	World Bank		I
16.2.2 Number of victims of human trafficking, per 100,000 population, by sex, age and form of exploitation	UNODC	UNICEF	II
17.3.2 Volume of remittances (in United States dollars) as a proportion of total GDP	World Bank		I

Source: UNSD, 2022.

and development, as countries now needed to report on a set of migration and development topics every year (see UNSD, 2017a; 2017b; IOM, 2018). These indicators meant that, in theory, a core list of comparable migration and development indicators would soon be regularly reported on across countries.

Eight years on, the effects of the 2030 Agenda on migration and development data are mixed. It is clear that the 2030 Agenda triggered impressive and relatively rapid advancements in relevant methodologies. As these indicators had to be used around the world, progress started and/or accelerated in conceptualising how some topics could be officially defined and measured. For example, the development of indicator 10.7.1 marked an important step towards having a new single, standardized way to measure recruitment costs, through efforts by KNOMAD and International Labour Organization (ILO). In some cases, the 2030 Agenda led to relatively innovative ways to measure migration and development topics. For example, due to a lack of official data, indicator 10.7.3 managed by IOM's Missing Migrants Project relies heavily on media reports and other non-traditional data sources to record migrant deaths, and similar progress was made in measuring migration governance with the Migration Governance Indicators project (IOM, 2016). Both the United Nations Office on Drugs and Crime (UNODC) and the Counter-Trafficking Data Collaborative (CTDC) leverage administrative data to learn more about human trafficking and the SDGs. Methodologies are improving; until 2020, all four migration-related indicators to monitor target 10.7 were classified as Tier II, in 2021, two of these moved to Tier 1, and as of 2023, three are Tier 1 and just one (10.7.1, Recruitment cost borne by employee as a proportion of monthly income earned in country of destination) remains Tier II. Beyond Target 10.7, out of the 12 key migration-related indicators in the SDG framework,[2] seven were Tier 1 and five were Tier 2; none were Tier 3 (UNSD, 2023). To be ranked a Tier 1 indicator, the indicator has to be "conceptually clear, has an internationally established methodology and standards are available, and data are regularly produced for at least 50 per cent of countries and of the population in every region where the indicator is relevant" (IAEG-SDGs, n.d). This is an example of progress in recent years in improving ways to monitor aspects of migration and development.

Nevertheless, actual data on migration and development in the context of the SDGs are patchy. Data availability is mixed; the global average of countries with data for migration-related SDG indicators varies by topic (see Figure 5.1). For example, data availability is complete for indicator 10.7.4 on countries' proportion of refugees and high for indicator 17.3.2 on remittances as a proportion of total GDP. However, it is low for indicator 8.7.1 on child labour. Often low data availability is due to relevant methodologies not yet being easy to roll out; for example, on indicator 10.7.1 on recruitment costs, for which there is the lowest data availability. There is country data available for at least one year since 2015 for most of the indicators (excluding 10.7.1), while most countries do not have data for at least two years before and after 2015 for these.

The SDGs' motto to "leave no one behind" (LNOB) urges governments to consider selected population sub-groups in policy and programming, such as migrants and migrant sub-groups that are especially vulnerable. SDG Target 17.18 calls to increase the availability of "high-quality, timely and reliable data disaggregated by income, gender, age, race, ethnicity [and] migratory status". This reflects a growing understanding that disaggregation of data is an important way to ensure inclusiveness for specific population sub-groups and leave no one behind. It is possible to disaggregate many other SDG indicators – such as those on poverty, health and many other topics – by migratory status, in order to see how migrants are faring in each. For example, SDG indicator 1.1.1, "the proportion of population below the international poverty line" can be disaggregated to show results for migrants and non-migrants separately. This is another theoretical opportunity the SDGs bring to improve migration and development data; showing how far migrants enjoy multi-dimensional development. However, in practice migrants are usually invisible in other SDG indicators: in 2020, only one officially reported SDG indicator was disaggregated by migratory status (IAEG-SDGs, n.d.; Mosler Vidal, 2021). This means that today, the wider situation of migrants in relation to the SDGs is largely unknown.

All this suggests that more work is needed to translate the SDG indicator framework into results on the ground. While theoretical conversations have progressed among UN agencies and countries on how to measure some

120 *Data availability on key migration topics*

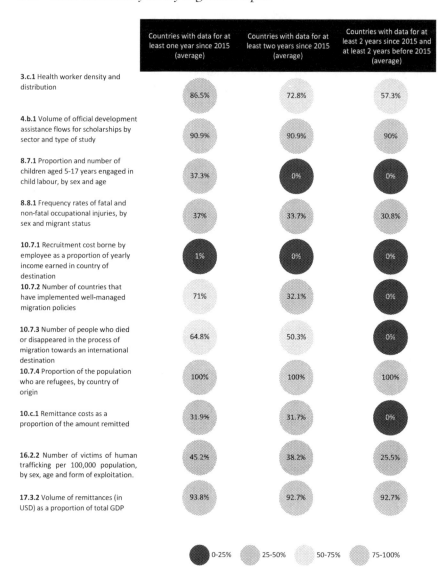

Figure 5.1 Average percentage of countries reporting migration-related SDG data by indicator, 2023.

Source: Based on data from SDG Global Database (DESA, n.d.).

migration and development topics, this has not yet been accompanied by practical progress. The SDG data architecture can be confusing and many countries struggle to produce appropriate datasets, with a large burden falling on under-equipped NSOs to respond to data requests from the international community. Overall, by creating many new regular and sometimes complex reporting requirements, the SDG framework has placed additional demands and increased pressure on NSOs to generate and share migration data, often unrealistically. In many ways, the indicator framework does not relate to capacities on the ground. This raises important questions about how such frameworks are designed and implemented. How can practitioners help ensure global frameworks are realistic for countries to implement? How can we help countries source the data needed? While comparable data is a key objective in the migration data community, how can we consider flexibility in these frameworks to see more progress in national statistics?

Around 2015 there was talk of a "data revolution" (UNSD, 2020) in the development world. As of 2023, it is not clear that this has happened. Further, though it is an achievement in itself that migration is integrated into a high-level global development reporting process, the revolution has definitely not yet taken place for migration and development data. Nevertheless, the 2030 Agenda can still help bring about progress. While the SDGs' reporting framework is imperfect, it represents a key opportunity to generate quality cross-country data on a few migration and development topics for the first time in a standardised way and to understand migrants' situations across a range of development areas.

The review process for the Global Compact for Safe, Orderly and Regular Migration (GCM), mentioned in preceding chapters, is intended to build on the 2030 Agenda. Thus, improving data on migration and the SDGs can also support GCM monitoring and more generally support and help follow up on other high-level frameworks and processes on migration.

5.4.2 Selected approaches: initiatives and examples

There is a clear need to improve the capacity of countries to collect, analyse, report and use data on migration and development. The growing world of statistical capacity building – which was given a boost by the 2030 Agenda – has included some relevant activities. Several initiatives, often using highly innovative methods, have improved the evidence base on migration and development in different contexts. Various examples of how to improve data have been presented throughout the text; the following presents a mix of approaches used by different actors to address specific challenges.

Box 5.3   Comprehensive approaches

- **Multi-site data collection and research.** Aligning Migration Management and the Migration-Development Nexus (MIGNEX) is a five-year research project (2018–2023) involving researchers at nine institutions in Europe, Africa and Asia. Its objective is to contribute to more effective and coherent migration management through evidence-based understanding of the linkages between development and migration (MIGNEX, n.d.). In 25 sub-national units of analysis (e.g. towns) across ten countries, the project aims to show how development processes affect migration and in turn how migration processes affect development. Data collection and analysis focus on assessing local drivers and consequences of migration, how combinations of factors interact to shape migration processes, the multi-level impacts of migration and more. The innovative project's design responds to many existing migration and development research gaps, challenges and opportunities and builds on existing theoretical frameworks to use a capabilities-oriented, multi-dimensional and multi-level approach. It also helps develop practitioners' own capacities as it publishes pieces on migration and development knowledge production, research typologies, ongoing related observations from implementing the project and more.
- **In-depth migration and development data assessment.** A comprehensive assessment of existing and missing data on migration and development in a country, tailored to their policy interests, can be a valuable tool to improve relevant data. For example, IOM helped develop the Armenian government's capacity to identify and monitor SDG targets on migration, by evaluating existing migration and development data across the country in different parts of the government and at different levels. The project, summarized in *Migration data in the context of the 2030 Agenda measuring migration and development in Armenia*, involved working with government counterparts to prioritize five migration-related SDG targets that were most relevant to the country and developing new indicators to monitor national progress made against the five selected targets, based on the in-depth data evaluation (Mosler Vidal, 2019). This led to the Armenian government successfully reporting the indicators on migration and development on an online database.

Box 5.4   Inclusive approaches: data disaggregation

A number of actors have increased their engagement on data disaggregation issues and data inclusivity, often in the context of LNOB – including within migration data (see UNSD, 2018, 2019;

Koch and Kuhnt, 2020). This has been done through publishing guidance and implementing capacity development activities, often focusing on how to disaggregate different types of data by country of birth and/or citizenship in order to identify migrants in datasets from different areas.

For example, IOM worked in close partnership with government stakeholders, the African Union Commission (AUC), African Union Institute for Statistics (STATAFRIC), and others to improve data disaggregation by migratory status and to overall strengthen data on migration and development. This included publishing a guide on gender and migration data for policymakers, NSOs and practitioners on how to promote gender-responsiveness when collecting, analysing, disseminating and using migration data (Hennebry et al., 2021), a report on disaggregated education data (Jeffers et al., 2018), and a guide to boost disaggregation and help make migrants more visible in development data (Mosler Vidal, 2021).

The Inclusive Data Charter (IDC), an initiative of the Global Partnership for Sustainable Development Data, aims to advance the availability and use of inclusive and disaggregated data, so that governments and organizations can better address the needs of marginalized people and ensure no one is left behind. By connecting over 30 organizations, it provides a useful way for actors in different sectors with similar objectives to connect and learn from each other in this space.

Box 5.5 Tailored approaches: specialized reporting and communications

Often initiatives that improve data collection on migration and development do not take special steps to ensure these data are used in policy. Effectively communicating data on migration and development can significantly improve their uptake. For example, some countries publish ad hoc or regular reports compiling data on various population sub-groups in the context of LNOB, and often include separate results on migrants. In Sweden, such a report was published using disaggregated data to show various development outcomes of migrants relative to those of non-migrants (Statistics Sweden, 2020). A report by the OECD and ILO (2018) similarly takes a targeted approach to integrate different data sources, instead focusing on migrants' contributions and impacts on destination economies.

5.5 What next?

5.5.1 Summary and implications

There is a need to understand much more about the links between migration and development to inform policy and development programmes around the world. Arguably, the only comprehensive global database relevant to migration and development is on economic remittances, one very small part of the puzzle. More and better data are needed to understand how migrants may support development, to better leverage these dynamics, as well as to reveal where migrants may be in situations of vulnerability, to improve their wellbeing, and where migration dynamics may negatively impact development, to halt or reverse these effects. There are important data gaps on migration and development, growing demands from governments and others for better data on this, and relevant conceptual advancements in academia. Taken together, this means there is high potential to make concerted efforts to improve data on migration and development in a way that is meaningful and more systematic.

There seems to be a disconnect between conversations on migration and development data both in the international community and academia, and concrete data availability at national level. Globally, many frameworks and processes pay lip service to the migration and development nexus, many high-level documents underline the urgent need to improve evidence on it, and many international organizations work to advance relevant methodologies. In academia, conceptual frameworks and evidence on migration and development have continued to evolve and today this is a lively area of scholarship. However, this all may mean little for actual data producers in countries where not much has changed, and it remains difficult to concretely understand and act on the links between migration and development. Quality and comparable data on migration and development today are insufficient, and what is collected at scale does not largely reflect current theoretical approaches. This divergence in some ways reflects the short history of migration and development data: as an area of development data with global standards, it is relatively young (Mosler Vidal and Laczko, 2022). Maternal mortality has been measured for decades; migrant recruitment costs have not and concepts like migrant aspirations and capabilities are being defined in real time today. Nevertheless, it is important to consider proactively how national data collection could be kept closer to and possibly help inform academic conversations on migration and development, and in turn how national perspectives on data needs and priorities can be considered by academia. A recent review showed that institutional and environmental development outcomes of migration, the development impacts of migration aspirations, failed migration attempts and involuntary immobility are under-explored (Andersson and Siegel, forthcoming; Andersson and Siegel, 2019). As scholars follow important new routes and explore different fronts of the migration and development nexus, countries should not be left behind. Improving migration and development data calls for cross-sectoral and inter-disciplinary exchange and collaboration and, necessarily, cooperation between countries.

Priorities around migration and development data are often predictable and reflect or follow policy agendas in countries based on their migration profile. For example, countries with a relatively large emigrant population typically prioritize data on diasporas and remittances, and countries with higher levels of immigration data on labour migrants' economic contributions. These in some ways reflect countries' perceived zero-sum scenarios when it comes to the development benefits and costs of migration. Often with some level of confirmation bias, countries investigate different aspects of migration and development, in different places and levels, separately. However, as transnational migration studies approaches have shown, it is necessary to explore dynamics in different sites to move towards a more comprehensive understanding of the development effects of migration.

Further, transnational approaches could actually improve the political economy of migration and development data production. For example, if a new cross-country initiative collected data on the different effects of migration in two countries in a migration corridor, these countries could be more likely to have a shared understanding of these and be able to create policies that are informed by evidence and coherent with each other's, and to further refine data collection priorities accordingly. Such collaborative transnational approaches to data could enable a virtuous circle to be formed between evidence and policy on migration and development. Today many practitioners generally find themselves stuck outside of that circle. For substantial advances to begin exploring the developmental effects of migration between countries, political will, currently missing, is needed. For the necessary political will to exist, some quality data on migration are development are needed to begin with.

Similar connections are yet to be made across themes and units of analysis. Often migration and development data focus on a specific sub-topic – for example, economic remittances – and a particular level of analysis – for example, national. Some important levels of analysis – for example, the city, where trends are often the most dynamic – are excluded. To gain a fuller understanding of the migration and development nexus in a particular context, it is important to work towards more integrated analysis, bringing together as far as possible evidence from different sub-topics and levels of analysis. While it is not conceptually possible to calculate the net development impact of migration, attempting to bring together different parts of the puzzle in a particular city, or sector – for example, considering together data on migrants' effects on healthcare provision, their health outcomes and those of their families back home, along with other data points – takes us closer to a more holistic understanding of the nexus. As the above between countries, this could support collaboration between different sectors and/or areas and levels of government in migration and development policymaking.

Working towards more transnational and integrated evidence on migration and development, as well as considering the bidirectional links between these together, would help bring about a more nuanced understanding of migration and development. Rodrik suggests that economists, fearing this would play into the hands of populists, were not transparent enough on the potential negative side effects of trade, and that this ultimately backfired (Rodrik, 2018). It is possible to make a similar argument about migration and its effects. The charged political atmosphere often hanging over migration has polarised debates. Some actors touting migration's development benefits may brush over some of its potential negative effects rather than address them, and some institutions have their own incentives to improve specific data (see de Haas, 2010 on economic remittance data); this can erode credibility and further divide audiences. Bringing together evidence on migration and development from different sites, sectors, units of analysis and more could help de-thorn some of these topics and move towards a shared and clear-eyed understanding of them, as well as pinpoint where and how policy can leverage any development benefits to be as a result of migration, and help reduce any potential negative effects.

Within migration and development, a conceptually broad and fluid field, there is clearly no one-size-fits-all regarding improving data. In any context, information needs and background factors are different, meaning that comparable, meaningful data are rare. Often, data comparability becomes more elusive the more refined the methodology. For example, there is a growing recognition that as migration occurs as part of many other processes and factors, there is a special need to accompany migration and development data with detailed background information on structural and environmental factors, for example on policy, to help contextualize it.

Some attempts to understand at global level broad progress or trends on migration and development are needed. There are opportunities. Data need to adhere to international standards where these exist – for example on labour migration – to make certain existing statistics more easily comparable. While the list of SDG indicators on migration is by no means comprehensive, it would still be very useful to have these monitored regularly around the world; this could be realistic given their relatively small number. Disaggregating other SDG indicators (that have internationally agreed methodologies) by migratory status would generate comparable data on migrants' situations across development areas. Further, experts across sectors could convene to discuss what particular global data needs are, and pool their expertise to measure phenomena in new ways. Some fundamental migration and development questions do not change through the decades: for example, what is the relationship between migrants and destination country economic growth? While perfectly assessing migrants' combined effects on a destination economy is nearly impossible, there are advanced analysis methods that could be consolidated, refined and regularly employed across countries using existing data; for example, estimating annually migrants' net fiscal contributions and impact on productivity by sector or industry. While conceptual clarity and robust methodologies are crucial, the perfect can be the enemy of the good. Regular, standardized and comparable estimates on a few migration and development topics, with working methodologies, could jump-start new policy conversations around the world and facilitate collaboration between countries. Again, this could help policymakers get beyond zero-sum thinking; data could help overcome the migration and development policy chasm between countries with different profiles and interests.

5.5.2 Practical ways forward

Migration and development is not only a vast area but also a moving theoretical target. Despite this, practical steps to improve data on it are possible. Many others have recommended thoughtful priorities for migration and development knowledge production and ways to get there, this chapter will not repeat these. Instead, it will summarize overarching priorities based on the above implications and list some practical ways forward by type of actor.

Overarching priorities:

1. Minimise the gap between government, academic, UN and other discussions on migration and development data, to work together in this space.
2. Increase transnational data collection, across sites.
3. Prioritize integrated data collection and analysis, across topics and/or units of analysis.
4. Generate and disaggregate comparable data on migration and the 2030 Agenda.
5. Make inclusive and concerted efforts to develop standardized reporting on selected persistent and policy-relevant data gaps.

For international organizations and the donor community, increasing capacity development and accompanying funding for data on migration and development are priorities. Activities can take demand-driven approaches; for example, using countries' existing data availability as a starting point. Capacity development could focus on enabling countries to learn from one another in this space, design targeted technical assistance to improve data in one particular sector or city, or support coordination of appropriate stakeholders across government. There is an opportunity to better integrate migration data into wider SDG or other development data initiatives. Because migration and development are cross-sectoral, efforts can and should be made, particularly by relatively new data funds such as the World Bank Global Data Facility and the Complex Risk Analytics Fund (CRAF'd), to include support for improving migration data.

Among NSOs and other country-level practitioners, much can be done practically to optimize key national data collection instruments to generate better information on migration and development. Migration modules could be attached to existing household surveys and include questions on, for example, transnational practices or use of remittances; specialized surveys could be rolled out. Many practical steps relate to migration data more broadly and are mentioned elsewhere in this book; for example, adhering to international data standards where these exist, combining data from multiple sources or exploring the potential of alternative sources of data to address data gaps. Disaggregating sectoral data by migratory status and other variables helps monitor multi-dimensional development outcomes of migrants; to this end, harmonized migration variables should be included in routine national data collection.

Further, so that academic debates on migration and development evidence do not become too divorced from realities in countries, it is worth considering on an ongoing basis how some national data collection could better reflect current theoretical approaches and how the latter can take into account the former. For example, academics could, where appropriate, include actionable recommendations directed at countries in research outputs, and include local and national authorities more often in large-scale research initiatives.

Notes

1 SDG indicators are classified under one of the following tiers. "Tier 1: Indicator is conceptually clear, has an internationally established methodology and standards are available, and data are regularly produced by countries for at least 50 per cent of countries and of the population in every region where the indicator is relevant. Tier 2: Indicator is conceptually clear, has an internationally established methodology and standards are available, but data are not regularly produced by countries. Tier 3: No internationally established methodology or standards are yet available for the indicator, but methodology/standards are being (or will be) developed or tested." For more, see https://unstats.un.org/sdgs/iaeg-sdgs/tier-classification/.
2 3c1, 4.b.1, 8.7.1, 8.8.1, 8.8.2, 10.7.1, 10.7.2, 10.7.3, 10.7.4, 10.c.1, 16.2.2, 17.3.2.

References

African Union. (2020). Factsheet: Leveraging the African diaspora for continental transformation. Available at https://au.int/documents/20200919/diaspora-division-factsheet

Aligning Migration Management and the Migration–Development Nexus (MIGNEX). (n.d.). About MIGNEX. MIGNEX. Available at https://www.mignex.org/our-research/about-mignex

Alvarez, P.S. et al. (2015). Remittances: How reliable are the data? *Migration Policy Practice*, V(2), 42–46.

Amuedo-Dorantes, C. (2014). The good and the bad in remittance flows. IZA World of Labor. 97. Available at https://wol.iza.org/uploads/articles/97/pdfs/good-and-bad-in-remittance-flows.pdf

Andersson, L. and Siegel, M. (2019). *Empirical Assessments of the Development Impacts of Migration*. MIGNEX Background Paper. Oslo: Peace Research Institute Oslo. Available at www.mignex.org/d024.

Ardittis, S. and Laczko, F. (2008). How are the costs and impacts of migration policies evaluated. Migration Policy Institute.

Carling, J. (2017). Thirty-six migration nexuses, and counting. Posted in jorgencarling.org. Available at https://jorgencarling.org/2017/07/31/thirty-six-migration-nexuses-and-counting/.

Carling, J. (2019). *Key Concepts in the Migration–Development Nexus, MIGNEX Handbook Chapter 2 (v2)*. Oslo: Peace Research Institute Oslo. Available at www.mignex.org/d021.

Carling, J. (2019). *Measuring Migration Aspirations and Related Concepts*. MIGNEX Background Paper. Oslo: Peace Research Institute Oslo. Available at www.mignex.org/d023.

Castles, S., de Haas, H., and Miller, M.J. (2014). *The Age of Migration: International Population Movements in the Modern World* (5th ed.). Hampshire and New York: Palgrave MacMillan.

Cernadas, P.C., LeVoy, M., and Keith, L. (2015). Human rights indicators for migrants and their families. KNOMAD Working Paper 5. Available at https://www.ohchr.org/sites/default/files/Documents/Issues/Migration/Indicators/WP5_en.pdf

Chappell, L. and Laczko, F. (2011) *What Are We Really Achieving? Building an Evaluation Culture in Migration and Development*. Washington, DC: Migration Policy Institute.

Clemens, M. and Hunt, J. (2019). The labor market effects of refugee waves: Reconciling conflicting results. *ILR Review*, 72(4), 818–857.

Clemens, M. and McKenzie, D. (2014). Why don't remittances appear to affect growth? World Bank Policy Research Working Paper No. 6856, Available at SSRN: https://ssrn.com/abstract=2433809.

Clemens, M.A., Özden, Ç., and Rapoport, H. (2014). *Migration and Development Research Is Moving Far beyond Remittances*. Washington, DC: Center for Global Development. Available at http://www.cgdev.org/publication/migration-and-development-research-moving-farbeyond-remittances-working-paper-365

De Haan, A. et al. (2000). *Migration and Livelihoods: Case Studies in Bangladesh, Ethiopia and Mali*. IDS Research Report 46. Brighton. Sussex: Institute of Development Studies.

de Haas, H. (2006). Engaging Diasporas: How governments and development agencies can support diaspora involvement in the development of origin countries. International Migration Institute (IMI). Available at https://www.migrationinstitute.org/publications/engaging-diasporas-hdh

de Haas, H. (2010). Migration and development: A theoretical perspective. *The International Migration Review*, 44(1), 227–264. JSTOR. Available at http://www.jstor.org/stable/20681751

de Haas, H. (2021). A theory of migration: The aspirations-capabilities framework. *CMS*, 9. https://doi.org/10.1186/s40878-020-00210-4

Genc, M. (2014). The impact of migration on trade. IZA World of Labor, 82.

Glick Schiller, N., Basch, L., and Szanton-Blanc, C. (1992). *Towards a Transnational Perspective on Migration: Race, Class, Ethnicity, and Nationalism Reconsidered*. New York: New York Academy of Sciences.

Global Forum on Migration & Development (GFMD). (2008). Roundtable 3: Policy and Institutional Coherence and Partnerships. Roundtable Session 3.1.

Global Migration Group (GMG). (2017). *Handbook for Improving the Production and Use of Migration Data for Development*. Washington, DC: Global Knowledge Partnership for Migration and Development (KNOMAD), World Bank. Available at www.knomad.org/publication/handbook-improving-production-and-use-migration-data-development-0

Hennebry, J., Hari, K.C., and Williams, K. (2021). *Gender and Migration Data: A Guide for Evidence-Based, Gender-Responsive Migration Governance*. Geneva: International Organization for Migration (IOM).

Hernandez, C. (2017). Chapter 14: Human rights of migrants. In *Handbook for Improving the Production and Use of Migration Data for Development*. Washington, DC: Global Knowledge Partnership for Migration and Development (KNOMAD), World Bank.

Inter-Agency and Expert Group on Sustainable Development Goal Indicators (IAEG-SDGs). (n.d.). Global indicator framework for the Sustainable Development Goals and targets of the 2030 Agenda for Sustainable Development. Available at https://unstats.un.org/sdgs/indicators/indicators-list/

International Organization for Migration. (IOM). (2016). *Measuring Well-Governed Migration: The 2016 Migration Governance Index, A Study by the Economist Intelligence Unit*. Geneva: IOM and Economist Intelligence Unit (EIU).

International Organization for Migration. (IOM). (2017). Migration Health Research to advance evidence based policy and practice in Sri Lanka. Available at https://publications.iom.int/books/migration-health-research-advance-evidence-based-policy-and-practice-sri-lanka

International Organization for Migration. (IOM). (2018). *Migration and the 2030 Agenda: A Guide for Practitioners*. Geneva: IOM.

International Organization for Migration. (IOM). (2020). *Diasporas. Migration Data Portal*. Berlin: IOM. Available at https://www.migrationdataportal.org/themes/diasporas

International Organization for Migration. (IOM). (2021). *How Countries Manage Migration Data: Evidence from Six Countries*. Geneva: IOM. Available at https://publications.iom.int/books/how-countries-manage-migration-data-evidence-six-countries

International Organization for Migration. (IOM). (2022). *Diaspora Mapping Toolkit*. Geneva: IOM. Available at https://publications.iom.int/books/diaspora-mapping-toolkit

International Organization for Migration. (IOM). (2023). Remittances. Migration Data Portal. IOM. Available at https://www.migrationdataportal.org/themes/remittances#:~:text=Remittances%2C%20usually%20understood%20as%20the,link%20between%20migration%20and%20development

Jeffers, K., Tjaden, J., and Laczko, F. (2018). *A Pilot Study on Disaggregating SDG Indicators by Migratory Status*. Geneva: IOM. Available at https://publications.iom.int/books/pilot-study-disaggregating-sdg-indicators-migratory-status

Koch, A. and Kuhnt, J. (2020). Migration and the 2030 agenda: Making everyone count. SWP Comment, No. 28. German Institute for International and Security Affairs (Stiftung Wissenschaft und Politik) (SWP), Berlin, July. Available at www.swp-berlin.org/fileadmin/contents/products/comments/2020C38_Migration2030Agenda.pdf

Levitt, P. (1998). Social remittances: Migration driven local-level forms of cultural diffusion. *International Migration Review*, 32(4), 926–948.
Levitt, P. and Glick Schiller, N. (2004). Conceptualizing simultaneity: A transnational social field perspective on society. *International Migration Review*, 38(3), 1002–1039.
Levitt, P. and Lamba-Nieves, D. (2011). Social remittances revisited. *Journal of Ethnic and Migration Studies*, 37(1), 1–22.
McDowell, C. and De Haan, A. (1997). *Migration and Sustainable Livelihoods: A Critical Review of the Literature*. Sussex: Institute of Development Studies.
Mendoza, D.R. and Newland, K. (2012). *Developing a Road Map for Engaging Diasporas in Development: A Handbook for Policymakers and Practitioners in Home and Host Countries*. Geneva and Washington, DC: IOM and MPI. Available at https://www.migrationpolicy.org/research/developing-road-map-engaging-diasporas-development-handbook-policymakers-and-practitioners
Migrant Integration Policy Index (MIPEX). (n.d.). What is MIPEX? MIPEX. Available at https://www.mipex.eu/what-is-mipex
Mosler Vidal, E. (2019). *Migration Data in the Context of the 2030 Agenda: Measuring Migration and Development in Armenia*. Armenia: IOM. Available at https://armenia.un.org/sites/default/files/2021-07/Migration%20data%20in%20the%20context%20of%20the%202030%20agenda_ENG.pdf
Mosler Vidal, E. (2021). *Leave No Migrant Behind: The 2030 Agenda and Data Disaggregation*. Geneva: IOM. Available at https://publications.iom.int/books/leave-no-migrant-behind-2030-agenda-and-data-disaggregation
Mosler Vidal, E. and Laczko, F. (2022). Introduction. In Elisa Mosler Vidal and Frank Laczko (Eds.), *Migration and the SDGs: Measuring Progress*. Geneva: IOM, 1–10.
Newland, K. and Plaza, S. (2013). *What We Know about Diasporas and Economic Development*. Migration Policy Institute (MPI). Available at https://www.migrationpolicy.org/research/what-we-know-about-diasporas-and-economic-development
Nigerians in Diaspora Organization Europe (NIDO). (n.d.). Global Database of Nigerians in Diaspora. Available at http://www.nigeriandiaspora.org/default.aspx
OECD and ILO. (2018). *How Immigrants Contribute to Developing Countries' Economies*. Paris: OECD Publishing. Available at www.oecd.org/migration/how-immigrants-contribute-to-developing-countries-economies-9789264288737-en.htm
Office of the High Commissioner for Human Rights (OCHR). (n.d.). Status of Ratification Interactive Dashboard. OCHR. Available at https://indicators.ohchr.org
Overseas Development Institute (ODI). (2018). Migration and the 2030 Agenda for Sustainable Development. Available at https://odi.org/en/publications/migration-and-the-2030-agenda-for-sustainable-development/
Plaza, S. and Ratha, D. (2017). Remittances. In Global Migration Group (Eds.), *Handbook for Improving the Production and Use of Migration Data for Development*. Washington, DC: Global Knowledge Partnership for Migration and Development (KNOMAD), World Bank, 65–78.
Ratha, D. (2007). *Leveraging Remittances for Development*. Migration Policy Institute (MPI). Available at https://www.migrationpolicy.org/research/leveraging-remittances-development
Rodrik, D. (2018). *Straight Talk on Trade: Ideas for a Sane World Economy*. Princeton, NJ: Princeton University Press.
Stark, O. and Bloom, D.E. (1985). The new economics of labor migration. *American Economic Review*, 75, 173–178.

Statistics Sweden. (2020). Leaving no one behind. Statistical review of the implementation of the 2030 Agenda in Sweden, October 2020. Solna. Available at https://scb.se/contentassets/093a4e6ee4004071815a5ec6773012e7/ mi1303_2020a01_br_x41br2101.pdf

Global Forum on Migration and Development (GFMD). (2008). Strengthening Data and Research Tools on Migration and Development. Available at https://www.gfmd.org/docs?search_api_views_fulltext=migration+data+development

Taylor, J.E. (1999). The new economics of labour migration and the role of remittances in the migration process. *International Migration*, 37(1), 63–88.

UNHCR and HelpAge International. (2021). A Claim to Dignity: Ageing on the Move. Available at https://ageingonthemove.org

UNHCR and World Bank. (2020). Understanding the socioeconomic conditions of refugees in Kalobeyei, Kenya. Results from the 2018 Kalobeyei Socioeconomic Profiling Survey. Available at https://documents1.worldbank.org/curated/en/982811613626800238/pdf/Understanding-the-Socioeconomic-Conditions-of-Refugees-in-Kenya-Volume-A-Kalobeyei-Settlement-Results-from-the-2018-Kalobeyei-Socioeconomic-Survey.pdf

United Nations Department of Economic and Social Affairs (UN DESA). (2017). Improving migration data in the context of the 2030 Agenda. United Nations Expert Group Meeting on Improving Migration Data in the Context of the 2030 Agenda, New York, 20–22 June. Available at https://unstats.un.org/unsd/demographic-social/meetings/2017/new-york--egm-migration-data/Background%20paper.pdf.

United Nations Development Programme (UNDP). (1997). Human Development Report 1997. Human Development Report. p. 15. ISBN 978-0-19-511996-1.

United Nations Economic Commission for Europe (UNECE). (2012). Measuring hard-to-count migrant populations: Importance, definitions, and categories. Working paper 9. Geneva. Available at www.unece.org/fileadmin/DAM/stats/documents/ece/ces/ge.10/2012/WP_9_UNECE.pdf.

United Nations General Assembly (UNGA). (1950). United Nations General Assembly resolution 429(V) of 14 December 1950. Available at http://www.unhcr.org/refworld/docid/3b00f08a27.html

United Nations General Assembly (UNGA). (2016). Resolution adopted by the General Assembly on 19 September 2016 A/RES/71. 71/1. New York Declaration for Refugees and Migrants. Available at https://www.unhcr.org/media/new-york-declaration-refugees-and-migrants-0

United Nations Network on Migration (UNMN). (n.d.). Repository of practices. Assessing the evidence: Country profiles on migration, environment and climate change. Migration Network Hub. Available at https://migrationnetwork.un.org/practice/assessing-evidence-country-profiles-migration-environment-and-climate-change

United Nations Statistics Division (UNSD). (2017a). ESA/STAT/AC.339/1 Improving migration data in the context of the 2030 Agenda.

United Nations Statistics Division (UNSD). (2017b). United Nations Expert Group Meeting Improving Migration Data in the Context of the 2030 Agenda New York Headquarters, 20–22 June 2017 Recommendations.

United Nations Statistics Division (UNSD). (2018). Overview of standards for data disaggregation. Working document. Available at https://unstats.un.org/sdgs/files/Overview%20of%20Standards%20for%20Data%20Disaggregation.pdf

United Nations Statistics Division (UNSD). (2019). Data disaggregation and SDG indicators: Policy priorities and current and future disaggregation plans. Prepared by the Inter-Agency and Expert Group on Sustainable Development Goal Indicators (IAEGSDGs). Background document. Available at https://unstats.un.org/unsd/statcom/50th-session/documents/BG-Item3a-Data-Disaggregation-E.pdf

United Nations Statistics Division (UNSD). (2020). Review of implementation of data revolution. Prepared by the United Nations Statistics Division for the High-level Group for Partnership, Coordination and Capacity-Building for statistics for the 2030 Agenda for Sustainable Development (HLG-PCCB). Background document. Available at https://unstats.un.org/unsd/statcom/51st-session/documents/BG-Item3a_Review-of-Implementation-of-Data-Revolution-E.pdf

United Nations Statistics Division (UNSD). (2023). Tier classification for global SDG indicators. Available at https://unstats.un.org/sdgs/iaeg-sdgs/tier-classification/

United Nations (UN). (2015). Transforming our world: The 2030 Agenda for Sustainable Development. Resolution adopted by the General Assembly on 25 September 2015. Available at https://documents-dds-ny.un.org/doc/UNDOC/GEN/N15/291/89/PDF/N1529189.pdf?OpenElement

Universal Declaration of Human Rights (UDHR). (1948). United Nations. Available at https://www.un.org/en/about-us/universal-declaration-of-human-rights

Vari-Lavoisier, I. (2020). Social remittances. In Skeldon, R. and Bastia, T. (Eds.), *The Routledge Handbook of Migration and Development*. London: Routledge, 125–135.

6 Data on migration and climate change
Making sense of the numbers

Over the last two decades, estimates suggesting that between 200 million and 1 billion people could be displaced by climate change during the next 40 years have fuelled the perception that climate change is likely to be associated with a new era of mass migration (Laczko and Warner, 2009). Many authors have criticized such estimates as artificially inflated and excessively alarmist (Kolmannskog, 2008). Despite the fact that many experts have dismissed such figures as, at best, "guesswork" (IPCC, 2007), these numbers have helped focus policymakers' attention on the subject of migration and climate change and have led to calls for better data and statistics on the topic.

Although interest in migration and the environment has grown significantly in recent years, the subject has been discussed for several decades. Indeed, the use of the term "environmental refugee" dates back to 1985 (El Hinnawi, 1985). Just over 40 years ago, the International Organization for Migration (IOM) published a report entitled "Migration and the Environment", which begins with the sentence:

> *Large numbers of people are moving as a result of environmental degradation that has increased dramatically in recent years. The number of such migrants could rise substantially as larger areas of earth become uninhabitable as a result of climate change from global warming, rising sea levels, drought, floods, and other geophysical effects.*
>
> (IOM, 1992)

More than 30 years ago, the Intergovernmental Panel on Climate Change (IPCC) also warned that "one of the gravest effects of climate change may be those on human migration" (McTegart et al., 1990). Over the last 40 years, a huge number of publications and a growing body of research have focused on the linkages between migration, environment and climate change (Selby and Daoust, 2021). In 2021, the UK government commissioned a review of English language studies on migration and climate change, which included nearly 300 studies. The University of Neuchatel in Switzerland developed a database to track the rising number of studies on this subject (Piguet and Laczko, 2014).

After some early attention to the topic in the 1980s and 1990s, interest in the subject waned. Indeed, in the 2005 report of the Global Commission on International Migration,[1] which was initiated by the United Nations (UN) Secretary-General, there is barely a mention of the topic as a major global issue linked to migration. Since 2005, references to migration and climate change have grown in UN documents dealing with disasters, displacement and mobility, and human mobility has been increasingly referenced in global responses to climate change. Human mobility was increasingly mentioned in the context of negotiations under the UN Framework Convention on Climate Change (UNFCCC) (Guadagno, 2022). In 2015, a special UNFCCC Task Force on Displacement under the Warsaw International Mechanism for Loss and Damage was created. Both the Global Compact for Migration and the Global Compact for Refugees highlight the need to address climate impacts as a driver of forced migration, together with other international policy documents dealing with disaster risk reduction, internal displacement and the achievement of development goals (ibid). These policy documents all highlight the need for better data on migration, environment and climate change to inform policy and practice. Answers are still being sought to basic questions, such as how many people are moving and will move, due to environmental changes. Where will they move to, how will they move and who will move? Data on all of these are urgently necessary for policy and programming.

Despite the growing research and policy interest, as this chapter will show, statistics on migration, environment and climate change remain very limited, with very few countries able to produce regular data on the subject. As explained below, there are several reasons for this, but part of the problem is conceptual and methodological: it is not always clear what needs to be measured and what terminology should be used.

This chapter therefore begins with a discussion of terminology and what needs to be measured when considering the linkages between migration, environment and climate change. It then discusses what the main sources of data and statistics on migration, environment and climate change are and what these data tell us. The chapter explains why data on this subject are often limited and suggests a way forward, drawing upon recent innovative examples.

6.1 Framing the data challenge – what needs to be measured?

It is difficult to collect statistics on environmental change and the movements of people because it is not always clear who and what should be counted. For many years, there has been considerable disagreement about how to conceptualize the relationship between migration, environment and climate change (IOM, 1992; Laczko, 2010; Piguet and Laczko, 2014). There is no single internationally agreed definition of "environmental migration", and some confusion and disagreement remain over the terms to be used to describe migratory movements linked to environmental change. Various terms have been introduced, such as "environmental refugees", "ecological refugees", "climate migrants", "environmental migrants" and "environmentally displaced persons" (see IOM, 2022).

More than a decade ago, the UK Government's Foresight Commission (UK Government, 2011), which investigated the implications of environmental changes for migration over the next 50 years, argued in its landmark report that it is difficult to identify who an environmental migrant is and hence difficult to collect data on this category of migrants.

> *It is almost impossible to distinguish a group of environmental migrants, either now or in the future – this is because a range of economic, social and political factors affect the movement of people and it will rarely be possible to distinguish individuals for whom environmental factors are the sole driver.*
>
> (Foresight report, "Migration and Global Environmental Change", 2011, p. 11)

Nonetheless, IOM developed a wide-ranging definition of environmental migrant, which emphasizes how adverse environmental factors impact the movement of people:

> *Environmental migrants are persons or groups of persons who, for compelling reasons of sudden or progressive changes in the environment that adversely affect their lives or living conditions, are obliged to leave their habitual homes, or choose to do so, either temporarily or permanently, and who move either within their country or abroad (IOM, 2019).*

This definition includes the possibility that such movements could be both forced and voluntary with some people choosing to adapt to adverse environmental conditions. The working definition developed by IOM encompasses population movement or displacement, whether it be temporary or permanent, internal or cross-border, and regardless of whether it is voluntary or forced, or due to sudden or gradual environmental changes.

It has also been common to describe those who move for environmental reasons as "climate refugees" or as "environmentally displaced persons" and to characterize such movements as forced migration. Popular with the media, the term "environmental refugees" has been used to describe the whole category of people who migrate because of environmental factors. However, this definition is not sufficiently precise to describe all the various types of movement, which may be linked to environmental factors (Laczko, 2010; Laczko and Aghazarm, 2019). In some situations, such as when disasters occur, people may have little choice but to move. In other places where environmental change is gradual, migratory movements are more likely to be voluntary, as people have time to weigh up their options, and environmental change may be one of many factors inducing them to move (ibid).

Although it is frequently assumed that environmental disruptions trigger only forced displacement, many experts also stress that environmental factors can induce voluntary migration. Many years ago, Professor Graeme Hugo suggested that it is more helpful to think of a continuum in relation to migration and environment:

"Population mobility is probably best viewed as being arranged along a continuum ranging from totally voluntary migration ... to totally forced migration, very few decisions are entirely forced or voluntary" (Hugo, 1996, p. 106).

United Nations High Commissioner for Refugees (UNHCR) rejects the use of the term "climate refugee", recognizing that most of those who move due to environmental factors tend not to cross international borders and that not all such movements are forced. UNHCR notes, for example, that:

> *The term "climate refugee" does not exist in international law. A refugee is a person who crosses international borders due to a well-grounded fear of persecution because of their race, religion, nationality, membership of a particular social group or political opinion (1951 Refugee Convention, see also Chapter 2). The majority of people displaced by climate change typically move within the borders of their own countries.*
>
> (UNHCR, 2021)

It has been suggested that the use of terms such as "climate refugee" could even potentially undermine the international legal regime for the protection of refugees (IOM, 2022). Nonetheless, there are clear linkages between refugees and climate change, as pointed out by UNHCR in several policy documents. "Refugees, internally displaced people (IDPs) and the stateless are on the front lines of the climate emergency. Many are living in climate 'hotspots', where they typically lack the resources to adapt to an increasingly hostile environment" (UNHCR, 2022).

The Asian Development Bank has suggested that other terms be used, such as "climate-induced migration" or "climate migrants" – although both of these terms are somewhat narrow, given that many movements linked to environmental changes do not necessarily result from climate change. For example, many changes in the environment, such as earthquakes, which are not necessarily linked to climate change, have an enormous impact on the movement of people.

Others have proposed further nuances when putting words such as climate and migration next to each other. Some have suggested that terms such as "climate-related migration" or "climate-change-related migration" should be used instead of "climate migration" (or climate-induced migration), to reflect the mediated, indirect ways in which climate change and climatic factors may influence migration (Selby and Daoust, 2021). Describing someone as a "climate migrant" might imply that climate change is the sole or main cause of their migration. This label does not seem to accord with existing evidence on the multi-causal character of migration and evidence of the frequently indirect and mediated nature of climate change impacts (ibid). Nonetheless, the authors of a recent major review of the literature on migration and climate change for the UK government noted that "we do not rule out the possibility that some climate change-related hazards may be so extreme, and so direct, as to render phrases like 'climate migration' appropriate in specific circumstances" (Selby and Daoust, 2021, p. 4).

Definitions matter not solely for the purposes of statistics and data collection. Without a clear definition, it is not always possible to identify which populations affected by environmental change are of most concern and may require assistance. Moreover, as the Asian Development Bank has remarked, typologies matter for the populations themselves because of the images and meaning they carry. For instance, empirical studies show that many people described as environmental refugees object strongly to the use of this terminology as they do not see themselves as "refugees" (ADB, 2012).

Discussions about definitions have helped to underline the importance of collecting data on different dimensions of the migration, environment and climate change nexus, but have not yet been incorporated into national statistical data systems. Few countries have set out to collect data on a regular basis on "environmental/climate migrants" or "environmental/climate refugees". UN guidance on this topic also remains somewhat vague, although, significantly, the UN now includes migration-related indicators in its guidance to countries on climate change statistics.

In March 2022, in a paper prepared for the UN Statistical Commission on "Climate Change statistics", the UN Statistics Division presented a "final draft of the global set of climate change statistics and indicators and metadata designed to support countries in preparing their own sets of climate change statistics and indicators" (UNSD, 2022). In Annex 2 of this paper, the UN Statistics Division presents a global set of climate change statistics and indicators, which could be potentially adopted by countries around the world. In total, 158 climate change statistical indicators are proposed, of which one specifically refers to migration – indicator number 43. Interestingly, the migration and climate change indicator is found under the heading "Hazardous events and disasters", highlighting an emphasis on capturing data on the impact of extreme environmental events rather than on slow-onset events. Under this indicator, it is proposed that countries should gather statistics on the "Number of climate refugees, climate migrants and persons displaced by climate change". In the absence of an agreed common definition of "environmental migration", this looks like an attempt to provide a broader set of options to countries. However, this approach might be quite confusing for national statistical systems to adopt and again implies direct causality between climate and movements of migrants and refugees. This indicator is currently ranked by the UN Statistical Division (UNSD) as a Tier 3 indicator, meaning that the indicator is relevant to climate change, "but not methodologically sound, and country data may not be available." (UNSD, 2022, p. 4).

When thinking about what data to collect on migration, environment and climate change, it is also important to keep in mind that migration is happening now, and many people are migrating to areas that are already environmentally vulnerable. Over a decade ago, the Foresight report noted that:

People are as likely to migrate to places of environmental vulnerability as from these places – this can create or add to vulnerabilities facing migrants... Migrants are particularly vulnerable as they tend to live in high-density settlements in areas prone to environmental risks. For example, in Dakar, Senegal, 40 per cent of new migrants arriving in the past decade have moved to zones with "high flood potential"

(Foresight, 2011, p. 19)

It has also been suggested that environmental change could have the effect of limiting migration opportunities and that some people might therefore be "trapped" because they cannot move (Foresight, 2011).

Environmental change is equally likely to make migration less possible as more probable"..."this is because migration is expensive and requires forms of capital, yet populations who experience the impacts of environmental change may see a reduction in the very capital required to enable a move"...." consequently, in the decades ahead, millions of people will be unable to move away from locations in which they are extremely vulnerable to environmental change...

(Foresight report, 2011, p. 13)

IOM has produced a useful glossary of key terms linked to migration, environment and climate change (IOM, 2019), which includes a definition of "Trapped populations". The IOM Glossary states:

Trapped populations: Populations who do not migrate, yet are situated in areas under threat, at risk of becoming "trapped" or having to stay behind, where they will be more vulnerable to environmental shocks and impoverishment. Note: the notion of trapped populations applies, in particular, to poorer households who may not have the resources to move and whose livelihoods are affected.

(IOM, 2019, p. 220)

However, it is not known how many people might be currently "trapped" or likely to be "trapped" in the future, and national data systems are generally not collecting data to estimate the size of this population. Another important consideration when thinking about data on migration, environment and climate change is that climate change might contribute to *less* migration.

Research published in an article in "Nature" in July 2022 provides new evidence to suggest that climate change, in fact, increases resource-constrained international immobility (Benveniste et al., 2022). In this article, the authors provide a quantitative, global analysis of reduced international mobility due to resource deprivation caused by climate change. The authors developed a model that includes both migration dynamics and within-region income distributions. The results of their research show that "climate change induces decreases of emigration in lowest-income levels by over 10 per cent in 2100 for medium development and climate scenarios compared with no climate change and by up to 35 per cent for more pessimistic scenarios" (ibid, p. 1). The authors suggest that this would leave these resource-constrained populations extremely vulnerable to both increased poverty and the impacts of climate change. This finding is consistent with the results of previous research, which suggests that the poorest groups have fewer opportunities to migrate. United Nations Development Programme (UNDP), for example, conducted research on migration patterns in Nicaragua during Hurricane Mitch in 1998, which found that rural families in the bottom two wealth quintiles were less likely to migrate than other families in the aftermath of Hurricane Mitch (UNDP, 2009).

The above has presented a glimpse of the complexity of the relationship between migration, environment and climate change and what this means for data. This shows that there is a need for many different types of data to inform policy and practice. In a special issue of "Migration Policy and Practice", published in January–March 2020, which focused on the state of data on migration, environment and climate change, the authors discussed what data are needed on migration, environment and climate change and how they can be obtained (Ardittis and Laczko, 2020).

The authors in this special issue argued that there is a need for a broad range of different types of data, including data on past, present and future migratory trends linked to environmental changes. In summary, they made the following points:

1 There is a need for data on the movement of people and how that impacts areas already affected by climate change.
2 There is a need for data on how many people are moving every year mainly although not necessarily solely for environmental reasons.
3 There is a need for data that are disaggregated, looking at different types of migrants – IDPs, labour migrants, refugees, etc. – to help identify which migrants are most likely to be forced to move due to environmental factors.
4 Data are required on both gradual changes in the environment and more sudden changes.
5 Collecting data to monitor national and regional policy responses is also required to understand how far migration considerations are factored into climate change plans and other relevant policies.

6 There is also a need for better data to help policymakers understand why some people cannot move and cannot use migration as a way to adapt to harsh environmental conditions.
7 Data also need to be collected on the contributions made by diasporas, such as the impact of remittances on communities badly affected by environmental changes. Diaspora groups can make a major contribution to the disaster response, both directly through financial contributions and by returning for temporary periods to assist their country. Remittances, for example, sent home by migrants assist individuals, households and communities in coping with disasters and help reduce risk or vulnerability in the face of such an event by enabling individuals to strengthen their economic base. In the aftermath of the tsunami in 2004 and later major disasters, there was a strong response by the diasporas linked to the affected countries (Naik et al., 2007; UNDP, 2009).
8 Last but not least, data are required to help policymakers forecast and prepare for likely future movements of people linked to climate change and the environment.

In addition, one could add to this list the data needed to understand the impact of relocation, re-settlement and adaptation programmes.

To sum up, climate change could have different forms of impact on mobility and immobility, and therefore, decision-makers will need a range of different forms of data to inform their policy responses. Currently, it remains difficult for national authorities to collect statistics on the movements of people linked to environmental change because of a lack of agreement on what to measure and, within this, on a common definition.

Box 6.1 provides an example of a global initiative to better understand the links between migration, environment and climate change.

Box 6.1 Migration, environment and climate change: comprehensive country analyses

Under the "Migration, Environment and Climate Change: Evidence for Policy (MECLEP)" project, implemented by IOM with six research partners, a series of country profiles were published on countries' situations regarding the migration, environment and climate change nexus. Each profile is based on a review of the links between migration, displacement, planned relocation, disasters, climate change and environmental degradation in each country and aims to answer questions such as how migration can be an adaptation strategy to environmental and climate change. It also examines relevant policy and legal frameworks and offers policy guidance. The profiles are produced in consultation with the national government and contribute to the capacity building of many actors in each country, as the profile production process involves bringing together those working in different parts of government in migration and environment, climate change, disaster management and development. These have led in some cases to concrete policy changes; for example, in Peru the study contributed to the development process of the Peruvian National Plan of Action on Climate Migration (Bergmann et al., 2021; United Nations Network on Migration, n.d.).

6.2 Main sources of data and global trends

There are essentially two main sources of data about global trends relating to migration, environment and climate change. These are first, data on disaster-related displacement, and second, data concerning likely projected migration trends linked to climate change, based on modelling techniques. In addition, a limited amount of policy data concerns the extent to which countries include human mobility in their climate change plans. Beyond these main sources of international data, some data are available from censuses and administrative sources for a limited number of countries. More countries are also exploring the potential of using "big data" and digital data to map and respond to migration trends linked to climate change.

A general problem here, as distinct from other chapters in this volume, is that these data sources generally focus on internal migration, because most migration linked to the environment is expected to occur within borders, and data on internal migration in general are quite limited. While the latest figure for the global stock of international migrants is for 2020, the latest figure for the global number of internal migrants is from 2005. Data on global patterns of internal migration are relatively limited and frequently out of date (UNDP, 2020). It is also difficult to compare internal migration data across countries because countries have differing numbers and sizes of administrative subregions or localities (ibid). The most recent data published by the UN Population Division draw together the available evidence on internal migration for a wide range of countries (Bell and Charles-Edwards, 2013). According to these estimates, in 2005 there were about 750 million internal migrants in the world, based on lifetime reported migration (UNDP, 2020).

6.2.1 Censuses

As discussed elsewhere in this book (Chapters 2–4), censuses are a key source of data about migration, but are conducted infrequently and may focus on a narrow range of questions. In the case of migration and climate change, a generic problem is that most censuses do not include a question about the reasons for migration (Mosler Vidal and Laczko, 2022). Even where such questions are asked, questions linked to environmental factors are rarely included. For example, a recent study in six Eastern Caribbean countries found that all the countries collect data on both international and internal migration. Censuses in these countries include questions on the numbers of foreign-born, reasons for moving and returning to the country (Serraglio et al., 2021). However, only one of the six countries, Grenada, included environmental factors in the options listed as reasons for moving and/or returning (ibid).

6.2.2 Administrative data

Administrative data on migration, environment and climate change tend to be limited because few countries have developed specific policies to grant work or residence permits to persons forced to move due to climate or environmental changes (Martin, 2013). Nonetheless, some data are available on those already residing in a country, who were given temporary protection, when an extreme environmental event occurred in their country. For example, the USA has granted temporary protection status to nationals of some countries already residing in the USA after a disaster has occurred in their country. Temporary protection status was granted to nationals of Honduras and Nicaragua following Hurricane Mitch in 1998 and migrants from El Salvador and Haiti following earthquakes in those countries (Martin, 2013).

In the Eastern Caribbean region, it was found that administrative records collected when disasters occur do not often include data on migration or displacement (see Box 6.2). Although the six Eastern Caribbean countries have designated agencies collecting data on disaster impacts, data on human mobility dimensions of climate change and disasters are very limited (Serraglio et al., 2021). The Caribbean Disaster Emergency Management Agency (CDEMA) is a regional intergovernmental agency for disaster management established in 1991. Although it has a key role in coordinating emergency response and relief efforts to member states, it does not collect data that account for or refer to the mobility dimensions of disasters (Serraglio, et.al, 2021).

As mentioned above, human mobility and climate change are often referenced in global policy documents and frameworks focusing on responses to disasters, internal displacement, international migration and climate change. Yet, no systematic monitoring mechanism has been developed at the international level to assess how far countries are integrating human mobility considerations into their national responses to climate change, and these references have not been accompanied by significant efforts to improve data collection on this nexus at large. Some studies, however, do provide useful data on the extent to which human mobility considerations are factored into climate change responses.

In a 2018 analysis of 82 national disaster risk reduction strategies, covering most regions of the world, it was found that over 80 per cent of these strategies contained references to displacement, migration, planned relocations or evacuation. Just over a third of these strategies also included references to migration, and 39 per cent included references to displacement (Guadagno, 2022).

Box 6.2 Migration, environment, disaster and climate change data in the Eastern Caribbean: regional overview: an example of data innovation

Data on migration, environment and climate change are often not fully accessible and shared within and between countries. Some data may be collected by national statistical offices, other data by migration authorities, other data by agencies responding to disasters and other data from agencies dealing with climate change. In a small pioneering study conducted in six countries in the Eastern Caribbean region between 2020 and 2021, IOM used a range of methods to conduct a systematic assessment of data sources relating to migration, environment and climate change in these countries (Serraglio et al., 2021). The study involved developing a standard template for data collection covering a range of different policy areas, migration, humanitarian response, climate change and disasters. The study combined desk research with in-depth interviews with "data stakeholders" from a range of different policy spheres. In addition to conducting individual interviews, the research teams also organized cross-departmental or multi-stakeholder validation workshops where the results of the data assessment exercise were presented and discussed. The study adopted a comprehensive approach involving not only collecting baseline statistics but also assessing the quality and use of data sources; gathered data on the migration, environment and climate change policy framework; and explored with policymakers or data stakeholders questions relating to how to quantify the impact of such data.

This process is intended to be one that is regularly repeated, increasing the likelihood that this may become a sustainable data initiative. While the study found that statistics on migration and environment are very limited, it was possible to identify various untapped data sources that could provide insights into migration and environmental trends. For example, the analysis of distinct household and other demographic (population-based) surveys across the six Eastern Caribbean countries found data that could be translated into statistics on human mobility in the context of climate and other environmental changes in the region. In at least four of the six countries, it was possible to identify surveys developed for other purposes that included relevant data on environmental variables and human mobility. The overall approach developed in this study provides a good way for data stakeholders from different policy domains to become more aware of data that are or are not collected relating to migration, environment and climate change, and this approach could help promote data sharing in the future.

IOM's Migration Governance Indicators project (IOM, 2022) also collects some data on the extent to which countries include references to displacement in their disaster risk reduction strategies. In the 84 countries in which IOM collected data, it was found that approximately a third of countries (28) have a national disaster risk reduction strategy with specific provisions for preventing and addressing the displacement impact of disasters (ibid).

The inclusion of references to human mobility in policy responses to climate change does not, however, mean that countries are systematically collecting data on migration and displacement and does not seem to have led to the establishment of more mechanisms to systematically collect data on migration and climate change (Guadagno, 2022). Furthermore, references to human mobility in policy documents dealing with plans to respond to climate change can be very diverse and suggest that migration is part of the problem and part of the solution (ibid).

6.2.3 Operational data

There are many agencies active on the ground in areas and regions exposed to climate change that collect operational data. IOM, for example through its "Displacement Tracking Matrix", has developed a system used to track and monitor disaster displacement and population mobility both within and between countries (see IOM, 2022). IOM has developed a capacity to collect data in areas of the world, especially those at risk of climate change. These data can often provide timely and disaggregated information on current and emerging trends in mobility linked to environmental change. In Madagascar, for example, IOM Displacement Tracking Matrix (DTM) data showed that the prolonged drought experienced in the south of the country since 2013 resulted in increased migration from the south to other regions, with some villages experiencing a 30 per cent decrease in their populations (Traore Chazalnoel and Randall, 2022). However, such data also have their limitations, as pointed out by the IOM in its latest "World Migration Report" (IOM, 2022). DTM's operational data

> *offer a partial snapshot of information related to slow-onset hazards... And the ad-hoc nature of operational data collected within the framework of time-bound projects that generally have a restricted geographical coverage, does not necessarily result in a long-term understanding of the patterns of recorded movements.*
>
> (Traore Chazalnoel and Randall, 2022)

Operational data may have their limitations, but they can certainly complement other sources of data on migration, environment and climate change. Given the scarcity of reliable national data on this, it is essential that policymakers draw on all available evidence.

6.2.4 Big data

There are several examples of innovative uses of big data to shed light on patterns of mobility linked to environmental change on the IOM Global Migration Data Portal, under the section focusing on data innovation (IOM, 2023). An interesting example is the case of "The impact of Hurricane Maria: Combining survey-based estimates and big data to produce migration estimates". The US Census Bureau combined survey-based estimates and big data to produce migration estimates for Puerto Rico after Hurricane Maria devastated the island in September 2017. The project showed that innovative data – in particular air passenger traffic data – could help estimate the impact of Hurricane Maria on migration to and from Puerto Rico more accurately than traditional survey-based methodologies. It demonstrated a large spike in Puerto Ricans flying to the USA during the latter months of 2017 and a corresponding return movement in 2018. The US Census Bureau noted that they will continue to integrate innovative data sources into the future production of migration statistics following this example.

Another example concerns the case of Bangladesh. The spread of mobile phones now makes it easier to study the mobility of people rapidly by analysing call detail records (CDRs). A study in the south of Bangladesh monitored the inflow and outflow of 6 million people after Cyclone Mahasen made landfall in the Bay of Bengal in 2013 (Xin Lu et al., 2016) (Vinke and Hoffmann, 2020). Using data collected during Cyclone Mahasen, which hit Bangladesh in 2013, researchers linked to Flowminder, a non-governmental organization (NGO) based in Sweden, used two datasets from six million de-identified mobile phone users to understand better mobility patterns. The researchers were able, using mobile phone network data, to quantify the incidence, direction, duration and seasonality of migration episodes in Bangladesh. Other studies have been innovative in combining big data on the environment, for example satellite data, data from cellular phones and data maps of climatic risks and vulnerabilities, with traditional sources of data on migration from censuses and surveys (Fussell et al., 2014; Chen et al., 2017).

Big data are already telling us a huge amount about the impact of climate change (WEF, 2018). The challenge is to harness this potential to learn more about the linkages between migration and climate change in the future. Big data can be used to create georeferenced datasets on factors affecting vulnerability and CDRs, and geospatial big data, such as remote sensing, can facilitate population mapping that can be used to study the risks of displacement linked to disasters (Ford et al., 2016). See Chapter 4 for more discussion on this topic.

6.2.5 Projections and forecasting data

Forecasts suggesting that millions of people could be forced to move due to climate change have frequently captured media headlines over the years, as mentioned at the beginning of this chapter. While many of these figures are based on rough guesstimates (Gemenne, 2011), more sophisticated models and forecasts have been developed in recent times, most notably by the World Bank. One of the most recent and sophisticated attempts to estimate and forecast future migration trends linked to climate change, which has received a great deal of attention, are the World Bank's "Groundswell" reports. These studies are especially important because they provide new data on how slow-onset climate change could contribute to significant increases in internal migration. The most widely available statistics on migration, environment and climate change tend to focus on extreme environmental events and the impact of disasters, as these kind of data is much more readily available, as explained in more detail in the next section of this chapter.

In 2018, the World Bank published the first Groundswell report (World Bank, 2018), which used a robust and novel modelling approach to help understand the scale, trajectory and spatial patterns of future climate migration within countries. The studies take a "scenario-based approach and implement a modified form of a gravity model to isolate the projected portion of future changes in spatial population distribution that can be attributed to slow-onset climate factors up to 2050" (World Bank, 2021, p. 1). The gravity model used in the reports provides indications of the relative importance of "push factors" (environmental or economic factors at origin that influence the decision to migrate) versus "pull factors" (similar factors at destination that influence the decision to migrate) over larger geographic areas. The reports recognize that future migration dynamics will be driven by several factors with varying degrees of uncertainty, from changes to local climate conditions to evolving political changes, social norms or technologies. To reflect this uncertainty, the reports suggest different scenarios for future climate-related internal migration, based on different assumptions.

The first Groundswell report focused on three regions: sub-Saharan Africa, South Asia and Latin America. The World Bank team examined how slow-onset climate change impacts water availability and crop productivity and how sea-level rise augmented by storm surges could affect future internal migration, modelling three plausible scenarios. The second Groundswell report (WB, 2021) extended the analysis to other regions: the Middle East and North Africa, East Asia and the Pacific, and Eastern Europe and Central Asia. The 2012 report also includes some qualitative research conducted in countries of the Mashreq and Small Island Developing States (SIDS). The two reports according to the World Bank "provide, for the first time, a global picture of the potential scale of internal climate migration" (World Bank, 2021, p. 1).

In 2021, the World Bank published a press release based on the calculations made in the two reports, which suggested that climate change could force up to 216 million people across six world regions to move within their countries by 2050. While this figure may seem like a very high number, the World Bank does point out in its main report, although not in the press release, that the 216 million figure represents less than three per cent of the likely total expected population in the affected regions. There are some significant regional variations, with higher percentages of the population likely to be affected in North Africa (9 per cent) and sub-Saharan Africa (4.2 per cent) compared with South Asia (1.2 per cent) and Latin America (2.6 per cent) (World Bank, 2021). Furthermore, the figure of 216 million could be an underestimate of the scale of migration linked to climate change, because the World Bank's study did not focus on estimating how many people might move voluntarily and how many might be displaced or relocated due to extreme environmental events. These studies also focus primarily on internal rather than international migration linked to climate change. The model developed by the World Bank team does not reflect the impact of rapid-onset climate change impacts, such as short-term climate variations and extreme weather events, except where successive shocks accumulate over multiple years (World Bank, 2021).

6.2.6 Limitations of forecasts and projections

Considerable literature in the migration field focuses on forecasting and the limitations of forecasting models (Sohst and Tjaden, 2020). As Sohst and Tjaden conclude after an extensive review of such literature, "Forecasting migration is no crystal ball. In fact, most forecasts turn out to be wrong ...As a general rule, the longer the forecast horizon, the greater the uncertainty" (Sohst and Tjaden, 2020, p. 11). The IPCC has also expressed some scepticism in using quantitative projections of changes in mobility to predict migration flows given the complex and multi-causal nature of such flows (IPCC, 2007).

One of the problems is that reliable data on current migration flows are often very limited, making it very difficult to forecast future trends, which may be affected by so many different factors. In a 2021 extensive review of studies on migration and climate change, for the UK government, it was found that climate and migration projections can vary hugely from one another, depending on the kinds of assumptions that are made (Selby and Daoust, 2021, p. 47). The authors of this review therefore conclude that "all estimates and projections are highly uncertain and all should be approached with caution" (Selby and Daoust, 2021, p. 63).[2]

For example, projections focusing on the expected impact of sea-level rise on migration and displacement can range from hundreds of millions to tens of thousands, depending primarily upon assumptions about potential in-place adaptations (ibid). Selby and Daoust (2021) conclude that projections are necessarily assumption-laden, and these assumptions need to be interpreted with care. Projections "must rely, first, on assumptions about future greenhouse gas emissions, and on climate scenarios of how these may affect temperatures, precipitation patterns, sea level rise and so on" (Selby and Daoust, 2021, p. 47). Projections of future climate-related migration rely second on models of population exposure to these projected climate-related changes and assumptions about how this exposure might translate into migration pressures. This includes assumptions about the causes and reasons for migration and about the potential for in-place adaptation. Moreover, projection studies rely on simplified models in which all future changes, except those associated with climate change, are held constant. For example, projections of future climate-related migration typically do not allow for or incorporate future technological or economic change, or improvements in adaptive capacities, nor adaptation measures taken in response to climate change specifically (ibid, pp. 48–49).

6.2.7 Displacement data and extreme environmental events

The most widely available statistics on migration, environment and climate change are produced on a regular basis by the Internal Displacement Monitoring Centre (IDMC), based on a variety of sources. The figures indicate that 21.6 million people were displaced by climate-related hazards worldwide in 2021 only (IDMC, 2022). In 2022, the number of internal displacements linked to disasters rose to 32.6 million (IDMC, 2023); see also Chapter 2. These figures are flow figures (new displacements registered in any given year), and the actual stock figure is considerably lower: according to IDMC, at the end of 2021, at least 5.9 million people, in 84 countries and territories, were living in displacement due to disasters that happened in previous years. The top five countries with the highest IDP stock numbers linked to disasters in 2021 can be seen in Table 6.1.

IDMC estimates highlight the importance of environmental changes in contributing to displacement each year. For example, of the 38 million "internal displacements" in 2021, 23.7 million were triggered by disasters (IDMC, 2022). Since 2008, IDMC has been publishing figures showing that there were on average 24 million new disaster displacements every year, totalling close to 320 million displacements, almost 90 per cent of which are due to weather-related hazards (IDMC, 2019). These figures mainly concern large disasters affecting areas with high population exposure (Guadagno, 2022). IDMC also collects a limited amount of data on the impact of slow-onset disasters. IDMC estimated that, in 2020, there were 46,000 new displacements due to extreme temperatures and 32,000 new displacements due to droughts. Between 2008 and 2020, IDMC statistics suggest that over 2.4 million new displacements were caused by droughts and 1.1 million by extreme temperatures (Traore Chazalnoel and Randall, 2022).

Table 6.1 Highest IDP stock numbers linked to disasters in 2021

Country	No. of IDPs due to disasters by the end of 2021
Afghanistan	1.4 million
China	943,000
The Philippines	700,000
Ethiopia	579,000
South Sudan	527,000

Source: IDMC, 2022.

6.3 Strengths and weaknesses of existing displacement figures

The IDMC figures are widely cited, but as recognized by IDMC itself and others, the data have several limitations and need to be interpreted with care. One of the challenges is that IDMC estimates are based on compilations of different sources of data at the national level, and countries do not all have a harmonized and consistent approach to data collection (IDMC, 2021; Selby and Daoust, 2021). For example, when data agencies use different methodologies to collect data on displacement within one country, this can result in different estimates of the number of IDPs. As Ginetti points out, "when actors use different methodologies to collect data on displacement within one country, this can result in multiple estimates of the number of IDPs or the volume of new displacements or returns" (Ginetti, 2020, p. 23).

Second, the data tend to refer mainly to short-term temporary movements: "much and perhaps most of this weather-related displacement comprises pre-emptive evacuations, and evidence suggests that most of it is temporary, though firm evidence on this question is lacking" (Selby and Daoust, 2021, p. 57). Time series data on the number of people displaced by disasters are limited, as usually data on displacement induced by disasters are collected for less than one month following the disaster event (Ginetti, 2020). There is a considerable lack of data on the number of people who experience protracted displacement for long periods due to disasters. Third, IDMC figures are likely to be an underestimate of the impact of the environment on displacement, because IDMC's methodology primarily captures "sudden-onset disasters", rather than "slow-onset" disasters linked to drought, desertification and sea-level rise. In addition, IDMC acknowledges that existing IDP data sources often do not fully capture the socio-economic and demographic profile of those who are displaced and their needs.

Summing up this section, there are several reasons for the paucity of timely, comparable data on migration, environment and climate change. First, it is difficult to separate the role of climate change from other economic, political and social factors that drive migration. Second, there is a basic lack of migration data (as seen in Chapter 2), and such data are particularly lacking in low- and middle-income countries, which are most vulnerable to climate change. Third, national statistical offices, the UN and governments have not agreed on a common definition of what needs to be measured for statistical purposes when collecting data on the impact of environmental changes on migration and displacement. Fourth, it is extremely difficult to forecast migration in general and migration linked to climate change in particular, as climate models and projections do not fully account for the impact of individual choice, the potential for international action and adaptation and the variability of future emissions and meteorological scenarios (Brown, 2008).

Box 6.3   Migration, environment, disaster and climate change data in the Eastern Caribbean: regional overview – an example of data innovation

Data on migration, environment and climate change are often not fully accessible and shared within and between countries. Some data may be collected by national statistical offices and other data by migration authorities, agencies responding to disasters and agencies dealing with climate change.

In a small pioneering study conducted in six countries in the Eastern Caribbean region between 2020 and 2021, IOM used a range of methods to conduct a systematic assessment of data sources relating to migration, environment and climate change in these countries (IOM, 2022). The study involved developing a standard template for data collection covering a range of different policy areas, migration, humanitarian response, climate change and disasters. The study combined desk research with in-depth interviews with "data stakeholders" from a range of different policy spheres. In addition to conducting individual interviews, the research teams also organized cross-departmental or multi-stakeholder validation workshops where the results of the data assessment exercise were presented and discussed.

The study adopted a comprehensive approach involving not only collecting baseline statistics but also assessing the quality and use of data sources; gathered data on the migration, environment and climate change policy framework; and explored with policymakers or data stakeholders questions relating to how to quantify the impact of such data. This process is intended to be one that is regularly repeated, increasing the likelihood that this may become a sustainable data initiative. While the study found that statistics on migration and the environment are very limited, it was possible to identify various untapped data sources that could provide insights into migration and environmental trends. For example, the analysis of distinct household and other demographic (population-based) surveys across the six Eastern Caribbean countries found data that could be translated into statistics on human mobility in the context of climate and other environmental changes in the region. In at least four of the six countries, it was possible to identify surveys developed for other purposes that included relevant data on environmental variables and human mobility.

The overall approach developed in this study provides a good way for data stakeholders from different policy domains to become more aware of data that are or are not collected relating to migration, environment and climate change, and this approach could help promote data sharing in the future.

6.4 Concluding remarks

Migration, environment and climate change have become a top issue of concern to researchers and policymakers around the world. The volume of studies and publications on the subject has increased enormously over the last two decades. International policy documents, such as the Global Compact for Migration and the Global Compact for Refugees, make prominent references to this topic, together with several other international processes (Guadagno, 2022). The availability of timely, reliable and comparable data on migration, environment and climate change has been recognized in several international policy documents as being vital for the development of evidence-based and holistic policies and strategies to address the impact of climate and other environmental changes and better understand the impact of mobility on the environment. The UNFCCC Task Force on Displacement, for example, has recommended to enhance research, data collection, risk analysis and sharing of information to better map, understand and manage human mobility related to the adverse impacts of climate change, in a manner that includes the participation of communities affected and at risk of displacement related to the adverse impacts of climate change (UNFCCC, 2019).

Despite growing recognition of the data challenges, in practice relatively little progress has been made in improving statistics on migration, environment and climate change over the last two decades, with the exception of some important research initiatives mentioned in this chapter. An extensive review of existing studies on migration, environment and climate change found that the strongest evidence of existing climate-related migration relates to shocks – flood, storms, droughts and short-term temperature and precipitation fluctuations (Selby and Daoust, 2021). Most countries in the world do not publish any kind of migration and environmental statistical report. It is difficult to find examples of countries that have developed an explicit strategy to improve the responsible collection and use of data on migration, environment and climate change. Such strategies could aim to integrate all relevant data sources and promote data collaboration and data sharing between actors responsible for addressing climate change and migration challenges.

At the global level, there are no comprehensive statistics on migration, environment and climate change. As this chapter has shown, the best available international data provide information on the numbers of people displaced, often for short periods, due to extreme environmental events, such as disasters. It is much more difficult to find data on the impact of slow-onset environmental changes on the movement of people or, conversely, on the impact of current migration flows on areas already vulnerable to climate change. It is also hard to find data on the extent to which environmental changes might make it more difficult for people to move and to adapt to climate change.

There are many reasons for the lack of data on migration, environment and climate change. Part of the problem is technical – it is difficult to identify the environment as a key driver of migration, and there is a lack of agreement on what needs to be measured, and how to describe those whose migration, whether forced or voluntary, is linked to environmental changes, but part of the problem is political and reflects the fact that although human mobility has been recognized as a factor by the IPCC, mobility considerations are not fully factored into national climate change responses, as evident in reviews, for example, of national adaptation plans and responses to climate change, as noted earlier.

Looking ahead, forecasting and projection data are improving. The first estimates about the likely global impact of environmental changes on migration were fairly rudimentary, as noted above, and often dismissed as no more than guesstimates. In recent years, the World Bank has developed more sophisticated models through its Groundswell project, which provides the international community with more solid projections of the likely impact of climate change on the movement of people in different regions of the world. The monitoring of policy responses has also seen some progress. For example, IOM's "Migration Governance Indicators" project gathers data on a regular basis on the extent to which mobility is factored into some aspects of environmental policy at the national level. Further, at the operational level important examples of data innovation exist – see Box 6.3, focusing on efforts to improve data collection in the Eastern Caribbean region.

Improving data on migration, environment and climate change will require action on both the technical and political levels. At the political level, initiatives such as the Eastern Caribbean project (Box 6.3) suggest that much can be achieved in the short term at a relatively low cost by creating a framework in which data actors from different policy spheres can come together to promote regular information exchange, identify shared priorities and foster technical improvements in data collection. The production of national "environmental migration profiles" could provide a useful means to bring together disparate sources of data on migration, displacement and the environment. IOM has worked with countries to produce a series of such profiles. However, too often these have been one-off exercises. Environmental migration profiles should be thought of as a process of regularly bringing together key actors at the national level to share and update data on migration, environment and climate change. The East Caribbean example also suggests that there is much scope to promote regional data-sharing initiatives and dialogue to improve the evidence based on migration and the environment.

At the technical level, the UN has a key role to play in providing technical guidance to countries to promote common definitions and terminologies and to assist in boosting data capacities. There is a need to develop a dedicated international programme to build the capacities of statistical systems to collect, analyse and use migration, environment and climate change data in a responsible way (Guadagno, 2022). Capacity-building programmes should also include the private sector and promote the use of non-traditional data sources. Such sources of data can complement existing sources of data from surveys, censuses and administrative units. The potential to leverage new technologies and big data to produce better data on migration, environment and climate change is considerable. In other policy spheres such as health and development, "data collaboratives" have been created (Chapter 4) to promote the innovative use of big data to inform policy.

Notes

1 "Migration in an interconnected world: New directions for action, report of the Global Commission on INTERNATIONAL Migration, 2005".
2 Selby and Daoust cite the example of a report from the Internal Displacement Monitoring Centre (IDMC), which projects that the risk of internal displacement due to flooding will double by 2090, especially in low-income countries. They suggest that, even if this projection is correct, based on current patterns, displacement is likely to mostly involve temporary evacuations and that the projected increases contrast with any equivalent present-day trend. Moreover, roughly half of the projected increase in displacement is likely to be a result of assumed population growth, not climate change. Furthermore, the projections do not factor in the impact of possible future adaptations (Selby and Daoust, 2021, p. 49).

References

Ardittis, S. and Laczko, F. (2020). Migration, the environment and climate change: What data do we need and how do we get it? In *Migration Policy Practice (January–March 2020)*. Geneva: IOM.
Asian Development Bank. (2012). *Addressing Climate Change and Migration in Asia and the Pacific*. Manila: Asian Development Bank.
Bell, M. and Charles-Edwards, E. (2013). Cross-national comparisons of internal migration: An update on global patterns and trends. *UN Population Division, Technical Paper; no. 2013/1*. New York: United Nations.
Benveniste, H., Oppenheimer, M., and Fleurbaey, M. (2022). Climate Change increases resource-constrained international immobility. *Nature Climate Change*, 12, 634–641.
Bergmann, J., Vinke, K., Fernandez Palomino, C.A., Gornott, C., Glexner, S., Laudien, R., Lobanova, A., Ludescher, J., and Schellnhuber, H.J. (2021). *Assessing the Evidence: Climate Change and Migration in Peru*. Potsdam/Geneva: Potsdam Institute for Climate Impact Research, and International Organization for Migration.
Brown, O. (2008). *Migration and Climate Change*. IOM Migration Research Series, Geneva: IOM.
Chen, J.J., Mueller, V., Jia, Y., and Tseng, S.K.H. (2017). Validating migration responses to flooding using satellite and vital registration data. *American Economic Review*, 107(5), 441–445.
El Hinnawi, Essam (1985). *Environmental refugees*. Nairobi: United Nations Environment Programme.
Ford, J., Tilleard, S., Berrang-Ford, L., and Bizikova, L. (2016). Big Data has big potential for applications to climate change adaptation, September, 27th, PNAS, Proceedings of the National Academy of Sciences. https://doi.org/10.1073/pnas
Foresight Report. (2011). *Migration and Global Environmental Change*. London: UK Government Office for Science.
Fussell, E., Hunter, L.M., and Gray, C.L. et al. (2014). Measuring the Environmental Dimensions of Human Migration: The Demographer's Toolkit. Global Environmental Change, 2014, September 1st; 28: 182–191.

Gemenne, F. (2011). Why the numbers don't add up: A review of estimates and predictions of people displaced by environmental changes. *Global Environmental Change*, 21(Supplement 1), 541–549. https://doi.org/10.1016/j.gloenvcha.2011.09.005.

Ginetti, J. (2020). Internal displacement data gaps and challenges: Why they matter for policy and operations. In *Migration Policy Practice*, Vol. X, Number 1 (January–March 2020). Geneva: IOM-Eurasylum.

Guadagno, L. (2022). Goal 13: Monitoring climate and migration topics. In Elisa Mosler Vidal and Frank Laczko (Eds.), *Migration and the SDGs: Measuring Progress*. 102–109. Geneva: IOM.

Hugo, G. (1996). Environmental concerns and international migration. *International Migration Review*, 30(1), 105–131.

Internal Displacement Monitoring Centre. (2019). *Disaster Displacement: A Global Review, 2008–2018, Thematic Report*. Geneva: IDMC.

Internal Displacement Monitoring Centre (IDMC). (2021). *GRID 2021: Internal Displacement in a Changing Climate*. Geneva: IDMC.

Internal Displacement Monitoring Centre (IDMC). (2022). *Global Report on Internal Displacement in 2022*. Geneva: IDMC.

Internal Displacement Monitoring Centre (IDMC). (2023). *Global Report on Internal Displacement in 2023*. Geneva: IDMC.

IOM. (1992, June). *Migration and the Environment*. Geneva: IOM and the Refugee Policy Group, IOM.

IOM. (2019). *Glossary on Migration*. Geneva: IOM.

IOM. (2022). *The World Migration Report*. Geneva: IOM.

IOM. (2023). *Harnessing Data Innovation for Migration Policy: A Handbook for Practitioners*. Geneva: IOM, Global Data Institute.

IPCC (Intergovernmental Panel on Climate Change). (2007). Climate change 2007: Synthesis report. In Core writing team, Pachauri, R.K. and Reisinger, A. (Eds.), *Contribution of Working Groups I, II, and III to the Fourth Assessment Report of the IPCC*. Geneva: IPCC 1–112.

Kolmannskog, V.O. (2008). *Future Floods of Refugees. A Comment on Climate Change, Conflict and Forced Migration*. Oslo: Norwegian Refugee Council.

Laczko, F. (2010). *Migration, the Environment and Climate Change: Assessing the Evidence*, Study-Team on Climate-Induced Migration. Washington, DC: The German Marshall Fund of the United States.

Laczko, F. and Aghazarm, C. (Eds.). (2019). *Migration, Environment and Climate Change: Assessing the Evidence*. Geneva: IOM.

Laczko, F. and Warner, K. (2009). Migration, Environment and Development: New Directions for Research, paper for IUSSP (International Union for the Scientific Study of Population) XXVI population conference, Marrakesh. Available at https://ipc2009.popconf.org

Martin, S. (2013). "Environmental Change and Migration: What We Know", Migration Policy Institute, Policy Briefs, September.

McTegart, W.J., Sheldon, G.W., and Griffiths, D.C. (1990). *Impacts Assessment of Climate Change*. Report of Working Group II. Edited by IPCC First Assessment Report. Canberra: Australia Government Publishing Service.

Melde, S., Laczko, F., and Gemmene, F. (Eds.). (2017). *Making Mobility Work for Adaptation to Environmental Changes: Results from the MECLEP Global Research*. Geneva: IOM.

Naik, A., Stigter, E., and Laczko, F. (2007) *"Migration, Development and Natural Disasters": Insights from the Indian Ocean Tsunami.* Geneva: IOM Migration Research Series, IOM.

Piguet, E. and Laczko, F. (Eds.). (2014). *People on the Move in a Changing Climate: The Regional Impact of Environmental Change on Migration.* Springer: Dordrecht, Netherlands.

Selby, J. and Daoust, G. (2021). *Rapid Evidence Assessment on the Impacts of Climate Change on Migration Patterns.* London: Foreign, Commonwealth and Development Office. Available at www.gov.uk

Serraglio, A.D., Adaawen, S., and Schraven, B. (2021). *Migration, Environment, Disaster and Climate Change Data in the Eastern Caribbean – Regional Overview.* Berlin: IOM GMDAC.

Sohst, R.R. and Tjaden, J. (2020). Forecasting migration: A policy guide to common approaches and models. In *Migration Policy Practice, Vol. X, Number 4 (September–December, 2020).* Geneva: IOM, 8–14.

Traore Chazalnoe, M. and Randall, A. (2022). Migration and the slow-onset impacts of climate change: Taking stock and taking action. *IOM World Migration Report 2022,* Geneva: IOM.

UK Government Office for Science. (2011). *Migration and Global Environmental Change,* final project report, the Government Office for Science, London. Available at www.gov.uk/government

UN Development Programme. (2009). *Human Development Report: Overcoming Barriers: Human Mobility and Development.* New York, NY: UNDP.

UN Development Programme. (2020). *Human Mobility, Shared Opportunities: A Review of the 2009 Human Development Report and the Way Ahead.* New York, NY: UNDP.

United Nations High Commissioner for Refugees (UNHCR). (2021). *How Climate Change Impacts Refugees and Displaced Communities.* Geneva: UNHCR.

United Nations High Commissioner for Refugees (UNHCR). (2022). *Climate Change and Disaster Displacement.* Geneva: UNHCR.

United Nations Framework Convention on Climate Change (UNFCCC). (2019). Migration, displacement and human mobility. *UNFCCC Task Force on Displacement.* Bonn: UNFCCC.

UN Statistics Division. (2022). Background document to the report of the Secretary-General on Climate Change Statistics, Global Set and Metdata. (E/CN.3/2022/17).

Vinke, K. and Hoffmann, R. (2020). Data for a difficult subject: Climate change and human migration. In *Migration Policy Practice (January–March, 2020).* Geneva: IOM-Eurasylum.

World Bank. (2018). *Groundswell Part 1: Preparing for Internal Climate Migration.* Washington, DC: World Bank.

World Bank. (2021). *Groundswell Part 2: Acting on Internal Migration.* Washington DC: World Bank.

World Economic Forum, WEF. (2018). *How Big Data Can Help Us Fight Climate Change Faster.* Geneva: WEF.

Xin, L., Wrathall, D.J., Sundsoy, P.R., Nadiruzzaman, Md, Wetter, E., Iqbal, A., Quereshi, T., Tatem, A., Canright, G., Engo-Monson, K., and Bengtsson, L. (2016, May). Unveiling Hidden Migration and Mobility Patterns in Climate Stressed Regions: A Longitudinal Study of Six Million Anonymous Mobile Phone Users in Bangladesh. *Global Environmental Change,* 38, 1–7.

7 Improving data on migration and health after the global pandemic

7.1 Introduction

The global pandemic raised awareness about the importance of obtaining timely health data. The pandemic also highlighted the close connections between migration and health. The World Health Organization (WHO) has for many years recognized that migration is a key determinant of health and well-being. For the WHO, health is defined broadly as a state of complete physical, mental and social well-being and not only the absence of disease or infirmity (WHO, 2006). Migration is often linked to many factors that can contribute to ill health, for example difficult and unsafe working conditions, overcrowded housing, prolonged periods in detention and embarking on dangerous journeys in search of safety and a better life. These risks are compounded by health policies and systems, which do not sufficiently include and address the special needs of migrants.

In the WHO's first-ever World Report on the Health of Refugees and Migrants published in 2022, the Director-General of WHO, Dr. Tedros Adhanom Ghebreyesus, states that "we must invest in strengthening and implementing policies that promote refugee and migrant health, guided by innovative data gathering and analysis" (WHO, 2022a, p. 1). Basic data about the health of migrants are often lacking. As noted in Chapter 5 of this volume, there is a lack of data disaggregation of key Sustainable Development Goal (SDG) indicators by migratory status, including those relating to health, making it very difficult to identify which migrants have the poorest health status.

This chapter seeks to answer three broad questions. First, what are the main sources of data on migration and health? Second, what are some of the key trends in international migration and health based on the available data? Third, what are some of the innovative measures that have been taken to improve the collection and responsible use of data on migration and health to inform policy and practice, and what may we learn from these? The chapter also includes a special section examining the impact of the global pandemic on migrants and on the collection of data on migration and health.

Research on the topic of migration and health has been growing in recent years, so much so that specialist academic journals focusing on the topic have

DOI: 10.4324/9781003266075-9

been launched (WHO, 2022a). The WHO systematically reviews this growing body of evidence in its global report (WHO, 2022a), explaining how migrants' physical and mental health can be adversely affected due to a range of factors linked to migration and the treatment of migrants, with different stages of the migration life cycle affecting health in different ways.

For example, migrants are often concentrated in what are called 3D jobs – dirty, dangerous and demanding – where they may be exposed to occupational injury. Many migrants and refugees may be vulnerable to ill health because they are forced to flee their homes for environmental reasons or due to conflict. Every year, thousands of migrants embark on dangerous journeys in search of a better life or safety. On these journeys, they are often exposed to enormous risks to their health, which can ultimately result in death. Since 2014, for example, the International Organization for Migration (IOM) has recorded the deaths of more than 50,000 migrants attempting to cross international borders around the world (IOM, 2022a). The WHO concludes that "at the broadest level being a refugee or migrant clearly carries significant health risks, to the extent that displacement or migration must itself be considered a determinant of health" (WHO, 2022a, p. 93).

As outlined later in this chapter, in many countries migrants lack access to health care, despite the fact that health has been recognized by the United Nations (UN) as a human right. For several years, the WHO and its member states across the globe have been advocating for universal health coverage; however, in practice migrants often lack access to health care, which contributes to a negative impact on their health (IOM, 2022b; 2022c). Migrants may face a number of barriers in accessing health services due to factors such as their legal status, lack of health insurance, language and cultural differences, lack of information about services and fear of detention and deportation, all of which make seeking health care difficult. Indeed, migration policies can also have an impact on migrant's health

> *many countries immigration laws require migrants to pass a medical exam to obtain residency status or a work permit. Testing positive for tuberculosis, HIV, a sexually transmitted infection, or even pregnancy can exclude migrants from obtaining a work permit or lead to their expulsion.*
>
> (GMG, 2017, p. 114)

Migration policies in some countries may place an emphasis on detention in closed facilities, jails and offshore. The length of detention can increase the severity of mental health disorders and psychosocial trauma.

However, migration alone is not necessarily associated with poor health. Several studies show that migration can have beneficial health consequences for a migrant, when, for example, someone moves from a poorer to richer country, which has a better healthcare system. Migration can also have many other benefits for health. For example, studies show that the families of migrants in countries of origin may be able to spend more on health care if they receive financial remittances from family members living abroad (Nathaniel, 2019; Kapri and Jha, 2020), and/or if positive health-related ideas, behaviours or information are transmitted among migrants and their transnational networks – also called "social remittances" (Levitt, 1998). As noted in Chapter 5, "Social remittances" are "the ideas, behaviours, identities, and social capital that flow from receiving to sending country communities" (ibid). Health systems in Organization for Economic Cooperation and Development (OECD) countries, as we shall outline below, also benefit enormously from the international migration of health workers, (OECD, 2019; WHO, 2022a).

In short, the relationship between migration and health is not straightforward. The impact of migration on health can vary between different migrant groups and according to the circumstances in which people migrate. In the worst cases, migrants may be deprived of their liberty and forced into trafficking, which can have damaging negative consequences for their physical and mental health. As we shall outline below, the recent global pandemic in many ways exacerbated the health risks faced by migrants.

7.2 COVID-19: data on its impact on migrants and migration

The coronavirus (COVID-19) global pandemic highlighted the linkages between mobility and health as never before. It showed not only how quickly global migration can be affected by a pandemic but also how traditional data collection efforts can be rapidly halted or delayed (Laczko, 2021). In April 2020, it was reported by the Pew Research Centre that 91 per cent of the world's population was living in a country which had imposed restrictions due to the pandemic on people arriving from other countries who are neither citizens nor residents (Connor, 2020).

The UN Department of Economic and Social Affairs (DESA) (2020a) estimates that due to the pandemic, the number of international migrants globally may have fallen by around 2 million. This figure corresponds to a decrease of approximately 27 per cent in the growth expected between July 2019 and June 2020 (Laczko, 2021). In a study of international migration trends for G20 countries, OECD, International Labour Organization (ILO), IOM and United Nations High Commissioner for Refugees (UNHCR) also concluded that "overall, 2020 is projected to be a historical low for international migration in the OECD and G20 countries" (OECD et al., 2021, p. 5). Before COVID-19, permanent migration flows to OECD countries reached 5.3 million in 2019. During the first half of 2020, recorded migration flows fell by 46 per cent compared with the same period in 2019. Figures for the second quarter of 2020 suggested an even sharper decline of 72 per cent (OECD, 2021). Refugee flows were also dramatically affected; for example, during 2020 the number of refugees resettled was 46 per cent lower than during 2019 (OECD, 2021).

It is difficult to know the full impact of the COVID-19 pandemic on migrants, not only because of a lack of disaggregated data but also because the work of national statistical offices (NSOs) was negatively impacted by the pandemic. Global surveys of NSOs conducted by the World Bank and the UNSD during the pandemic showed that COVID-19 caused serious disruptions to data collection, especially in low- and middle-income countries, with many having to cancel or postpone censuses and surveys. In May 2020, for example, 96 per cent of NSOs reported that they had stopped face-to-face data collection (UN DESA, 2020b).

Available data suggest that some migrants were more vulnerable to the spread of the virus than other groups in society. Many migrants especially face risks during a global pandemic; it is well documented that they often lack access to health care, are more likely to live in overcrowded and substandard housing and many work in low-paid jobs, which cannot be done remotely from home. Furthermore, migrants are usually more exposed to health risks as they are over-represented in jobs in the healthcare sector and sectors such as services and construction (Laczko, 2021). According to data from Eurostat, 30 per cent of foreign citizens in European countries lived in overcrowded households in 2018 compared with 18 per cent of citizens (see IOM, 2022b).

Some evidence suggests that where data were available, the incidence of COVID-19 was higher among migrants than non-migrants. For example, in Norway, Sweden and Denmark, migrants seem to be more likely to have been infected by COVID-19 (OECD, 2020). In the case of Norway, among the confirmed cases of COVID-19, it was found that 31 per cent were foreign-born, which is almost twice as high as their share of the population. However, in the case of Italy, only five per cent of cases concerned foreigners, or only about half of their share of the population (OECD, 2020).

Given the different demographic profiles of countries and differences in COVID-19-related data collection, it is not easy to make comparisons between them. Few countries collect data on the number of people who died from COVID-19 disaggregated by migratory status, but some countries do. Such data for France, Sweden and the Netherlands indicate higher death rates among migrants during the first wave of the pandemic in 2020. Drawing together this information, the OECD concluded that:

> *Immigrants are disproportionately affected by COVID-19. In virtually all countries for which data are available (Canada, Denmark, France, Germany, Italy, the Netherlands, Norway, Portugal, Sweden, the United Kingdom and the United States) – with the exception of Ireland – immigrants were much more likely than their native-born peers to catch the disease, to develop severe symptoms, and to face higher mortality risks.*
> (OECD, 2022, p. 1).

Further evidence from a review of studies in 82 high-income countries suggests that migrants were at high risk of exposure to, and infection with,

COVID-19. It was also found, based on analysis of datasets available in these countries, that there was a disproportionate representation of migrants in reported COVID-19 deaths (Hayward et al., 2020).

Despite being at higher risk of infection and death from COVID-19, migrants were in many countries less likely to be fully included in national vaccination plans in response to the pandemic. In surveys of the National Deployment and Vaccination Plans in response to COVID-19, the WHO and IOM found that while the majority of migrants in a legal situation were included in national vaccination programmes, this was the case for less than half of migrants in an irregular situation. In a survey conducted by the IOM, only 28 per cent of countries included irregular migrants, and only 45 per cent included refugees in their COVID-19 vaccination plans (IOM, 2021).

IOM collected data from January and December 2021 from nearly 200 of its offices around the world. IOM found that in 45 countries surveyed, it was not clear what level of access to the vaccine migrants had. Sometimes, this was due to a lack of disaggregated data and sometimes because policymakers prefer to avoid publicizing the government's intention to include migrants in the national vaccination campaigns to avoid xenophobic reactions from the general population. Of the 180 IOM country offices providing data, 149 (83 per cent) reported that migrants with legal status have access to COVID-19 vaccines in practice, while only 84 offices (46 per cent) reported that migrants in irregular situations have access. In some countries, IOM reports that certain laws and regulations prohibit some categories of migrants from having access to public health services. Some countries require specific documents to prove legal status in a country before someone can be included in the vaccination programme. In some countries, undocumented migrants may fear that data shared with health authorities may be shared with immigration authorities and used to deport them. In some countries, migrants may lack information in their own language about the procedures that need to be followed to gain access to COVID-19 vaccines (IOM, 2021).

In response to this challenge, the WHO produced an extensive guide titled *Strengthening COVID-19 vaccine demand and uptake in refugees and migrants* (WHO, 2022b). The guide was designed to support policymakers and provides guidance on data collection, coordination of policy and planning, implementing communication strategies, social media monitoring, community engagement and capacity-building monitoring and evaluation.

During the pandemic, there were also reports of increased anti-migrant sentiment, which may have had a negative impact on migrants' health. In the WHO's "Apart Together" survey of 30,000 migrants in 170 countries, nearly 30 per cent of respondents aged 20–29 reported that anti-migrant sentiment had worsened (WHO, 2020).

To sum up, the pandemic increased the public's awareness about the importance of having solid, reliable, timely and actionable data. The latest statistics about COVID-19 and the use of technical terms such as "R" numbers received widespread publicity. Indeed, the UN has commented that data were the first line of defence against the pandemic before vaccines were developed (UN, 2022). The pandemic also raised awareness about the linkages between migration and health and highlighted the risks and vulnerabilities that migrants are exposed to. While COVID-19 had a negative impact on traditional data collection methods, it also contributed to more data innovation and data partnerships between the public and private sectors in an effort to better track mobility trends (IOM, 2023).

7.3 Overview of key sources of data on migration and health

The data required to inform migration and health policies and practices are varied, and no one data source can provide all the information needed by policymakers. The migration and health "data ecosystem" includes a range of different types of data, coming from various sources, which need to be integrated and managed to inform effective policy responses.

This includes gathering data on the health status of different groups of migrants, some of whom may be easier to reach than others with data collection methods. It includes gathering data on a range of different health indicators, which may cover both physical and mental well-being. It involves gathering data on both communicable and non-communicable diseases (NCDs). It includes gathering data on health policy responses and their impact, and the access migrants have two different types of health care. It also entails gathering data for global health monitoring frameworks, such as the WHO's Triple Billion targets and SDG targets focusing on migration and health. It also involves collecting data on the movement of health workers – and data on many other areas.

Collecting these data is challenging because migrants may often be part of so-called "hidden populations" and may be frequently uncounted. The WHO notes that "fewer data are available about hard-to-reach populations, such as irregular migrants, refugees not living in camps, victims of trafficking, deportees, stateless individuals and people perpetually on the move" (WHO, 2022a, p. 250). Another special challenge when collecting data on migration and health concerns data protection. As personal data about someone's health can be very sensitive, it is essential that adequate safeguards are in place when sharing and using such data to inform policy and practice. In the Global Migration Group's first handbook on data on migration and development, this point is underlined: "Caution is advised regarding how data on migrants' health are collected and disseminated, as data can be used to stigmatize and discriminate against migrants, especially data related to communicable diseases" (Lopez et al., 2017, p. 115).

An agreed and functioning global health and migration indicator framework has yet to be developed, partly because this would be a very complex exercise. To be comprehensive, such a framework might need to gather data on migrants' access to healthcare services, provide data on the health status of migrants and provide indicators of the broader impact of migration on health,

Improving data on migration and health after the global pandemic 163

for example, through the sending of different types of remittances or the hiring of health workers.

At the global level, little data are available on migration and health that could be used to develop standardized indicators. It is difficult, for example, to report on the extent to which the health of migrants is improving in relation to the health targets identified under the SDGs, as noted in Chapter 5. SDG 3 calls upon states to "ensure healthy lives and promote well-being for all at all ages". Relatively little can be said about the SDGs and health and migration if one looks at other indicators. The challenge is not simply a lack of disaggregation of health indicators by migratory status, as data, even if disaggregated, are generally of poor quality. As the WHO points out in its global report, most administrative data collected by health systems are fragmented, not easy to access and often of poor quality and reliability (WHO, 2022a, p. 213).

7.3.1 Sources of data on health and migration

The picture of migration and health is skewed because most data come from a small set of countries as we show below. The best data on the health risks faced by migrants tend to come from middle-income and high-income countries (Brian, 2021). Yet, migrants may face greater health risks in the poorest countries and in countries dealing with humanitarian crises or emergencies. Risks may be greater in these countries due to the lack of health care and labour market regulation. However, even in the richer European region, the WHO reports that only 25 of its 53 member states' health and information systems collect refugee and migrant health data (WHO, 2022a). Although health information systems are the major source of data on the health status of the population in many countries, this kind of administrative data is rarely disaggregated by migratory status.

7.3.1.1 Censuses

Population censuses are a key source of data on international migration, providing comparable and reliable data on the characteristics and well-being of migrants (Chapter 2). Most censuses include a question on country of birth, or less commonly, as seen in preceding chapters, on country of citizenship, which can be used to measure the number of migrants residing in a country, but few censuses collect much information about the health status of respondents, as seen, for example, in the international database on censuses compiled by IPUMS, which has collated census data from 103 countries (Mosler Vidal, 2022). One recent exception is the UK, which included a number of health questions in its 2021 census; data are collected on general health, long-lasting health conditions and illnesses, activity restriction and provision of unpaid care.

Even if censuses do not provide direct information about health indicators, they can provide very useful data on the social determinants of health. For example, in a pilot study using IPUMS data, IOM explored how far it is possible to disaggregate census data relating to SDG target 8.6.1 (the proportion of youth not in employment, education or training) from census data, using the variables "nativity", "native-born" or "foreign-born" as indicators of migratory status (Jeffers et al., 2018).

7.3.1.2 Surveys of migrants

Relatively few countries conduct specialized nationally representative surveys focusing on questions on migration and health. Surveys can shed light on many different aspects of health and migration, including the health status of migrants, their access to health services and the factors that influence their health status. However, several international household surveys do include health-related questions. The WHO reviewed relevant evidence from surveys in five major surveys – the "Multiple Indicator Cluster Survey" (MICS), the "Demographic and Health Survey" (DHS), the "European Social Survey", the Household Survey Data Bank, "BADEHOG", and the "Programme for International Student Assessment" (PISA). The review found that each of the surveys uses a slightly different definition to identify migrants, making it sometimes difficult to draw comparisons between these surveys. None of these surveys were designed specifically to study population movement, but all provide some important data on migration and health, especially for low-income countries where such data are scarce. The MICS and the DHS are the largest international surveys, which include data on migrants.

DHSs are comparable nationally representative household surveys that have been conducted in more than 85 countries since 1984. The DHS collects a wide range of objective and self-reported data with a strong focus on indicators of fertility, reproductive health, maternal and child health, mortality, nutrition and self-reported health behaviours among adults. The DHS therefore provides a potentially rich source of data on migration and health, where surveys disaggregate data by migratory status. Migrants can be identified in these surveys, which collect data on citizenship, country of birth and length of stay or date of entry. The surveys are usually designed to meet the data requirements of a particular country but also include basic common questions asked in all countries. DHSs can also be used to understand trends in internal migration between rural and urban areas and international migration between countries. A 2012 review of 85 national DHSs found detailed information that only 12 countries included a specific module focusing on migration (WHO, 2022a).

Surveys can also tell much about the social determinants of health that may be related to migration. For example, the BADEHOG surveys collect data on overcrowding, as measured by the number of people sleeping in a single bedroom. This information is highly relevant to migration and health, as overcrowding is associated with an increased risk of transmission of communicable diseases, and can contribute to greater levels of domestic violence and poor mental health.

In seven of the nine countries in Latin America and the Caribbean covered by BADEHOG surveys, a relatively larger proportion of international migrants lived in households where three or more people shared a bedroom (WHO, 2022a).

In 15 of 25 countries surveyed by MICS and DHS, international migrants were considerably less likely to have health insurance coverage than the host populations. This was also true in eight of the nine selected Latin American and Caribbean countries in the BADEHOG surveys. To give but one stark example, data from 2018 suggest that only just under a quarter (24.5 per cent) of Venezuelan migrants in Colombia were part of the health insurance system, compared with 93 per cent of those born in Colombia. In Chile, migrants are 7.5 times more likely to report not having health insurance than the Chilean-born population (WHO, 2022a).

To sum up, although well-established international survey instruments exist, the largest household surveys currently provide relatively little robust, comparable information about the health of migrants, and these data are available for only a small number of countries and only a few migration and health indicators (WHO, 2022a). Therefore, a new specialized international migration and health survey is needed, together with a programme to add more health questions to existing migration-related surveys.

7.3.1.3 Administrative data

Health information systems are the major source of data on the health status of the population in many countries. However, these data are often not readily compiled, not disaggregated by migratory status and not easily accessible due to data protection requirements. It is also difficult to compare such data across countries because national health information systems tend to use different definitions of migration and collect data over different time periods. Even the best health information system may not collect data on certain hard-to-reach populations, such as homeless migrants or undocumented migrants. In short, health and information systems often collect a great deal of administrative data on health, but very little specifically on migrants and refugees.

Administrative records can be a valuable source of data on certain aspects of migration and health, for instance when it comes to collecting data on hidden populations such as victims of human trafficking. Human trafficking is clearly also a health issue and is addressed in dedicated SDG targets: SDG target 8.7 calls for immediate and effective measures to eradicate forced labour and end modern slavery and human trafficking, and SDG target 16.2 calls for an end to child trafficking. Monitoring progress in achieving the targets related to human trafficking in the framework of the SDGs requires countries to report the number of trafficking victims per 100,000 population, by sex, age and form of exploitation, whether people cross borders or not.

Human trafficking survivors often need a range of health services to respond to their immediate physical and emotional health care concerns to longer-term mental health issues. Health issues can include sexually transmitted infections, physical injuries, burns, anxiety, post-traumatic stress disorder and some form of trauma. In recent years, data on human trafficking have improved, and the number of studies has increased (see Galez-Davis et al., 2022). A specialist guide titled "Caring for Trafficked Persons: A Guide for Health Providers" has been published in recent years by IOM (IOM, 2017).

Gathering data on human trafficking is a very challenging task as this is a hidden crime. However, many counter-trafficking agencies providing support to victims of trafficking routinely collect data on the people they assist. These administrative and operational data constitute a key source of data about trafficking, providing a wealth of detailed information about a population that would be otherwise hard to reach (Galez-Davis et al., 2022). These data are collected regularly and at relatively little extra cost, as they are part of an agency's existing operations. In the absence of other sources of data on trafficking and health, administrative data are a key source of information about victims of trafficking. To make such data more accessible, IOM and other partners established the "Counter-Trafficking Data Collaborative" (CTDC), the first global repository of primary case data on human trafficking, which brings together anonymized administrative data from different organizations around the world (ibid). CTDC provides a platform for front-line organizations to share their data safely and in a standardized format. The platform includes information on over 156,000 cases, of which 73 per cent are women and girls.

However, one of the challenges of working with administrative data is that these can be very diverse. Different organizations may use different methods and concepts when collecting operational trafficking data. In response to this challenge, IOM and partners have been developing an "International Classification Standard for Administrative Data on Trafficking in Persons" (ICS-TIP). The aim is to provide standard guidance to front-line agencies on trafficking data collection, data analysis, data protection and data sharing (ibid).

7.3.1.4 Operational data

Another potentially useful and rich source of data on migration and health comes from the operational data collected by UN agencies such as IOM and UNHCR, which have health programmes targeting migrants. For example, IOM conducts migration health assessments that capture a great deal of information about the health of migrants. In 2016, it reported that it conducted 400,000 health assessments of migrants and refugees. This information, as noted by IOM, could be used to better understand the prevalence of diseases such as tuberculosis (TB) and conditions such as malnutrition among migrant populations. In 2021, IOM provided over 109,000 COVID-19 tests worldwide and performed more than 75,800 tests in emergency settings around the world. UNHCR has an "Integrated Refugee Health Information System" (IRHIS), which is used to monitor refugee health status where services are provided specifically to refugees. UNHCR used IRHIS to collect and analyse health information in 22 countries (UNHCR, 2021).

7.3.1.5 Big data and new technologies

As noted at the beginning of this book and in Chapter 4, we are living in a new era when it comes to thinking about migration data. Due to technological advancements, the growth in data has been exponential. One estimate suggested that every person on earth had created 1.7 MB of data every second by 2020 (see Chapter 4). Technology has also increased our capacity to analyse data. Furthermore, the global pandemic accelerated interest in using these non-traditional data sources.

Big data platforms have been widely used to provide information on the health and well-being of populations around the world. In the early literature on big data, there was quite a lot of focus on health issues (Harford, 2020). There was much discussion about the potential of using big data to inform health policy, for instance demonstrating how early detection of seasonal influenza epidemics could be improved by monitoring the volume of relevant queries on search engines, although later research found that such predictions can be inaccurate if not complemented with other sources of data (ibid).

Several examples of how big data can be used to improve our understanding of migration and health can be found in IOM's Data Innovation Directory (IOM, 2023). For example, in Namibia a project measured the effectiveness of social distancing measures using mobile phone data. The project used anonymized and aggregated data from call detail records provided by mobile network operators (MNOs) to analyse the mobility patterns of populations during the COVID-19 pandemic in Namibia. In response to the pandemic, there has been a growth in the number of "data collaboratives", which aim to strengthen public–private partnerships to harness the potential of big data as explained in Chapter 4. An example of a migration and health collaborative is the "COVID-19 Mobility Data Network", which is a network of researchers who have agreed to collaborate with technology companies to produce situation reports on COVID-19 (GovLab, 2022).

7.4 Data on migration and health policies and access to health services

Data on migration and health policies and programmes are often easier to find than data on the health status of migrants, especially for higher-income countries. Quite a lot is known about national health policies and the extent to which they address the needs of migrants. In recent years, several new initiatives have been launched, which are described below, which collect data on migration and health policies and programmes. Nonetheless, even in a high-income region such as Europe, the WHO reported as of 2017 that only 11 of 42 countries had developed national immunization plans, which included refugees and migrants (WHO, 2022a).

168 *Data availability on key migration topics*

7.4.1 Migration Governance Indicators

IOM developed a set of nearly 100 Migration Governance Indicators in 2015, in partnership with the Economist Intelligence Unit. Some of the data collected by IOM provide information on the extent to which countries grant universal access to health care for all, including migrants. Data collected between 2018 and 2021 in 84 countries show that only half of the countries report that all migrants have access to government-funded health services under the same conditions as nationals, regardless of their migratory status (WHO, 2022a). Just over one-third of countries reported that access depends on migratory status, and in eight per cent of countries, it was reported that migrants only have access to emergency health care services; in five per cent of countries, migrants have no access to any government-funded health services. As mentioned above, UNHCR also collects data on refugees' access to health care through its "Integrated Refugee Health Information System (IRHIS)".[1]

7.4.2 The Migrant Integration Policy Index (MIPEX)

The MIPEX project has been collecting data on the integration of refugees and migrants since 2004. MIPEX has expanded to cover 56 countries across six continents. In addition to including all European Union (EU) member states, MIPEX also gathers data from countries with very large populations including China, India, Russia and Brazil. MIPEX has some distinctive features including its breadth of coverage and regular updates, which make it possible to make comparisons between countries over time using the same set of indicators.

MIPEX asks the basic question – Is the health system responsive to immigrants' needs? It ranks countries health systems according to a set of "migrant-friendly" indicators. MIPEX finds that there are significant differences between countries in terms of migrant access to health services with many countries failing to take the specific needs of migrants into account in their health systems[2] that "major differences emerge in immigrants' healthcare coverage and ability to access services between countries; policies often fail to take their specific health needs into account" (MIPEX, 2020, (Health) p. 1).

The MIPEX health strand is an example of a metric (38 indicators) that aggregates multiple indices defined by a broad expert group (over 100 experts were involved in the development, piloting and implementation), for 48 countries as a benchmark for measuring the equitability of a country's policies relating to the health of migrants. The index is not, however, based on information collected directly from the WHO member states and reviewed by them. It is an index based on an assessment made by academics and civil society experts.

Administrative barriers often prevent migrants from obtaining their full healthcare coverage. These barriers can include requirements for documents that may be difficult for migrants to obtain, or discretionary decisions about how urgently their treatment is needed and whether they are able to pay for it themselves. In all countries, undocumented migrants face the greatest barriers

Improving data on migration and health after the global pandemic 169

to accessing health care, according to MIPEX data. Only two of the 56 countries covered by MIPEX impose no administrative barriers for undocumented migrants: where coverage for this group is limited to emergency care (MIPEX, 2020). Based on this information, MIPEX asserts that health systems are least inclusive in countries such as most of Central and Southeast Europe, Brazil, China, India, Indonesia, Jordan, Russia and Saudi Arabia (MIPEX, 2020). The latest data were gathered in 2019 before the global pandemic.

7.4.3 United Nations Inquiry Among Governments on Population and Development

This global survey has been conducted by the UN since 1963. The survey gathers data for monitoring the Programme of Action of the International Conference on Population and Development and other international agreements, including the 2030 Agenda for Sustainable Development. To date, 13 surveys have been conducted. As of November 2021, data on SDG indicator 10.7.2 were available for 138 countries, equivalent to 70 per cent of all countries globally (from the 12th and 13th surveys, conducted from 12 September 2018 to October 2019, and the 13th inquiry, conducted between November 2020 and October 2021).

The vast majority of countries (93 per cent) reported having policies to provide non-nationals with equal access to essential or emergency health care (UN DESA, 2021). Nearly all (90 per cent) provided such services to all non-nationals, regardless of their immigration status (ibid).

In the past, response rates to the migration module were not high, with less than half of the countries surveyed responding. However, since UN DESA entered into a partnership with IOM, response rates have increased, and more than half of the countries responded. The inquiry also includes a separate module focusing on reproductive health, which makes it possible to correlate response to this part of the survey to responses to migration-related questions. The module on reproductive health contains questions about government policies, laws and regulations relating to maternal health, sexual and reproductive health, family planning, sexually transmitted infections, including human immunodeficiency virus/acquired immunodeficiency syndrome (HIV/AIDS), and induced abortion.

The UN Population and Development Inquiry includes a migration module, which features several questions relating to migration and health. These include, for example, "Does the Government provide non-nationals equal access to the following services... Essential and/or emergency health care", regardless of immigration status or only for those with legal immigration status. Also, "Does the Government take any of the following measures to respond to refugees and other persons forcibly displaced across international borders – contingency planning for displaced populations in terms of basic needs such as food, sanitation, education and medical care?" Seventy-six per cent of countries responding to the 13th inquiry reported using contingency planning for displaced populations to meet basic needs such as food, sanitation, education and medical care.

More recently, during the global pandemic, the United Nations Population Division (UNPD) added a new module focusing on the impact of COVID-19. The module in the survey includes questions such as "Has the Government taken any of the following policy measures in response to the COVID-19 pandemic?", "providing access to testing and treatment for COVID-19, regardless of migration status".

While the UN Population and Development Inquiry now covers more countries, questions remain about the quality of the data that are collected through this survey. As UN DESA itself points out, different countries may interpret the questionnaire in different ways, and national survey responses may vary because of this (UN DESA, 2021).

7.4.4 Health Inclusivity Index: monitoring progress towards good health for everyone

This new index prepared by "Economist Impact" in November 2022 aims to measure "health inclusivity" in different countries. Health inclusivity is defined as "the process of removing the personal, social, cultural and political barriers that prevent individuals and communities from experiencing good physical and mental health, and a life fully realized" (Economist Impact, 2022, p. 7). Poor health for some sections of society, the authors note, is bad news for society overall. The Health Inclusivity Index collects data on the barriers to good health for 40 countries across all regions of the world, using an index comprising 37 indicators. The index recognizes that the healthcare system alone in a country cannot guarantee good health for everyone. There are extensive disparities in health outcomes within and between countries, which cannot be explained solely by comparing healthcare systems. "Inclusivity in health requires that a society values health so highly that it pervades all areas of national policy, strategy and programmes" (Economist Impact, 2022, p. 9). The index includes one indicator that focuses specifically on migration and "migrant healthcare coverage". The findings suggest that, overall, one in five of the 40 countries included in the index "exclude people from accessing healthcare systems based on characteristics such as migration status". Examples of countries covered in the survey that limit access to health care for migrants and asylum-seekers can be found in Table 7.1.

7.5 Data on the health status of migrants: some key figures

What can be said about the physical and mental health status of migrants based on international sources of data on migration and health? NCDs are the leading cause of death worldwide, accounting for nearly 70 percent of recorded deaths

Table 7.1 Health Inclusivity Index: countries with policies of exclusion against migrants and asylum-seekers

	Excluded group
Israel	Migrants and asylum-seekers, except when they are of Jewish origin
Poland	Limited access for immigrants
Russia	Migrants
Sweden	Undocumented migrants and asylum-seekers
UK	Asylum-seekers whose applications have been rejected

Source: Adapted from Economist Impact (2022).

(IOM, 2017). In lower- and middle-income countries, nearly half (47 per cent) of premature deaths were from NCDs in 2015. Many migrants originate from such countries with high NCD rates. Furthermore, difficult conditions linked to the migration process may increase exposure and vulnerability to NCD risk factors. The data on this subject are patchy and mixed. There is no major international source of data on this subject. In reviewing the evidence from a wide range of research studies, the WHO recently concluded that:

"NCDS are an increasing health burden among refugee and migrant populations, …Cancer (for example) is often diagnosed at later stages among refugees and migrants, who often have lower uptake of or access to preventive measures" (WHO, 2022a, p. 115).

However, the evidence varies across regions. For example, data from the USA show a lower prevalence of cardiovascular events such as heart attack and stroke among the foreign-born compared with the host population (ibid). However, evidence from Gulf countries, such as the United Arab Emirates, where migrants often work long hours in very difficult conditions, shows a much higher prevalence of hypertension among migrant workers from South Asia (ibid).

7.5.1 *Mental health*

Certain groups of migrants and refugees, especially those fleeing conflict or those forced to move quickly for environmental reasons, are likely to have a higher prevalence of mental health problems. "Conflict and war affected refugees and migrants display higher levels of PTSD and other mental health issues, particularly younger migrants and adolescents" (WHO, 2022a, p. 124). "Evidence shows that the incidence of psychoses is higher among migrant populations in a number of countries linked to the cumulative effect of social disadvantages before, during and after migration" (ibid).

Some studies suggest that although migrants are, at least initially, healthier than the non-migrant population in the receiving country, they tend to be more vulnerable to certain communicable diseases and poor mental health, especially in the case of those fleeing conflict situations (IOM, 2022b).

7.5.2 Migrant deaths

It is now well documented that thousands of migrants die each year when they embark on dangerous journeys in search of a better life or safety. Since 2014, IOM has been collecting data on the deaths and disappearances of migrants worldwide through its "Missing Migrants Project". Since 2014, IOM has documented more than 50,000 deaths and disappearances of migrants. Drawing on a range of sources from coastguards, medical examiners, media reports, non-governmental organizations, UN agencies and surveys and interviews with migrants, IOM produces estimates of the number of migrants who die on migration journeys worldwide. The data may not be fully representative of the realities on the ground across the globe. For example, the majority of deaths and disappearances of migrants documented have been recorded on maritime routes to Europe, and this may have greater media attention in this region. As missing migrant data are partially based on media reports, it is likely that deaths in other more remote regions of the world are underreported.

Migrants also face many health risks during their journeys, which may not be fully documented. Long journeys across difficult terrains without adequate protection often expose migrants to many health risks, due to a lack of food, dehydration, exhaustion and lack of adequate shelter. There are also many cases of migrants being subjected to violence and intimidation during such journeys from smugglers, host communities and other migrants. In addition, these problems may be compounded by the fact that undocumented migrants often have little access to health services during such journeys.

7.5.3 Occupational injuries

Most international migrants are migrant workers. The ILO estimated that in 2019 there were 169 million migrant workers globally. Migrant workers are more likely to work in 3D jobs – dirty, dangerous and demanding – and are more prone to occupational accidents, injuries and work-related health problems. This is especially likely if they come from lower-income and middle-income countries where they are frequently employed in low-wage or low-skilled occupations (WHO, 2022a).

> *Migrant workers can frequently face negative health outcomes, resulting from workplace hazards, exposure, discrimination, lack of insurance (or loss of insurance when it is not portable), an absence of safety measures, or abuse in jobs in which they face higher risks to their safety and well-being*
> (WHO, 2022a, p. 95)

The incidence of work-related fatalities is much higher for migrants, according to research conducted in 73 per cent of countries where such data are available (Gammarano, 2020). In 22 of the 26 countries that collect data on migrants and occupational fatalities (SDG indicator 8.8.1), migrants had higher average rates of work-related fatalities during the period 2000–2009 (UN DESA, cited in IOM, 2022b). In 25 of 35 countries reporting data on non-occupational injuries by migratory status, migrants experienced higher rates of work-related casualties. The majority of countries reporting on this indicator by migratory status, 22 of 25, are in Europe, while none are in Africa and Oceania (UNSD, 2020).

7.5.4 Disability

There are no official international statistics on the global prevalence of disability among migrants and those who are forcibly displaced (IOM, 2022d). In addition to existing impairments, people on the move may acquire or develop impairments during the migration process. Some people do not disclose disabilities to police, social services or migration authorities for fear that it may affect their asylum application or opportunity to benefit from family reunification.

The WHO and World Bank estimated in 2011, in a World Report on Disability (WHO and World Bank, 2011), that about 15 per cent of the world's population lives with some form of disability, of whom 2–4 per cent experience significant difficulties in functioning. This figure is higher than earlier estimates made by the WHO in the 1970s, when the figure was around ten per cent (WHO, 2011). Taking the 15 per cent figure and applying it to the 82.4 million persons who are forcibly displaced, IOM calculated that approximately 12.4 million of the 82.4 million persons who were forcibly displaced at the end of 2020 were persons with disabilities,[3] but this figure is likely much higher today, partly because the number of forcibly displaced has surpassed the 100 million figure (UNHCR, 2022) and partly because the prevalence of disability among those forcibly displaced may well be higher than for the average population. If we applied the 15 per cent figure to all migrants, we would obtain a figure of just over 36 million migrants with a disability, but the figure for migrants could be lower as they are generally younger.

Several individual studies suggest that the incidence of disability among forcibly displaced populations can be very high – see, for example, the Syria Disability Impact and Prevalence Study (UNHCR, 2020): 27 per cent of people, aged 12 and above, within Syria, were found to have a disability, in a country where 6.8 million were internally displaced as of end June 2022 (approximately 1 in 3 of the 18.2 million Syrian population is internally displaced). The report notes that households fleeing violence frequently lose access to essential socio-economic safety nets. The prevalence of disability within the migrant population may be underreported for several reasons:

- Data collection relies heavily on the migrant themselves or family members to identify and report on disability, but migrants may not always self-report their or a family member's disability for various reasons.
- Non-standard data collection tools fail to identify the population of interest due to poorly constructed questions that do not address the full range of potential disabilities.
- Those collecting data may not be trained well and may only identify the "visible" characteristics that the data collector determines are disabilities (Mosler Vidal, 2022; IOM, 2022d).

In sum, while there are no official data sources on the global prevalence of migrants with disabilities, several national studies have been conducted by UN agencies such as UNHCR, IOM and United Nations International Children's Emergency Fund (UNICEF), which suggest higher levels of disability among those who are forcibly displaced (Mosler Vidal, 2022).

7.5.5 Health of migrant children

Several studies have documented that migrant children are exposed to different types of health risks. Migrant newborns and infants under five often have higher mortality rates due to their poor living conditions, such as overcrowding in low-quality housing, poor sanitation and inadequate nutrition, and these factors are compounded by a lack of access to good health care (IOM, 2022b). Data from across the world show that infant mortality rates are higher among immigrant populations in several countries (WHO, 2022a).

There is also evidence that migrant children are especially vulnerable to hunger, food insecurity and malnutrition (IOM, 2022b), but being a migrant per se may not be the main source of disadvantage. Much depends on the socio-economic situation of the migrant household. A comprehensive review of studies from Europe, North America and Australia, for example, found a strong correlation between migration and both child obesity and stunting (IOM, 2022b).

Immunization plays a key role in ensuring the healthy lives of children and is a key SDG indicator for many developing countries. MICS and DHS provide data on five vaccines received by children who are international migrants in host countries. The surveys show that migrant children are often less likely to be vaccinated. For example, data from 8 of 15 countries or areas show that the percentage of international migrant children who received the measles vaccine was lower than for non-migrant children (ibid).

The reasons why migrant children may lack access to vaccines include limited vaccine coverage assessment upon entry into the country, living in border areas with highly mobile populations, incomplete migrant-specific data in immunization programmes in some countries, language barriers and low levels of health literacy among caregivers or lack of knowledge about how to access vaccines (WHO, 2022a).

7.5.6 Migrant health workers

Most of the international data on migrant health workers come from the OECD and focus on migration to OECD countries. Nearly a quarter of all doctors in OECD countries are born abroad, and nearly a fifth are trained abroad (OECD, 2020). In recent years, the number of foreign-born and foreign-trained nurses in OECD countries has increased significantly and on average 16 per cent of the nursing workforce is foreign-born, and 7 per cent of the nursing workforce was trained abroad (OECD, 2020).

Nearly one-third of foreign-born nurses in OECD countries originate from within the OECD area and a quarter are from upper-middle-income countries (non-OECD). The lower-income countries account for approximately another third and low-income countries for six per cent of foreign-born nurses. By far, the largest numbers of foreign-born and foreign-trained nurses originate from the Philippines, India and Poland. Emigration rates to OECD countries, defined as the ratio between the number of native-born or home-trained nurses working in (other) OECD countries and the sum of all nurses born or trained or working in the country of origin, are generally much lower than for the native-born or home-trained doctors, but a few countries still experience a significant loss of skilled health workers according to the OECD.

For example, for 20 of the 188 studied countries – predominantly in Africa and Latin America – the emigration rates for native-born nurses exceed 50 per cent. However, when considering the number of nurses per 1,000 population, analysis reveals that the global health workforce shortage is by no means solely linked to migration. Relatively few of the countries of origin would significantly increase the number of nurses per 1,000 population by additionally having all migrant nurses born or trained, respectively, in that country to also work in that country.

The proportion of migrant doctors employed in OECD countries' health systems has risen during the past twenty years. Approximately two-thirds of all foreign-born or foreign-trained doctors originate from within the OECD area and upper-middle-income countries and one-third from lower-middle-income countries. Only 3–4 per cent of foreign-born or foreign-trained doctors working in OECD countries' health systems originate from low-income countries (Socha-Dietrich and Dumont, 2021), but for some of the poorest countries, the emigration of doctors represents a significant percentage of their health workforce.

There is a paucity of data on migrants' contributions to the health of low-income countries through diaspora contributions. Some evidence shows that financial and other remittances and the return of trained and more experienced health workers can contribute to the improvement of health conditions in the country of origin (UNDP, 2020).

In sum, international migration and health data seem to be much more comprehensive, comparable and abundant regarding data on the movement of health workers and much more limited with respect to data on the health status of migrants.

7.5.7 *Migration and health data innovation examples*

This chapter has highlighted many gaps in data on migration and health, but it is important to note that, in recent years, many new initiatives have been launched to improve the collection, understanding and use of migration and health data. Indeed, although there has been much focus on new technologies and big data, data innovation has often concerned the use of traditional data sources. Below are some examples of initiatives that have been taken in recent years to improve data on migration and health.

Box 7.1 Data management: WHO's Information Platform on Health and Migration in the Americas

In May 2022, the WHO launched an "Information Platform on Health and Migration in the Americas". The platform systematizes information to facilitate the storage, dissemination and exchange of knowledge to guide the development of policies, public health interventions and other health and migration initiatives. The platform provides easy access to a huge amount of qualitative and quantitative evidence on health and migration gathered from the Americas. It includes interactive dashboards on policy, legal and regulatory frameworks, as well as scientific literature on health and migration, where data can be explored through dynamic panels and various filters can be used for analysis. The information compiled in the platform is a result of collaboration with various actors in the Americas, including those with years of expertise on issues related to health and migration.

Box 7.2 Data management: IOM's Migration and Health Evidence Portal

In response to growing demands for data on migration and COVID-19, IOM launched the "Migration and Health Evidence Portal for COVID-19". This portal comprises three types of evidence to guide policy and decision-making.

1 An interactive, searchable (and downloadable), open-source repository of research publications on COVID-19 in relation to migrants, migration and human mobility.
2 A quantitative analysis of publications on COVID-19 and migration health – the analysis includes information on studies' scope and aims to identify research gaps.
3 Evidence briefs – these synthesize key information relevant to IOM's COVID-19 strategic preparedness and response plan and contain key messages relevant to priority areas in the field of migration health and COVID-19 that will be produced in collaboration with relevant stakeholders.

Box 7.3 Data management: the migrant health country profile tool

IOM, in partnership with academia and country-level partners, has developed a tool to bring together disparate sources of national migration and health data in one place. Drawing on data from a range of different sources, IOM has worked with five countries (Morocco, Egypt, Libya, Tunisia and Yemen) in a feasibility phase, to develop a migration and health country profile. The profiles compile data from routine health information systems, disease surveillance systems, national public health registries, demographic and health surveys, health insurance data and relevant data from the private sector. Evaluations of this new tool show that it contributed to improving the understanding of the sources and types of migration-related health data and migrant health-related national policies. The tool is being developed further in a second phase across the Middle East and North Africa region (IOM, 2022d).

Box 7.4 Harnessing new technologies: the electronic personal health record to foster access to health and integration of migrants

The electronic personal health record (e-PHR) was developed in 2016 by the European Commission in response to large numbers of arrivals of refugees and migrants in Europe. After a pilot phase in four countries, IOM implemented and consolidated the use of the e-PHR as a single tool for health assessments in EU countries. The tool has also been extended to several non-EU European countries. The tool supports health professionals to enable them to obtain a comprehensive view of a person's health status and needs during clinical encounters and/or treatments. For authorized users, records are retrievable from multiple locations across Europe. As of 31 January 2019, over 24,000 health assessments have been made using e-PHR. The tool can be used to generate tailored reports, which highlight the main disease trends and needs across various migrant populations and provide important aggregate-level information about migration and health trends for decision-makers (IOM, 2022b).

> **Box 7.5   Data for policy: data to engage the health diaspora of the Eastern Mediterranean region**
>
> IOM and WHO conducted a review of available data on existing health diaspora organizations and institutions and challenges in relation to the emigration of health professionals in 2021 in the Eastern Mediterranean region. The review revealed that engaging the diaspora brings about opportunities to help strengthen the health workforce and health systems and that it needs to be anchored on well-coordinated and supported government programmes to yield a sustainable impact.

7.6   Concluding remarks and way forward

This brief review of international data on migration and health has highlighted many gaps in knowledge, but also some promising new data initiatives. Based on existing data sources, it is very hard to monitor global progress in meeting health and migration targets. As the WHO points out, "data do not currently permit accurate measurement of the progress made by and for refugees and migrants towards achieving the SDG targets" (WHO, 2022a, p. 297). Nonetheless, there is enough evidence available to suggest that many migrants often have poorer physical and mental health due to the difficult conditions in which they live and work. Moreover, the global pandemic exposed further the vulnerabilities that migrants face around the world (World Bank et al., 2022). As the WHO points out, the existing data present a mixed picture:

> *It is clear that refugees and migrants face poorer health outcomes than people in host countries around the world if the conditions they live and work in are not conducive to good health. However, the threats, risks and vulnerabilities often differ between regions and among groups. It is also clear that poorer health outcomes for refugees and migrants are not universal; research has revealed deviations from this rule in some regions and for some diseases.*
>
> (WHO, 2022a, p. 153)

Data on migration and health tend to be much more widely available and of better quality in high-income countries. As discussed in more detail in Chapter 2, there is also a chronic lack of data capacities in many of the poorest countries in the world where the health situation of migrants may be most acute. Furthermore, evidence suggests that, in some contexts, migrants often support the health of their families and others in their networks, as well as health systems more broadly both in destination and origin countries. More information on this is needed, so that policy and programming can support these dynamics.

Improving data on migration and health after the global pandemic 179

From a global perspective, there are few migration and health datasets that cover most countries in the world. Some exceptions are IOM's global database on missing migrants, the UN's Population and Development Inquiry and IOM's Migration Governance Indicators project, but none of these data collection initiatives are solely focused on collecting and analysing data on migration and health. There is currently no global survey focusing on collecting data on different aspects of migration and health. Although well-established international survey instruments exist, the largest household surveys currently provide relatively little robust, comparable information about the health of migrants, and these data are available for only a small number of countries and only a few migration and health indicators (WHO, 2022a).

While there is an abundance of administrative data relating to migration and health, these are often not disaggregated by migratory status; even if they were, they might not be comparable because each country uses different definitions and time periods to collect data on migration and health. Censuses could provide more insights into the relationship between migration and health, but few countries currently include in-depth health questions in their census, and censuses are conducted infrequently and can be costly. While the pandemic boosted interest in using big data to inform health policy responses, collaboration between the public and private sectors in the use of migration and health data is still in its infancy, as discussed in Chapter 4. Many ethical concerns also remain about the use of big data, particularly when it comes to sharing data about people's health (Chapter 4).

A more general problem is the fact that global-level, comparable data on health indicators are often quite limited around the world, and the data that do exist are fragmented and not shared effectively. In recognition of this issue, a new international "Health Data Collaborative" has been created to promote the collection of health data worldwide (GovLab, 2022). In the case of migrants, it is difficult to protect migrants and health systems when basic data pertaining to the number of migrants who need to be vaccinated do not exist.

This chapter has shown that there are many different sources of data on migration and health and no one source is likely to provide all the information needed to inform policy and practice. This means that efforts need to be made to promote migration and health data integration, and indeed, there is a case for developing "Migration and Health Data Collaboratives", which would bring all key stakeholders together at the country level to share data and discuss priorities for future data collection. In short, most countries lack an explicit migration and health data strategy.

From a global perspective, there is also a need for new international migration and health initiatives. Several different measures could be considered. In the absence of any World Health Survey, consideration should be given to launching a regular specialized international survey focusing on collecting data on the health of migrants. There is also scope to do much more to build migration and health data capacities, by, for example, encouraging countries to add more health questions to migration-related surveys and censuses, as discussed in Chapter 3.

Finally, we have seen in this chapter that a considerable amount of data innovation in the migration and health field has happened in recent years. The examples that we have presented by no means focus solely on the use of technologies and big data. In fact, there has been considerable innovation in the use of traditional sources of data on migration and health. Many of these relatively low-cost initiatives could potentially be replicated by other countries and regions around the world.

Notes

1 Integrated Refugee Health Information System (iRHIS) – relaunched in 2020, the iRHIS is an interactive web based application designed to collate and analyse a comprehensive set of health and nutrition data that visualizes trends over time and generates a range of reports. iRHIS provides country and global updates on standard indicators to inform programming and comparative analysis with host communities across all subsections of public health. For more information see www.UNHCR.org/Strategic Health Information.
2 See www.mipex.eu for further details
3 See https://www.migrationdataportal.org/themes/disability-and-human-mobility (last accessed on 9 June 2023).

References

Brian, T. (2021). *Occupational Fatalities among International Migrant Workers*. Geneva: IOM.

Connor, Philip. (2020). More than nine-in-ten people worldwide lives in countries with travel restrictions amid COVID-19, Pew Research Institute, 1 April. Available at www.pewresearch.org/fact-tank

Economist Impact (2022). *The Healthy Inclusivity Index*. London: The Economist Group.

Galez-Davis, C., Cook, H., Laursen, S., Jasi P., and Todorova, I., et al. (2022). Leveraging administrative data to fight human trafficking. In Mosler-Vidal, E., & Laczko, F., *Migration and the SDGs: Measuring Progress*. Geneva, Berlin: IOM, 90–96.

Gammarano, R. (2020). Covid-19 and the new meaning of safety and health at work. ILO blog post. 30 April. Available at https://ilostat.ilo.org

GMG (Global Migration Group). (2017). Handbook for Improving the Production and Use of Migration Data for Development, United Nations. Available at http://knomad.org/publications

GovLab. (2022). *Data Collaboratives: Creating Public Value by Exchanging Data*, The Governance Lab, New York University, Tandon School of Engineering.

Harford, T. (2020). *How to Make the World Add Up: Ten Rules for Thinking Differently about Numbers*. London: Little Brown.

Hayward, S., Deal, A., Cheng, C., Crawshaw, A., Orcutt, M., Vandrevala, T.F., Norredam, M., Carballo, M., Ciftci, Y., Requena-Mendez, A., Greenaway, J.C., Knights, F., Mehrotra, A., Seedat, F., Bozorgmehr, A.V., Veizis, I., Campos-Matos, F., Noori, T., McKee, M., Kumar, B., and Hargreaves, S. (2020). Clinical outcomes and risk factors for COVID-19 among migrant populations in high-income countries: A systematic review. *Journal of Migration and Health*. https://doi.org/10.1016/jmh.2021.10041

Health Data Collaborative. (2022). Available at www.healthdatacollaborative.org

IOM, International Organization for Migration. (2017). *Caring for Trafficked Persons: A Guide for Health Providers*. Geneva: IOM.

IOM. (2021). Migrant inclusion in COVID-19 vaccination campaigns. Available at www.iom.int

IOM. (2022a). IOM missing migrants project. Available at www.missingmigrants.iom.int

IOM. (2022b). *Migration and the SDGs: Measuring Progress*. eds E. Mosler-Vidal and F. Laczko, Geneva: IOM.

IOM. (2022c). Migration Governance Indicators (MGI), a Key Tool for the Global Compact for Safe, Orderly, and Regular Migration Implementation. Geneva: IOM.

IOM. (2022d). IOM migration data portal. Available at https://www.migrationdataportal.org

IOM. (2023). *Harnessing Data Innovation for Migration Policy: A Handbook for Practitioners*. Geneva: IOM.

Jeffers, K., Tjaden, J., and Laczko, F. (2018). A Pilot Study on Disaggregating SDG Indicators by Migratory Status. Geneva: IOM.

Kapri, K. and Stuti, J. (2020). Impact of remittances on household health care expenditure: Evidence from the Nepal living standards survey. *Review of Development Economics*, 24(3), 991–1008; https://doi.org/10.1111rode.12666

Laczko, F. (2021). Covid-19 and migration in 2020: Five key trends. In *Migration Policy Practice, Vol. xi, Number 1 (January–February)*. Geneva: IOM and Eurasylum, 5–10.

Levitt, P. (1998). Social remittances: Migration driven local-level forms of cultural diffusion. In *The International Migration Review, Vol. 32, Number 4 (Winter, 1998)*, pp. 926–948. New York, NY: Sage Publications.

Lopez, A., Crespo, M., and Rijks, B. (2017). "Health" in Global Migration Group. *Handbook for Improving the Production and Use of Migration Data for Development*. Geneva: United Nations.

Migration Policy Practice. (2021). Vol. xi, Number 1, January–February, Geneva: IOM and Eurasylum.

MIPEX. (Migrant Integration Policy Index) (2020). Available at https://www.mipex.eu

Mosler Vidal, Elisa. (2022). Data on disability and migration – What do we know?, blog, February 4th, Global Partnership of Sustainable Development Data.

Nathaniel, O.A. (2019). Impact of remittances on healthcare utilisation and expenditure in developing countries: A systematic review, *Rwanda Journal of Medicine and Health Sciences*, 2(3), September. https://doi.org/10.4314/rjmhs.v2i3.15

OECD, ILO, IOM, and UNHCR. (2021). *2021 Annual International Migration and Forced Displacement Trends and Policies Report to the G20*. Paris: OECD.

OECD. (2020). Contribution of migrant doctors and nurses to tackling COVID-19 crisis in OECD countries. OECD, 13, May, Paris. Available at http://www.oecd.org

OECD. (2021). *International Migration Outlook*. Paris: OECD.

OECD. (2022). *What Has Been the Impact of the COVID-19 Pandemic on Immigrants? An Update on Recent Evidence*. Paris: OECD.

Organization for Economic Cooperation and Development (OECD). (2019). Recent trends in international migration of doctors, nurses, and medical students. OECD Publishing, https://doi.org/10.1787/5571ef48-en

Socha-Dietrich, K. and Dumont, J.C. (2021). *International Migration and Movement of Doctors to and within OECD Countries -2000 to 2018: Developments in Countries of Destination and Impact on Countries of Origin*. OECD Health Working Papers 126, Paris: OECD Publishing.

UN (2020 and 2022). *The Sustainable Development Goals Report*. New York, NY: United Nations.
UNDESA. (2020a). *International Migration Trends*. December, New York, NY: United Nations.
UNDESA. (2020b). Survey of National Statistical Offices (NSOs) during COVID-19. Availableathttps://covid-19-response.unstatshub.org/statistical-programmes/covid19-nso-survey.
UNDESA, IOM, and OECD. (2021). *SDG Indicator 10.7.2 – Number of Countries with Migration Policies to Facilitate Orderly, Safe, Regular and Responsible Migration and Mobility*. Policy Brief 2, December, New York, NY: United Nations.
UNDP (United Nations Development Programme) (2020). *Human Mobility, Shared Opportunities: A Review of the 2009 Human Development Report and the Way Ahead*. New York, NY: UNDP.
UNHCR. (2021). Integrated Refugee Health Information System (IRHIS). Available at https://his.unhcr.org
UNHCR. (2022). 103 million Forcibly displaced people worldwide. Refugee Data Finder. Available at www.unhcr.int Geneva.
UNHCR (United Nations High Commissioner for Refugees) (2020). *Disability Prevalence and Impact: Syrian Arab Republic*. IDP Report Series, Geneva: UNHCR.
World Health Organization (WHO) (2006). *The World Health Report: 2006: Working Together for Health*. Geneva: WHO.
World Health Organization (WHO) and World Bank (2011). *World Report on Disability*. Geneva, WHO.
WHO. (2020). *Apart Together Survey*. Preliminary overview of refugees and migrants self-reported impact of COVID-19, Geneva: WHO.
WHO. (2022a). *World Report on the Health of Refugees and Migrants*. Geneva: WHO.
WHO. (2022b). *Strengthening COVID-19 Vaccine Demand and Uptake in Refugees and Migrants*. Geneva: WHO.
World Bank, UN, and Global Partnership for Sustainable Development. (2022). *Unlocking Data For a Better, Greener, Safer Future*. New York, NY: United Nations.

8 Way forward
Four key recommendations

8.1 Introduction

This book shows that significant progress has been made in recent years in improving data on migration. For example, 30 years ago there was no global database on human trafficking, or global reports gathering data from all countries on this subject. A decade ago, no global database on migrant deaths and disappearances. The "Missing Migrants" project that compiles data on this topic was launched in 2014.

Nonetheless, major gaps in our knowledge about global migration patterns persist. It is often said that good migration data are essential if migration is to be managed effectively. The reality is that global data on migration are often scarce, inaccessible, not comparable or several years old, or perhaps it is simply the case that the data are poorly communicated or misunderstood. Even though more data are being collected on migration and mobility than ever before, we still struggle to answer basic questions about migration, such as how many migrants arrived or left a country in the previous year, or what their profiles are. Beyond disaggregation by sex, data about gender and migration are widely unavailable, which affects the ability of practitioners and policymakers to address their specific needs and ensure their fundamental rights. It remains difficult to monitor progress towards the achievement of the objectives of the Global Compact for Safe, Orderly and Regular Migration (GCM) or Sustainable Development Goal (SDG) migration-related targets due to a lack of data. Even where data do exist, they may not be shared or used effectively.

The three chapters of this book that focused on specific policy themes, migration and development, migration and climate change, and migration and health, all highlighted major gaps in data.

As explained in Chapter 5, there is a clear need to improve the capacity of countries to collect, analyse, report and use migration and development data – a broad and quickly evolving area. Very few SDG indicators are disaggregated by migratory status. It is difficult to know, for example, to what extent poverty rates are higher among migrants and how far progress is being made in reducing poverty among migrants due to a lack of disaggregated data. However, the SDGs boosted migration data innovation in several areas. For example, new

DOI: 10.4324/9781003266075-10

pilot surveys were launched by the International Labour Organization (ILO) and World Bank to gather data on migrant recruitment costs, and there has been progress in collecting data on migration governance. To improve data in this area, it is important to increase transnational data collection and prioritize integrated data analysis that is across topics and/or units of analysis. Furthermore, it is key to generate and disaggregate comparable data on migration and the 2030 Agenda and make inclusive and concerted efforts towards standardized reporting on selected persistent and policy-relevant migration and development data gaps. As also mentioned in Chapter 2, tools such as the IOM report on Gender and Migration Data (Hennebry et al., 2021) could be used to boost capacity-development efforts to collect gender-responsive migration data.

Regarding climate change and migration, most countries do not produce, on a regular basis, any statistics specifically on migration and its linkages to the environment and climate change (Chapter 6). The United Nations (UN) has only very recently begun to produce guidance on what statistics relating to climate change might be collected by each country, but few countries have adopted a clear definition of what would count as a "climate migrant" for statistical purposes. The best available data provide information on extreme environmental events when people are displaced often for short periods of time. There are fewer data on the impact of slow-onset environmental changes, which could likely affect much larger numbers of people as suggested by recent projections. Most of the data relating to migration and climate change focus on what might happen in the future, based on projections, rather than how climate change is affecting migration patterns now. Given that the data available today are poor, it is difficult to predict future trends with accuracy.

Concerning migration and health, the global pandemic highlighted many gaps in data about the health of people on the move. For example, data on migrant COVID-19 infection and mortality rates are only available for a small number of countries. When countries launched national vaccination programmes to combat COVID-19, many of them struggled to identify how many migrants needed to be vaccinated in their country. Much of the data available on migration and health are collected in high-income countries. Yet, the risk of ill health is much greater for migrants in lower-income countries. There has, however, been some progress in collecting more data on migration and health policies through initiatives such as MIPEX (Migrant Integration Policy Index), which collects data in 56 countries, and the MGI (Migration Governance Indicators) project, which collects data in 84 countries. These data initiatives show that in many countries, migrants often have much more limited access to health care than the native population.

More generally, in earlier chapters of this book, we highlighted some of the main obstacles to collecting data on migration. The technical challenges relating to the limitations of traditional migration data sources such as censuses, administrative records and surveys, and novel data sources such as big data are many and well known (Dumont et al., 2018). Indeed, there is no shortage of recommendations and guidance on how to improve migration statistics. The UN has been issuing recommendations on international migration statistics since 1954, but UN recommendations are not binding, and the UN has little capacity to support countries in operationalizing these recommendations, as spending on migration statistics remains low. Thus, there are still significant differences in the way in which countries define and collect data on migration (IOM, 2021a).

However, too often the data challenges are presented as mainly technical challenges. The Global Compact for Safe Orderly and Regular Migration tends to present the issues in this way. However, as we noted in Chapter 1, governments can suppress data findings and manipulate data if they fear that the release of the data might have negative political or financial consequences. They may also be reluctant to share data with other countries for these reasons. Improving data on migration also means promoting greater transparency in the use of data. Promoting more "open data" – meaning data that are openly accessible and shared by anyone for any purpose – is essential. Data need to be accessible to all, to ensure that decision-makers can be held to account for their decisions.

Little political priority is often given to collecting timely reliable data on migration. Few countries have an explicit migration data strategy or road map, which spells out how they plan to improve the collection, analysis, sharing and use of migration statistics (IOM, 2021a). A study based on interviews with key officials responsible for migration data in six countries found that it was often unclear what the overall migration data priorities are at the national level and how the country plans to manage migration data effectively (ibid and Chapter 3). The same study also found that while many government agencies publish statistics based on the operational or statistical data they collect, examples of integrated databases on migration are rare to find, making it difficult to obtain a comprehensive picture of migration patterns across countries and even within the same country.

In this concluding section, we consider what could be done in the short-to-medium term and longer term to improve data on migration. Our aim here is to suggest specific actionable recommendations building on some of the examples of data innovation presented in earlier chapters. This book provides concrete examples of innovative ways in which the collection, analysis, communication and use of migration data can inform policy and practice. In short, the chapter advances an ambitious, yet realistic proposal to improve the collection and responsible use of timely, comparable, disaggregated migration data over the next decade. To phrase it another way, what measures might be required to achieve a real *migration data revolution* – a significant improvement in realizing the value of migration data and their impact on people's lives?

Below, we highlight *four key recommendations*. These recommendations are specific and measurable, and build on previous migration data recommendations, noting that currently resources devoted to improving data on migration are limited. However, before outlining these, it is important to highlight the need for much greater investment in collecting, analysing and using migration data given the current lack of spending in this area.

8.2 The need for greater investments in migration data

Spending on migration data, like spending on development statistics more generally, remains quite low, although it is difficult to identify how much is actually allocated to improving migration statistics and how countries compare in this respect (Chapter 3). About one-third (32 per cent) of development funding assistance devoted to improving statistical capacities in low- and middle-income countries in 2016–2018 was spent on improving demographic and social statistics. Exactly how much of this spending was channelled to migration statistics is unknown (Jenkins and Mosler Vidal, 2022). More generally, spending on statistics has not been a top priority for development donors. Many commentators have lamented that too little is dedicated to improving data in poorer countries, making it very difficult to track progress towards SDG targets.

As Espey explains,

"Current resources allocated to data and statistics are woefully inadequate to ensure all countries have the systems in place to track progress on sustainable development and achieve the SDGs" (2019). "The share of total development assistance devoted to statistics has ranged from 0.35 per cent and 0.4 per cent in recent years or USD 693 million in 2018".

(World Bank, 2021, p. 66)

The scale of additional investment required for national statistical systems to realize the data revolution and monitor progress on the SDGs is relatively modest (IOM, 2022). It has been estimated that an additional US$100–200 million in overseas development assistance, alongside increased domestic contributions, could significantly help the world's lower-income countries to put in place the building blocks of an effective SDG monitoring system, improve data governance and service delivery and drive progress towards sustainable development (ibid).

Partly in response to this challenge, in 2022, the World Bank launched a new "Global Data Facility", a new fund to support statistical capacity building and good data governance in lower- and middle-income countries. The World Bank describes the "Global Data Facility" as an innovative global funding instrument "that enables long-term support and durable transformation of data systems and data capital in low and middle-income countries to improve lives and safeguard the planet" (World Bank, 2022). This new fund was launched to implement the key recommendations of the World Bank's 2021, "World Development Report: Data for Better Lives", which calls for a "new social contract for data" grounded in the principles of value, trust and equity.

One of the main reasons for the lack of investment in development data over the years has been that the case for investing in data has not been made strongly enough (Espey, 2019):

We, the international data community, have not provided a short and compelling pitch for why data is so crucial for international development ... If we are going to get people's attention, we need clear and compelling advocacy messages, like investing in data will save x people's lives, or will generate cost efficiencies of y.

(Espey, 2019)

The Global Partnership for Sustainable Development Data (GPSDD), in response to this challenge, has recently calculated that "every US dollar invested in data systems creates an average of USD 32 in economic benefits" (GPSDD, 20 September 2022). The research, conducted by Dahlberg, "shows that stronger data systems drive a diverse range of powerful benefits, improving quality of life, livelihoods, and leading to greater efficiencies in social programmes" (ibid).

A strong case for greater investment in data was also made by senior UN officials at the UN General Assembly in 2022 at a side event entitled "Unlocking Impact: Data with Purpose". They cited many reasons for investing in data, noting, for example, that data will be the first line of defence against future pandemics, and better data can be used to forecast and respond more effectively to humanitarian crises. They cite many concrete examples of cases where investing in data has brought benefits. For example, in 2020, an early warning weather system in Bangladesh enabled a faster emergency response to record-breaking floods at half the cost, generating savings of over USD 5 million (UN/GPSDD, 2022).

An International Organization for Migration (IOM) report with McKinsey, entitled "More Than Numbers" (IOM, 2018), attempted to demonstrate, through seven case studies, the potential value of investing in migration data (IOM, 2018). For example, the report shows that using data to match migrants' qualifications with adequate jobs could increase the income of highly skilled migrants by EUR 5–7 billion in the EU alone. The report also shows that data-driven interventions could double the number of cases of human trafficking identified. The authors of the report argue that policymakers need a clear sense of the tangible outcomes they can expect and which risks they can address through their investments in migration data, and countries need to identify and prioritize the value dimensions most relevant to them, depending on their respective migration situation. In short, to maximize migration's potential and mitigate its risks, each country needs to develop a tailored migration data strategy focusing on the specific objectives of that country. There is also a need to agree on some quantifiable, public goals that help the international community track progress in building national migration data systems (ibid).

8.3 Four key recommendations

A plethora of recommendations have been made over the years on how to improve migration statistics, but there has been little systematic monitoring of the implementation of these recommendations. For example, the 2008 final report of the Commission on International Migration Data for Development Research and Policy advanced five key recommendations (CGD, 2009).

1 *Ensure that more censuses include basic questions on migration.*
2 *Use administrative data on international migrants more extensively.*
3 *Make better use of the migration data collected in labour force surveys.*
4 *Integrate migration modules into existing household surveys.*
5 *Make publicly available microdata from migration surveys and censuses.*

These recommendations remain important and relevant today. However, there is no agreed international framework in place to monitor progress towards the achievement of these. Moreover, since the formulation of this list in 2008, considerable changes have occurred in the migration data field – not least a huge increase in the volume and timeliness of data due to new technologies, together with new global reporting requirements following the endorsement by countries of the SDGs and GCM.

To address the political challenges outlined above, the UN could establish, with the support of a group of "champion countries", a Global Migration Data Commission. This body could include representatives from the private sector, civil society, national authorities and international agencies and could be tasked with developing a plan on how best to improve data on international migration and human mobility over the next decade. Below, we suggest some key elements that could be included in such a plan. The recommendations are inter-linked and based on some of the key examples of data innovation that have been discussed in this book. All of these recommendations will also require a significant investment in different forms of migration data capacity building.

It is important to keep in mind that every data source has its strengths and weaknesses; hence, an integrated approach that combines data sources is likely to work best. Moreover, migration is a cross-cutting issue affecting many different policy domains; therefore, an integrated data strategy that brings together often disparate sources of data is most likely to be effective. Efforts to improve migration data should also be aligned with broader initiatives to strengthen national statistical capacities. Many countries have national statistical strategies and specific measures in place to improve reporting on development indicators such as the SDGs. Proposals to enhance data on migration are also more likely to succeed if they are included in broader data plans. This involves plans to improve data on different sub-groups of people on the move such as internally displaced people (IDPs), refugees and other migrants – see, for example, Box 8.1, which highlights the cross-sectoral work being done by the International Data Alliance for Children on the Move (IDAC). Finally, the examples of data innovation presented below are intended to be illustrative rather than exhaustive.

Box 8.1 International Data Alliance for Children on the Move (IDAC)

IDAC is a cross-sectoral global coalition comprised of governments (including experts from national statistical offices (NSOs) and migration-relevant line ministries), international and regional organizations, non-governmental organizations (NGOs), think tanks, academics and civil society. Formally launched in March 2020, by the United Nations

International Children's Emergency Fund (UNICEF), Eurostat, IOM, United Nations High Commissioner for Refugees (UNHCR) and Organization for Economic Cooperation and Development (OECD), IDAC aims to improve statistics and data on migrant and forcibly displaced children with the goal to support evidence-based policymaking that protects and empowers them.

Why data on children on the move matter

At the end of 2020, an estimated 35.5 million children in the world were counted as international migrants – one in eight of all international migrants and the highest figure recorded. Around 1 in 66 children worldwide living outside his or her country of birth was counted as migrant. At the end of 2021, some 36.5 million children were forcibly displaced – 40 per cent of the total. In 2021 alone, there were an estimated 14.1 million children newly displaced within countries, more than half driven by disasters. Displacement figures are expected to rise significantly in the future due to the impact of climate change.

Children on the move face a unique range of deprivations, challenges and risks that require targeted intervention, through policies and programmes that take their age, gender and other key demographics into account. However, migrant and displaced children are often overlooked in data collection efforts, and the limited data available are further hindered by large gaps that obscure the most basic information about them: their age, sex, precise location, condition and needs, and other critical details to ensure they receive the appropriate support and assistance.

IDAC response

IDAC has adopted a three-pronged action plan for 2021–2023 geared towards:

1 Strengthening national data systems and capacities to protect migrant and forcibly displaced children, through the provision of sustainable capacity-building support.
2 Promoting and establishing collaborative, innovative methods for child-specific data work, for example through an annual conference, annual report and working groups.
3 Improving data visibility, availability, accessibility and usability by developing a global database and dashboard on children on the move, as well as a dedicated online IDAC hub.

Source: Adapted from UNICEF, 2023, International Data Alliance for Children on the Move.

8.3.1 Use existing data sources more effectively

In any given country, a considerable amount of migration data is collected already. However, this is often of limited value to policymakers, because of its high degree of fragmentation. A lack of intragovernmental coordination and systematic sharing of data collected by different parts of governments is a common issue, as noted in Chapter 3. The lack of comparability and interoperability of migration data collected by different actors is a further challenge. Many individual government agencies publish statistics based on the operational or statistical data they collect; however, integrated databases or even publications featuring diverse data on migration are rare.

New large-scale migration data collection initiatives are not necessarily the answer. It would be enough, or at least a significant step, to comprehensively map out what is collected already, and to evaluate steps to make analysis of this information available to policymakers or even to the public, by cleaning, linking up different datasets or simply disseminating aggregate versions of the statistics (as discussed in Chapter 3).

This book has identified some concrete examples of initiatives, which have been taken in recent years to enhance the use of existing migration data.

Migration profiles

Migration profiles were first proposed by the European Commission in 2005 as a means of encouraging migration stakeholders to bring together disparate sources of migration data in one place. From the outset, preparing a country migration profile was not conceived to be merely a statistical exercise. The process of bringing different actors together from different ministries, civil society and UN agencies was intended to facilitate discussions about data gaps, data priorities and data capacity-building needs. By 2020, there were nearly 300 country migration profiles, which could be found on IOM's Migration Data Portal. Some regions, such as West Africa, have also produced regional migration profiles. Although conceived as a flexible and country-specific tool, IOM encouraged a common approach to preparing such profiles using a standardized template and report structure (Borgnas, 2018). While the preparation of migration profiles was conceived to be the start of an ongoing inter-ministerial process of cooperation, in practice only a minority of countries have updated their migration profile on a regular basis, often due to a lack of resources. However, some countries have managed to incorporate migration profiles into their information processes by preparing "light", shorter profiles, which are more easily updated (ibid). Encouraging countries to develop and update migration profiles is one of the action points mentioned specifically under GCM Objective 1. Migration profiles bring together a wealth of data about migration but as yet there is no common database that pools together in one place all the information that is available. Instead, it is necessary to consult each national profile separately.

Regional migration data networks

As mentioned earlier in this book, much migration happens at the regional level between neighbouring countries in one region. These countries therefore often have a common interest in promoting the sharing of migration data at the regional level. One example of data innovation at the regional level, already mentioned in Chapter 5, is the "Africa Migration Data Network". This network launched by the African Union in 2021, with support from IOM, OECD and Statistics Sweden, covers 53 countries in Africa. Each country has nominated a migration data focal point in their NSO and/or migration-relevant ministry. The objectives of the network include promoting data harmonization, sharing innovative data practices and developing joint data capacity-building programmes. This type of relatively low-cost regional data initiative could potentially be replicated in other regions of the world. As this initiative is essentially embedded in NSOs, it also has the potential advantage of aligning migration statistical work with broader national data initiatives.

Compiling data from media reports and other sources – the Missing Migrants Project

A relatively low-cost and high-impact data initiative is IOM's Missing Migrants Project. The project, described in Chapter 2, is another example of migration data innovation. With a handful of staff, IOM boosted reporting on the number of migrant deaths worldwide by systematically monitoring media reports of migrant deaths and disappearances. The project draws upon other sources of data, such as national administrative data, and data from organizations involved in search and rescue, but essentially compiles existing sources of data. As there is a dearth of official data on migrant deaths and disappearances, because countries tend not to publish statistics on this subject, the Missing Migrants Project has become a key source of data on migrant deaths worldwide (Brian and Laczko, 2014; Black, 2018). Data from the project are widely cited in the media and the UN Secretary-General's annual reports on migration. Since 2014, when the project was launched, it has recorded over 50,000 deaths worldwide and has become a recognized key source of data relevant to monitoring SDG 10.7, as outlined in Chapter 5.

Making it easier to find and understand migration data

More migration data are being collected than probably ever before from both traditional and non-traditional data sources. Yet, misperceptions about the scale and impact of migration are widespread (IOM, 2018). With large amounts of data available from such disparate sources, it is increasingly difficult but also all the more important for policymakers to know where they can find the most reliable and up-to-date statistics about international migration.

In May 2022, the World Health Organization (WHO) launched an "Information Platform on Health and Migration in the Americas". The platform

192 *Data availability on key migration topics*

systematizes information to facilitate the storage, dissemination and exchange of knowledge to guide the development of policies, public health interventions and other health and migration initiatives. The platform provides easy access to a huge amount of qualitative and quantitative evidence on health and migration gathered from the Americas. It includes interactive dashboards on policy, legal and regulatory frameworks, as well as scientific literature on health and migration, where data can be explored through dynamic panels and various filters can be used for analysis. The information compiled on the platform is a result of collaboration with various actors in the Americas, including those with years of expertise on issues related to health and migration.

The Global Migration Data Portal launched by IOM in December 2017 in collaboration with several other UN agencies is an excellent example of a concrete response to the challenge outlined above. A key objective of the portal is to help policymakers, experts, the media and anyone interested in migration find and understand key sources of data on international migration. The portal includes a user-friendly interactive world map, sections explaining the strengths and weaknesses of migration data by over 40 themes, a data innovation section and a section including guidance on migration data capacity building.

Harness the potential of big data – expand data collaboratives

The data world has changed significantly since 1993 when the "Age of Migration", written by Stephen Castles and Mark J. Miller, was first published. It is different not only because of the growth in the number of migrants but also because of the increase in the amount of data about migration in the digital age. Unlike in the past, when most data came from national authorities, today much data relevant to migration and human mobility are collected by the private sector.

As seen in Chapter 4, these new data sources offer huge potential benefits but also significant risks, if not managed carefully. On the plus side, this vast and ever-increasing amount of data, generated in real time across the globe, has the potential to inform decision-making across a range of different policy areas, including migration. New technologies also make it easier to store and analyse these vast quantities of complex data. Chapter 4 provided several concrete examples of specific projects and initiatives, which demonstrate the advantages of using such new data sources to understand migration patterns and inform related policies and programmes. For example, mobile phone data can help policymakers track the number and location of displaced persons in the aftermath of disasters, facilitating fast and targeted humanitarian response, if handled responsibly.

The recent global pandemic further highlighted the potential benefits of using such data sources when traditional data collection efforts were interrupted. As noted in Chapter 4, the relevance and importance of new digital data sources increased during the pandemic as it became more difficult to collect migration data through traditional methods such as face-to-face surveys.

The European Commission has highlighted the potential policy gains of using Big Data – *"We have an extraordinary opportunity to use the enormous amount of privately held data available for the benefit of our society and future generations ....business-to -government data sharing for the public interest can become a game-changer in this respect".*

Thierry Breton, European
Commissioner for the Internal Market,
B2gG report, (European Union, 2020, p. 1).

Recent UN data strategy documents, such as IOM's migration data strategy and the UN Secretary-General's UN data strategy also argue that it is essential to harness the potential of new technologies and data innovation (IOM, 2020). However, IOM also warns that such data need to be managed carefully. IOM's migration data strategy notes the importance of "ensuring consistent application of guidance on data privacy, data protection and data ethics in IOM work" (IOM, 2020, p. 1).

Using private sector data, which are already being collected, could help NSOs in a number of ways. It may be more cost-effective in some circumstances for NSOs to access and use private sector data rather than generating new data through costly surveys or other means. This also reduces the burden on public authorities to administer data collection. Using existing data could also be an easier way to obtain data within a short time frame to inform policy responses (Bither and Ziebarth, 2020).

While new data sources and technologies offer many opportunities, they also come with challenges and complexities. For example, "big data" are being generated faster than ever before, making it increasingly difficult to assess the quality and reliability of such data. Chapter 4 highlighted a number of these challenges such as how to access, make sense of and harness data owned by the private sector for the public good, while safeguarding the rights of migrants.

Data ethics has become a major concern in the digital era. Research shows, for example, that the unconscious biases of algorithm designers can reproduce racial, ethnic and gender discrimination (Gilbert, 2021). These biases, if not corrected, may skew thinking about migration policy responses.[1] Furthermore, greater volumes of data do not automatically translate into answers to key migration policy questions. It is often difficult to interpret and use such data, especially given that the data were not collected first and foremost to inform migration policy and practice.

As a way forward, we would like to recommend one promising type of approach that can be applied to any policy area and any country – data collaboratives. As explained in Chapter 4, data collaboratives are currently being developed to foster data dialogue and cooperation between the public and private sectors. Data collaboratives are defined as "an emergent form of public-private partnership that allows for collaboration and information sharing" between the public and private sectors (Verhulst and Young, 2023). Data collaboratives can help to define business models and compelling reasons for public–private data partnerships, which may vary in form. For data collaboratives to succeed, public and private sector partners need an effective agreed framework to collect, process, analyse and use data (ibid). For example, this might include an agreement on when and how to share data and how to do so in a responsible manner.

Verhulst and Young (2023) suggest four ways in which to develop a data collaborative framework. First, there needs to be a discussion and agreement on what is the purpose of data collection and what are the key migration policy areas where better data are needed. Second, dedicated "data steward" positions need to be introduced in collaborating organizations, to facilitate structured data cooperation. Data stewards could have several responsibilities, including ensuring that data protection guidelines are fully respected and that data are shared and communicated effectively. Third, data stewards could help to develop new governance models for data collaboratives and advise on the pros and cons of adopting different frameworks. Fourth, data collaboratives could help to promote the development of "data responsibility guidelines" to ensure that private–public data sharing does not create undue risks for migrants. Developing an agreed ethical framework for the collection, sharing and use of such data can be an important part of the work of data collaboratives. In recent years, numerous examples of data collaboratives have been developed in different regions of the world, although to date only a few of them focus on migration (IOM, 2023).

8.3.2 Launch a new global migration survey and leverage existing surveys

It has often been argued that one of the best ways to boost understanding of global patterns of migration is to launch a dedicated World Migration Survey (Bilsborrow, 2016). This would mean that each country would conduct a nationally representative survey of migrants (and non-migrants) using at least a standard set of core questions. While there might be some variations in the questions asked depending on each national context, a major aim of such a global survey would be to ask the same set of questions to make it easier to make real comparisons between countries. Conducting a World Migration Survey could have many potential advantages. These include providing information on subjects that traditional migration sources fail to capture well, such as emigrant stocks and migrant flows, return migration and temporary migration (Cerruti et al., 2021). The survey could also collect retrospective and biographical information that can be used to understand better why some people migrate and others do not. The survey would make it possible to make comparisons between different population groups, such as emigrants, immigrants, return migrants and non-migrants. A World Migration Survey could inform policy responses by collecting a great deal of data on the causes and consequences of migration (ibid). Cerruti et al. (2021) suggest that a World Migration Survey could provide data on:

Individual drivers of migration
Contextual factors influencing migration
Opportunities and linkages at destination
Migration, gender and the life cycle
Migration and change in origin countries
Migrant inclusion in destination countries

A World Migration Survey might be very welcome, but despite several years of discussions, it has not been possible to even begin pilot work on such a survey. Part of the problem is that launching a survey of this kind could be very costly, especially compared to adding more migration questions to existing household surveys. Conducting specialized nationally representative surveys can cost hundreds of thousands of dollars, and if all countries conducted such surveys, the budget for the World Migration Survey could be tens of millions of dollars. A second concern is that policymakers may be reluctant to invest in launching such a survey for fear that it might result in the production of "league tables" where countries might be ranked according to their treatment of migrants. The advocates of the World Migration Survey have recognized such a potential problem and suggested that the value of investing in a World Migration Survey (WMS) would need to be carefully explained to policymakers (Cerruti et al., 2021).

Another more feasible and less costly option in the short term that could complement preparations for a WMS might be to add more migration questions to existing surveys. ILO, for example, has developed substantial new guidance for NSOs on how to add questions relating to migrant recruitment costs to existing labour force surveys (ILO, 2019; Benes et al., 2022; Mosler Vidal and Laczko, 2022). As noted in Chapter 5, the SDGs call for a reduction in high recruitment costs, but few countries currently gather systematic data on this subject. The ILO and the World Bank have conducted pilot surveys to gather data on migrant recruitment costs, but information on this topic remains limited. Adding questions to existing labour force surveys, however, may not produce the data required, given that the sample sizes of these surveys are not always large enough to identify a representative sample of migrants (Benes et al., 2022). Thus, there may also be a need for specialized migrant surveys to gather data on recruitment costs.

A WMS could also be complemented by other sources of data. For example, a great deal of data about national migration policies is already being collected through an existing example of data innovation – the "Migration Governance Indicators" (MGI) project (IOM, 2022). As discussed in Chapters 2 and 5, the MGI has become a key source of information about global migration governance trends, providing data on migration policies in over 80 countries using a standard set of indicators. The advantage of the MGI project is that it has buy-in from national authorities and is adapted to national contexts. Each report is first presented and discussed with a range of migration stakeholders at the national level before being published.

A further advantage of the MGI is that it is an indicator framework, which can be used to monitor GCM objectives. In a 2022 report entitled "Migration Governance Indicators Data and the Global Compact for Safe, Orderly and Regular Migration: A Baseline Report" (IOM, 2022), IOM demonstrates how data collected through the MGI process in 84 countries between 2016 and 2021 can provide relevant data for each of the 23 GCM objectives. For example, regarding Objective 10 of the GCM – "Prevent, combat and eradicate trafficking in persons", MGI data show that even though most countries have a strategy to combat human trafficking, only one-third of them regularly publish information on counter-trafficking activities (ibid). Regarding GCM Objective 15 – "Provide access to basic services for migrants", MGI data show that equal access to all government-funded health services is contingent on migrants' legal status in about four of ten MGI countries (ibid).

As discussed in Chapter 4, there is also considerable scope to gather data cheaply and quickly through online surveys, social media analysis, Google search analysis and many other digital tools. Any programme to develop a new World Migration Survey using traditional survey methods should be completed by novel sources of migration data, which are being produced in real time by the private sector. Non-traditional data sources and methods often have considerable scope to provide new insights into many different aspects of human mobility and migration, which are often hard to study using traditional survey methods. For example, temporary and repeat movements of people, which may be undocumented, are not easily captured in a national survey conducted at one point in time. New technologies and digital platforms can also be used to sample migrant populations and administer cross-country surveys in a fast and cost-efficient manner.

Create a global migration data programme to boost data capacities and strengthen migration data governance

One recommendation highlighted under GCM Objective 1 is the call to develop a global migration data capacity-building programme. Such a programme would help:

> *to build and enhance national capacities in data collection, analysis and dissemination to share data, address data gaps and assess key migration trends, that encourages collaboration between relevant stakeholders at all levels, provides dedicated training, financial support and technical assistance, leverages new data sources, including big data, and is reviewed by the United Nations Statistical Commission on a regular basis.*

While there seems to be a widespread consensus in favour of supporting data capacity-building programmes, there is as yet no comprehensive, coherent global programme in this area. As outlined in Chapter 3, a great deal of new guidance has been produced on how to improve migration data, strengthen migration data protection and ethics and encourage countries to develop national data capacity-building strategies. Chapter 3 identified many examples of good data practice in this area. These include, for example, encouraging countries to conduct baseline assessments, create inter-ministerial groups to identify data gaps and needs and develop a coherent national migration data strategy.

Key elements of a global migration data capacity-building programme

In this section, we suggest what could be some of the key elements and features of a future global migration data capacity-building programme.

First, given the huge needs and the likely resource constraints, it is essential to make the best use of existing guidance materials. It would be useful to produce an overall guide to these materials and to organize this guidance in such a way to make it easily accessible to policymakers and practitioners. A dedicated *migration data capacity-building portal* could be created at a relatively low cost to facilitate the sharing of such materials. The portal could be regularly updated and provide a broad range of materials relating to data collection, governance, protection, ethics, disaggregation, etc.

Second, it is essential to invest in and develop more migration data training courses. Too often, guides are being produced but not being fully used because of a lack of investment in providing training to officials and others working with migration data.

Third, it is important to target both data collectors and data users when developing migration data capacity-building programmes. One evaluation of the World Bank's data capacity-building programmes, for example, showed that only a few programmes focused on building the capacity of policymakers to use data effectively (World Bank, 2017).

Fourth, migration data capacity programmes need to target those countries where the needs are greatest. Needs are especially acute in some of the poorest countries in the world, where it has been several years since a census was last conducted, and other sources of data remain limited.

Fifth, any new global migration data capacity-building programme needs to focus on strengthening migration data governance, especially in lower- and middle-income countries. In its flagship World Development Report 2021 "Data for Better Lives", the World Bank notes that "data governance arrangements to facilitate greater use of data while safeguarding against misuse remain in their infancy… the legal and regulatory frameworks for data are in lower-income countries inadequate" (World Bank, 2021, p. 13). As the World Bank points out "data protection needs to go beyond asking for the consent of the data user, data service providers also need to be responsible pointing out that – "it would take 76 days a year to thoroughly read data disclosure documents" (World Bank, 2021, p. 13). Migration data governance raises questions such as "what kind of data arrangements are needed to support the generation and use of data in a safe, ethical and secure way while also delivering value equitably" (ibid).

Sixth, there should be a strong regional dimension to a global migration data capacity-building programme, given that so much migration happens between countries in one region. The establishment of regional training centres can help training and research services be more efficient by delivering services as close as possible to the countries themselves. Examples of existing regional migration observatories that provide data training are presented in Chapter 3.

Seventh, it is essential to build capacities to support data disaggregation. As noted in Chapter 5, it is difficult to know whether migrants are being "left behind" in a country if key indicators of well-being are not disaggregated by migratory status. Chapter 5 that focuses on data on migration and development shows that migrants are largely invisible in official global SDG data, as only one of the recommended SDG indicators at the global level is disaggregated by migratory status.

One example of data innovation is the growing amount of guidance, which is being produced to help national authorities disaggregate data by migratory status (UNHCR, 2020;[2] IOM, 2021c; IOM, Asia, 2022). IOM, for example, published in 2021 its first dedicated guide on how to disaggregate SDG indicators by migratory status – "Leave No Migrant Behind" – the 2030 Agenda and Data Disaggregation. At the end of 2020, UNHCR published a guide on how to disaggregate SDG indicators by forced displacement.

IOM's guide explains why SDG indicators need to be disaggregated by migratory status and shows how this can be done, using a range of different data sources such as surveys, censuses and administrative data. A review of the availability of published disaggregated SDG indicators and to assess the feasibility of estimating them based on existing data and … to encourage National Statistical Offices (NSOs) and custodian agencies to improve the availability of data on forced displacement aligned to the SDGs (UNHCR, 2020).

The challenge now is to ensure that such guides are used to promote more disaggregation of key development and other indicators by migratory status. This recommendation is closely related to our final recommendation concerning how to boost efforts to build data capacities in lower- and middle-income countries.

Lastly, a significant investment of funds in migration data capacity building is required. There is a case for developing a new "global migration data facility", which could be managed by the UN to provide greater data capacity-building assistance to countries. This could also help to ensure better coordination between different agencies providing different forms of data capacity-building assistance to countries. Some countries face a confusing plethora of UN-driven capacity development efforts with duplicating or overlapping aims and activities.

In sum, much guidance is already available on how to improve migration statistics, and there are many examples of national and regional migration data capacity-building programmes, as discussed in Chapter 3. The challenge in the future is to develop a global, coherent and targeted programme that will help build migration data capacities. To gain support for such a programme, it will be necessary to communicate to relevant stakeholders how and why particular investments in migration data would be beneficial.

A new global migration data capacity-building programme needs to provide assistance at different levels—local, national, regional and global. It should also include guidance on how to work with the private sector to leverage new data sources. The programme needs to be balanced, focusing as much on data use, communication and analysis as data collection. In order for such a programme to be sustainable over the longer term, it may be necessary to create dedicated migration data units in NSOs. For example, some countries have created dedicated migration units within their statistical offices (Djibouti, Egypt and South Africa). Others have established inter-ministerial working groups on migration data – for example in Nigeria – the "Working Group on Migration Data Management" (IOM, 2021a).

8.3.4 Develop a global migration data monitoring framework

Many recommendations have been made on how to improve data on international migration (UN, 1998; CGD, 2009; GCM, 2018), but it is difficult to assess how much progress is being made in improving data on migration globally, because there is no global framework in place to monitor how far such recommendations are being implemented.

GCM Objective 1, for example, includes 11 action points, but these are fairly generic and have not been translated into measurable indicators.[3] Also, countries have not yet reported, in a systematic way, on how much progress they are making in addressing these recommendations. Some 60 countries have reported on the progress that they have made in implementing GCM objectives, including objective 1 according to the GCM website.[4] These reports contain a wealth of information about new data measures implemented at the national level, but generally do not provide much information on how far a country is collecting data according to UN recommendations, and the extent to which it produces statistics on even basic migration indicators, such as the number of foreign citizens or number of migrants returning to the country.

While the GCM reports do not provide us with an overall indication of the "state of migration data", they do offer important examples of data innovation in several countries and, in some instances, highlight important data gaps. These reports could therefore form the basis for better monitoring of migration statistics in the future, and such materials could be included in an annual short report on the "State of Migration Data".

The GCM country reports overall indicate that a great deal of migration data innovation has occurred in recent years. For example, Albania reports that it launched its first "Home Migration Survey" in 2019 with the participation of more than 20,000 households, the biggest survey of its kind ever conducted in the country. Kenya mentions that it launched a "Demographic Health Survey" survey in 2022, which includes a migration module (Government of Kenya, 2022). Belgium is developing a website dedicated to facts and data on migration in Belgium, including sections on "fact checks", to improve the way in which migration data are communicated and interpreted.

The GCM country reports also highlight some key data challenges, which need to be addressed. For instance, the challenges identified by Belgium – which are shared by many countries – are, first, the need for better disaggregation of migration data by gender, so that, for example, gender-specific violence occurring on migration routes could be better identified; second, the need to promote data integration and make better use of existing data by ensuring that migration data are shared widely.

> *Due to the Belgian state structure, many actors are involved in collecting data at different levels of government. This results in data being scattered over various databases*
>
> (Government of Belgium, 2022, p. 4)

Third, the importance of investing in the analysis of data is to improve the way data are used to inform policy.

> *While having adequate and reliable data is vital and a crucial element for implementing evidence-based policies, it is certainly not sufficient… the added value of data collection… also lies in the in-depth analysis of those data, to inform concrete actions in the strengthening of science-based policy, especially in a domain as sensitive as migration.*
>
> (Government of Belgium, 2022, p. 4)

The GCM Objective 1 action points are also limited in scope. Few of the 11 action points, for example, deal directly with the need to harness the potential of big data or novel data sources. No mention is made of encouraging the public and private sectors to work more closely together to leverage big data and new analytical methods for official statistics, although this aspect is addressed in several UN and other initiatives, as seen in Chapter 4. Another limitation of the GCM Objective 1 framework is that it focuses solely on international migration and includes few references to other forms of mobility, such as internal displacement and refugee movements. It is also not clear what criteria should be used to measure data progress.

A key recommendation advanced by this book is to develop an agreed set of indicators, which could be monitored on an annual basis to broadly assess whether migration data are improving at the global level (Laczko, 2017, p. 20). There might have to be an agreement on a core set of migration data indicators, which would need to be monitored on a regular basis, such as

> Does the national census include migration questions?,
> Does the government publish migration statistics regularly?,
> Do surveys include migration modules?,
> Are administrative data disaggregated by migratory status?,
> To what extent are data shared, and are there any national or regional fora for sharing data?
> How far are globally-recommended concepts, definitions and other standards applied? What measures are in place to protect migration data?

Agreement on a common set of "core" data indicators which could be monitored over time would help to raise awareness among states and other actors about the importance of improving the collection of timely, reliable, disaggregated migration statistics.

8.5 Concluding remarks – time for a global migration data action plan

Over the last decade, at the political level, the importance of improving data on migration has been underlined in many international policy documents. For example, the majority of countries in the world agreed in 2018 to make improving data on migration the first objective of the "Global Compact on Safe Orderly and Regular Migration". Across the UN system, data have become a higher priority. The UN launched its first data strategy in 2021, and in the same year, IOM launched its first-ever migration data strategy. At the regional level, the African Union launched the first "Africa Migration Observatory" in 2021 to improve the collection, analysis and responsible use of data to inform policy and practice. The private sector has also launched a number of initiatives to make its migration-related data more available to policymakers, such as META's "Data for Public Good" programme outlined in Chapter 4.

There has also been progress at the technical level. For example, as we have shown in previous chapters, there have been significant improvements in the collection of migration data on topics such as migrant deaths, migration governance, human trafficking, remittances, recruitment costs, migration and the environment. This book has also highlighted many examples of data innovation using both traditional and non-traditional data sources.

While there are many good ideas and recommendations on how to improve data on migration, these have yet to be translated into a global action plan to improve migration data. Unlike in the field of development, the international migration community has yet to agree on a way forward. A decade ago, there were calls for a "development data revolution". In a high-level report to the

UN Secretary-General (UN, 2014), experts argued that it was time to invest in development data to improve the lives of poor people around the world. "Data champions", such as Bill Gates, made a powerful case for investing in the "development data revolution".

> *Few people believe in the power of data in the way I do. When you're trying to reach a goal, data not only tells you if you are succeeding, but it also suggests which activities you should do more of, in order to improve your results. Ultimately, the better the data available in the development field, the higher the quality of people's lives in poor countries.*
>
> (Bill Gates, 2013, p. 32)

Calls for a development data revolution led to the creation of the "Global Partnership for Sustainable Development Data" (GPSDD), the organization of the first UN World Data Forum in Cape Town in 2019 and the launching of the "Global Action Plan for Sustainable Development Data". In the migration field, there is no such plan. IOM's migration data strategy provides an excellent starting point for developing such a plan, but it has yet to be fully implemented and a global plan needs to be developed in partnership with several different agencies and stakeholders.

The International Forum for Migration Statistics (IFMS), the largest global conference focusing on how to improve migration statistics, could be a good place to develop and monitor the implementation of an action plan for migration data. We hope that this book can help to stimulate more discussions about how to develop and implement such an action plan. If carefully managed, data have the potential to significantly improve migration policy and practice and the lives of migrants. As a final reminder, investing in migration data could bring many benefits including the following:

Better protecting children on the move at risk of exploitation and harm
Better identifying victims of trafficking
Boost development through lower remittance costs
Better integration of migrants
Better matching supply and demand for migrant labour
Better understanding who may need to move due to climate change
Better identifying migrants who cannot access health services.

The time for action is now. We hope that this book will add ideas and stimulate fresh thinking to create some real momentum to advance the global migration data agenda.

Notes

1 Facebook has an internal tool called "Fairness Flow" that measures how algorithms affect specific groups; Google has released the "What-if Tool", which is intended to help developers identify biases in datasets and algorithms (Gilbert, 2021, p. 249).

2 Data disaggregation of SDG indicators by forced displacement, UNHCR (2020).
3 At the first International Migration Review Forum, countries were asked to report on the progress that they have made in implementing the 23 GCM indicators, but no systematic reporting framework has yet been developed in relation to GCM Objective 1.
4 See www.gcm.org.

References

Benes, E., Gallotti, M., Habi, Y., and Plaza, S. (2022). 10.7 supporting evidence-based policymaking on fair recruitment. In Mosler-Vidal, E., & Laczko, F. (Eds.), *SDGs and Migration: Measuring Progress*. Geneva: IOM, 19–25.

Bilsborrow, R. (2016). The Global Need for Better Data on International Migration and the Special Potential of Household Surveys, conference paper, Improving Data on International Migration: Towards Agenda 2030 and the Global Compact on Migration, Berlin, 2–3 December, Ministry of Foreign Affairs, Germany. Available at www.gmdac.iom.int

Bither, J. and Ziebarth, A. (2020). *AI, Digital Identities, Biometrices, Blockchain: A Primer on the Use of Technology in Migration Management*, Migration Strategy Group on international cooperation and development, Bertelsmann Stiftung, German Marshall Fund, Robert Bosch Stiftung, Berlin.

Black, J. (2018). *Migrant Deaths and Disappearances*. Data Bulletin Series - Informing the Implementation of the Global Compact for Migration. Geneva: IOM.

Borgnas, E. (2018). Migration profiles. In *Data Bulletin Series: Informing the Implementation of the Global Compact for Migration*. Geneva: IOM.

Brian, T. and Laczko, F. (2014). *Fatal Journeys*. Geneva: IOM.

Castles, S. and Miller, M.J. (1993). *The Age of Migration*. London: Macmillan.

Cerruti, M., Fargues, P., and Awumbila, M. (2021). *The Case for a World Migration Survey*, IUSSP (International Union for the Scientific Study of Population), Policy and Research paper.

CGD. (2009). *Migrants Count: Five Steps towards Better Migration Data*. Washington, DC: Center for Global Development.

Dumont, J.C., Hovy, B., Osaki, K., and Laczko, F. (2018). Improving data for safe, orderly and regular migration. In *Data Bulletin Series*. Informing the implementation of the Global Compact for Migration, Geneva: IOM.

Espey, J. (2019). "The World we want" for data: Articulating clear, compelling goals on data for development, February 25. Available at www.sdsntrends.org/blog, Bern-dialogue-data-goals.

European Union. (2020). *Towards a European Strategy on Business-to-Government Data Sharing for the Public Interest*, Final report prepared by the High-Level Expert Group on Business-to Government Data Sharing, Brussels: European Union.

Gates, Bill (2013). Improving the lives of the poor will take a steady thoughtful revolution in development data, Development Asia. Available at www.development.Asia

GCM. (2018). *Global Compact for Safe, Orderly and Regular Migration*. New York, NY: United Nations.

Gilbert, S. (2021). *Good Data: An Optimists Guide to Our Digital Future*. London: Welbeck Publishing.

Government of Belgium (2022). Global compact on migration action plan: Belgium" – Voluntary global compact for migration reviews. Available at www.UN.org

Government of Kenya. (2022). "Kenya Voluntary Review Report on Implementation of the Global Compact for Safe, Orderly and Regular Migration", National

Coordination Mechanism on Migration for the Government of Kenya, May, 2022, - "Voluntary Global Compact for Migration Reviews". Available at www.UN.org.

GPSDD (Global Partnership for Sustainable Development Data) (2022). September 20th, "New analysis shows every dollar invested in data systems creates an average of USD32 in economic benefits".

Hennebry, J., H. KC and K. Williams, 2021. Gender and Migration Data: A Guide for Evidence-based, Gender-responsive

Migration Governance. International Organization for Migration (IOM). Geneva. Available at https://publications.iom.int/books/gender-and-migration-data-guide-evidence-based-gender-responsive-migration-governance

ILO, International Labour Organization. (2019). *ILO Operational Manual on Recruitment Costs- SDG 10.7.1.* Geneva: ILO.

IOM and McKinsey & Company. (2018), More than Numbers: How Migration Data Can Deliver Real-Life Benefits for Migrants and Governments. Geneva: IOM. Available at https://publications.iom.int/system/files/pdf/more_than_numbers.pdf

IOM. (2020). *IOM Migration Data Strategy.* Geneva: IOM.

IOM. (2021a). *How Countries Manage Migration Data: Evidence from 6 Countries.* Geneva: IOM.

IOM. (2021c). *Leave No Migrant Behind: The 2030 Agenda and Data Disaggregation.* Geneva: IOM.

IOM. (2022). *Asia-Pacific Migration Data Report 2021.* Bangkok: IOM.

IOM, (2023) "Harnessing Data Innovation for Migration Policy: A Handbook for Practitioners", eds M. Rango, N Sievers, and F. Laczko, Geneva, IOM.

Jenkins, C. and Mosler-Vidal, E. (2022). Migration data capacity-building. In *Migration and the SDGs: Measuring Progress.* Geneva: IOM.

Laczko, F. (2017). *Improving data on migration: A 10-point plan.* In *Migration Policy Practice, Vol. VII, Number 1 (January–March 2017)*, Geneva: IOM-Eurasylum.

UN. (1998). *"Recommendations on Statistics of International Migration".* Statistical Papers Series M, No 58, Rev. 1 Department of Economic and Social Affairs, Statistics Division. United Nations, New York.

UN. (2014). "A World That Counts", report prepared at the request of the UN Secretary-General by the Independent Expert Advisory Group on a Data Revolution for Sustainable Development. New York: United Nations.

UNHCR. (2020). *Data Disaggregation of SDG Indicators by Forced Displacement.* Geneva: UNHCR.

Verhulst, S. and Young, A. (2023). Operationalizing data collaboratives for migration. In *Harnessing Data Innovation for Migration Policy: A Handbook for Practitioners.* Geneva: IOM.

World Bank. (2017). *An Evaluation of World Bank Support for Data and Statistical Capacity.* September, Washington, DC: World Bank.

World Bank. (2021). *Data for Better Lives.* World Development Report, Washington, DC: World Bank.

World Bank. (2022). *The Global Data Facility at a Glance.* Washington, DC: World Bank.

World Bank. (2023). *Migrants, Refugees and Societies.* World Development Report, Washington DC: World Bank.

Index

Note: **Bold** page numbers refer to tables and page numbers followed by "n" denote endnotes.

acute humanitarian crisis 89
adaptation programmes 141
administrative data 50, 114, 142–145, 165–166
Africa Migration Data Network (AMDN) 61, 191
Africa Migration Observatory 201
African Union Commission (AUC) 123
African Union Institute for Statistics (STATAFRIC) 123
2030 Agenda for Sustainable Development (2030 Agenda) 17, 74, 75, 116–121, 169, 184
air passenger traffic data 92, 146
Aligning Migration Management and the Migration-Development Nexus (MIGNEX) 122
Application Public Interfaces (APIs) 80
Article 12 of the Universal Declaration of Human Rights 58
artificial intelligence (AI) 73, 88
Asian Development Bank 137, 138
asylum seekers 23, 44, 83, 89

big data 7, 10, 51, 72–78, 142, 146; data collaboratives 192; internet-based data 80–85; for migration and human mobility 86–92, 94; mobile phone-based data 78–80; and new technologies 167; online search data 85; satellite imagery 86; social media 80–85
Big Data for Migration Alliance (BD4M) 74, 95
border data collection systems 50

call detail records (CDRs) 73, 146
capacity and practical challenges 54–57
capacity-building programmes 59, 61, 94, 153
Caribbean Disaster Emergency Management Agency (CDEMA) 143
Caring for Trafficked Persons: A Guide for Health Providers 166
censuses 5, 79, 92, 114, 142–143, 163–164, 184
citizen-generated data (CGD) 51
citizenship 6, 27, 47
civil registration system 111–112
climate change 1, 19, 87, 106, 113, 134, 139, 140, 142, 143, 184; human mobility 142, 143; international mobility 140; migration dynamics 140; mobility and immobility 141; refugees 136
Climate Change statistics 138
climate migrants 136, 137, 138, 184
climate-related migration 86, 137
Commonwealth of Independent States (CIS) 6
Continuous Reporting System on International Migration in the Americas (SICREMI) project 32
1951 Convention relating to the Status of Refugees 110
Corporate Social Responsibility 77
Counter-Trafficking Data Collaborative (CTDC) 5, 90, 118, 166
country of birth 47
COVID-19 3, 11, 63; data collection 160; impact on migrants and

migration 159–162; infection and mortality rates 184; migratory status, 160; Mobility Data Network 167; national vaccination plans 161; pandemic 77, 84, 87, 92; vaccines 112
cross-sectoral partnerships 92

data: accessibility 112; administrative data 143–145; availability 119; capacity-building activities 63–67; censuses 142–143; collaborative framework 87, 94–95, 152, 193, 194; disaggregation 122; displacement data 149; ethics 193; extreme environmental events 149; forecasts and projections limitations 148–149; gaps 37–38; and global trends 142; governance 43–44; innovation application 5, 72, 95; integration 55; life-cycle 51; management 176; minimization 88; operational data 145; projections and forecasting data 146–148; protection legislation 58, 91; responsibility guidelines 194; revolution 75, 121; sceptics 7; stewards 95
data collection 115, 173; data protection principle 88; foster technical improvements in 153
data disaggregation 119, 122–123, 157, 198, 203n2
Data Innovation Directory 74, 146, 167
data sources: administrative data sources 50–51; alternative sources 51; data theft/loss 57; intragovernmental coordination 53; regional and international data sources 51–52; statistical data sources 46–49
decision-makers 1, 2, 77, 96, 141, 185
decision-making 90, 96, 176, 192
demand-driven approaches 127
Demographic and Health Survey (DHS) 18, 48, 112, 164, 200
Demographic Yearbook data collection system 28, 31
Department of Economic and Social Affairs (DESA) 6
diaspora 109, 110
digital devices 8, 51
digital self-determination 96
digital trace data 72

disability 173–174
disaster management 143
discrimination 88, 89
Displacement Tracking Matrix (DTM) data 52, 145
domestic workers 114
"do no harm" principle 57–58
duration of stay concept 20

Eastern Caribbean region 143, 144
Eastern Mediterranean region 178
economic remittances 108, 110
education/health 19, 106
electronic personal health record (e-PHR) 177
environmental change 140, 145, 149
environmental/climate migrants 134, 136, 138
environmental migration 38, 135, 153
ethics and data protection 57–58, 92–93
ethnic minorities 89
EU General Data Protection Regulation (GDPR) 93
European Commission 49
European Social Survey 164
European Union (EU) 168
Expert Group on Migration Statistics 21, 23
Expert Group on Refugee, IDP and Statelessness Statistics (EGRISS) 23, 45

Facebook 80, 81, 82, 87, 202n1
family migrants 29
family migration **34**
family reunification 44
forced and voluntary migration 23
forced migration/displaced populations **35–36**
forecasts and projections limitations 148–149
foreign citizenship 6, 28
fundamental human rights 87–88, 89

gender 18, 36–37, 38, 64, 78, 113, 119, 123, 189, 195; gaps in public transport 87; gender data 65; gender identity 88; and income groups 78
General Data Protection Regulation 89
Global Compact for Safe, Orderly and Regular Migration (GCM) 4–5, 17, 22, 74, 75, 121, 183, 185, 201–202

Global Compact on Refugees (GCR) 9, 18
global diaspora populations 109
Global Forum on Migration and Development (GFMD) 106
Global Knowledge Partnership on Migration and Development (KNOMAD) 52, 111
global migrant stock statistics 29
global migration data 2; action plan 201–202; capacity-building programme 197–199; monitoring framework 199
Global Migration Data Portal 62, 146, 192
global migration data programme 196
global migration survey 194
global pandemic 8, 157
Global Partnership for Sustainable Development Data (GPSDD) 123, 187
Google 85
Google Trends data 83, 85
Google Trends Index (GTI) 82
gravity model 147
Groundswell project 147, 153
"ground truth" data 83
Guidance for the Integrated Data Ecosystem Assessment and Strengthening (IDEAS) Tool 60
Guidelines for Developing Statistical Capacity 66
Guiding Principles on Internal Displacement 24

hard-to-reach migrant groups 115, 162
health 162–163; administrative data 165–166; big data and new technologies 167; censuses 163–164; inclusivity 170; information systems 165; operational data 166; surveys of migrants 164–165; workers 105
healthcare system 158
Health Data Collaborative 179
Health Inclusivity Index 170, 171
health insurance coverage 165
high-income countries 113, 184
2013 High-Level Dialogue on International Migration and Development 106
homeless migrants 114
household surveys 48, 55, 85, 92, 112, 114, 146, 164, 193
humanitarian crises 1, 19

Humanitarian Open Street Map Team (HOT) 96
human mobility 2, 8, 21, 72, 73, 78, 92, 135, 142, 143, 145; data 23; dynamics 2, 21; phenomena 74
human right 158
human security 88
human trafficking 5, 38, 44, 52, 90, 114, 165, 166

Immigration and Customs Enforcement (ICE) Agency 91
Immigration Service Delivery (ISD) 45
Inclusive Data Charter (IDC) 123
Information Platform on Health and Migration in the Americas 176
innovative analytical methods 73
innovative approaches 5
integrated data systems 55; Data Innovation Directory 146; Data Protection Manual 58; Global Migration Data Analysis Centre 167; Global Migration Data Portal 192; migrant deaths 172; migration governance indicators 168; Migration Governance Indicators 153; Missing Migrants Project 191
Integrated Public Use Microdata Series (IPUMS) 163
Integrated Refugee Health Information System (iRIHS) 168, 180n1
inter-disciplinary: collaborations 75; exchange 125
Intergovernmental Panel on Climate Change (IPCC) 134, 148
internal displacement 143
Internal Displacement Monitoring Centre (IDMC) 149, 150, 154n2
internally displaced people (IDPs) 137, 188
internally displaced persons (IDPs) 23, **35**, 52
internal migration 142, 147
International Classification Standard for Administrative Data on Trafficking in Persons (ICS-TIP) 166
international community 4, 121
International Covenant on Civil and Political Rights or the European Convention on Human Rights 93
International Data Alliance for Children on the Move (IDAC) 62, 188, 189

International Forum for Migration Statistics (IFMS) 63, 202
International Labour Organization (ILO) **33**, 118, 159, 172, 184
international migrants 2, 3, 22, 24, 25, 142, 172; definition of 20; quality data on stocks and flows 32
international migration 2, 3, 22, 53, 74, 83, 143, 163; quality statistics on 17
international mobility 22, 78, 140
International Organization for Migration (IOM) 9, 60, 134, 146, 158, 167, 190
international public law 110
International Recommendations on Internally Displaced Persons Statistics (IRIS) 24, 61
International Recommendations on Refugee Statistics (IRRS) 24, 61
international students **34**
international temporary mobility 22
internet-based platforms 51, 74
interoperability 91
involuntary immobility 124
irregular migrant status 89
irregular migration 3, 22, 38

Joint Data Center on Forced Displacement (JDC) 115
Joint Labour Migration Programme (JLMP) **33**

labour force surveys (LFS) 48
labour market 19, 37
Labour Market Information System (LMIS) 111
labour migrants 29, 125
labour migration 21, 44, 107, 111
Labour Migration Module 49
Leave No One Behind (LNOB) 119, 197
legal framework 89
long-term migrant 20
low-income countries 56, 86, 94, 175

machine learning 73
maternal mortality 124
mental health 171
methodology 126
Microsoft, *Open Data Campaign* 77

Migrant Integration Strategy Data Group (MISDG) 45
migrants: characteristics of 32, **36–37**, 46; children health 174; conceptualization of 28; deaths/disappearances 38, 172; definition of 20, 23; Facebook advertising platform 81; global data and trends 4; groups 114; healthcare coverage 170; health country profile tool 177; health status of 170; health workers 174–175; labour rights violations of 106; migration policymakers 28; personal data on 58; populations 2; recruitment costs 124; rights 111; selected categories of 32, **33–36**; smuggling 38; surveys of 164–165; workers **33**
migrant stocks 17; data summary 28–30; definition of 24; global trends 25–28
migration: causal impacts of 116; and climate change 134; comprehensive statistics on 151; conceptual framework on 21; definitions of 3, 6; development implications of 106; environmental changes on 152; global data and trends 4; and health data innovation 112, 175–178; and human mobility phenomena 74; management 55; multi-causal character of 138; policies and programmes 1, 44; policymakers 115; political economy of 125; process 107, 110; profiles 190; public perceptions of 7; statistics 1, 59
Migration and Health Data Collaboratives 179
Migration and Health Evidence Portal for COVID-19 176
migration data 2, 5–7, 17–18, 74; assessment of 59; comparability and interoperability of 6; concepts and definitions 19–24; data gaps 37–38; data protection 58; fragmentation of 54; governance 43; investment in 185–187; migrant stocks 24–30; migration flows 30–32; privacy safeguards 58; revolution 185;

stakeholders 54; statistical sources of 46; strategy 65
migration-development nexus 105–106; common challenges 113–116; diaspora contributions 109–110; economic remittances 108–109; initiatives and examples 121–123; migrant rights 110–111; migration and development data topics 108; migration and development debates 107–108; practical ways forward 127–128; summary and implications 124–127
"Migration, Environment and Climate Change: Evidence for Policy (MECLEP)" project 141
migration flows 50; data summary 31–32; definition of 30; global trends 30–31
"Migration Governance Indicators" (MGI) project 145, 153, 168, 184, 195
Migration Health and Development Research Initiative (MHADRI) 112
Migration Integration Policy Index (MIPEX) 112, 168, 184
migration trends 18, 74
migratory movements 2, 3
migratory status 119, 123
Missing Migrants Project 52, 118, 172, 183, 191
mixed migration flows 23
mobile network operators (MNOs) 78, 167
mobile phone network data 92, 146
mobile positioning data (MPD) 73, 78
mobility 21; types of 22
Multiple Indicator Cluster Survey (MICS) 164
multi-site data collection and research 122

national data systems 139
National Deployment and Vaccination Plans 161
national household survey 31
National Human Trafficking Resource Center (NHTRC) 5
nationality (foreign citizenship) 2
national migration data dynamics 44–45, 59

national stakeholders 56, 59–60
National Statistical Office (NSOs) 21, 44, 114, 159, 189
national statistical systems 186
native-born population 109
non-communicable diseases (NCDs) 162
non-governmental organization (NGO) 146, 172, 189
non-normative frameworks 91
non-standard data collection tools 173
non-traditional data 57, 72, 73, 77, 93
non-traditional methods 92
normative frameworks 93
novel data sources 72

occupational injuries 172–173
online search platforms 85
Open Data Campaign 77
open street mapping 51
operational data 145, 166
Organization for Economic Co-operation and Development (OECD) 6, 159
Organization for Migration (IOM) 187
Organization of American States' (OAS) 32

participatory data 51
partnerships and data access 94–95
Pew Research Centre 82
place of birth (foreign-born) 2
policymakers 2, 7, 8, 17, 19, 53, 74, 106
political instability 2
political values 110
population censuses 46, 112
population mobility 137
population movement 19
poverty 106, 109
practical progress 121
privacy safeguards 58
private–public data sharing 194
private sector 93
Programme for International Student Assessment (PISA) 164
Programme of Action of the International Conference on Population and Development 169
projections and forecasting data 146–148
public emergency 93
public–private data partnerships 194

210 *Index*

qualitative data 116

Recommendations on Statistics of International Migration 19, 21
refugees 23, 29, 44, 171; *see also* asylum seekers; migrants; data landscape 24; international legal regime 137
regional and globallevel migration data 18, 45, 191
regional intergovernmental agency 143
Remittance Prices Worldwide 108
remittances 17, 19
remote-sensing data 86
Report on Labour Migration Statistics in Africa 33
re-settlement programmes 141

satellite imagery 86
Sendai Framework for Disaster Risk Reduction 2015–2030 18
sensor-based data 86
short-term migrant 20
SIM (Subscriber Identity Module) card 78, 87
"slow-onset" disasters 150
Small Island Developing States (SIDS) 147
social media 74, 80–85
social media data 80, 83, 87
social remittances 110, 159
South-South migration 113
statistical capacity development 59–63, 66
Statistical Capacity Indicator (SCI) 66–67
statistical definitions, implementation of 52–53
sudden-onset disasters 150
survival migration 23
Sustainable Development Goal (SDG) 1, 11, 116, **117,** 128n1, 157, 183; data architecture 121; definition of 116; monitoring system 186
Syria Disability Impact and Prevalence Study 173

Technical Working Group on Migration Statistics (GTT) 45
temporary (non-resident) population 22, 23, 143

traditional data collection systems 72, 78, 114, 184
"Training of Trainers" (ToT) 60
transnationalism 78, 107
Trapped populations 139

UN Committee of Experts on Big Data and Data Science for Official Statistics (UN-CEBD) 76
UN Complex Risk Analytics Fund (CRAF'd) 66
UN Department of Economic and Social Affairs (DESA) 25, 159
UNFCCC Task Force on Displacement 152
UN Framework Convention on Climate Change (UNFCCC) 135
UN General Assembly 1, 187
UN Guiding Principles on Business and Human Rights, the OCHA Guidance 93
UN Interagency Working Group on AI (IAWGAI) 76
United Nations (UN) 169, 184
United Nations Development Programme (UNDP) 140
United Nations Economic Commission for Europe (UNECE) 61
United Nations High Commissioner for Refugees (UNHCR) 115, 137
United Nations International Children's Emergency Fund (UNICEF) 174
United Nations Office on Drugs and Crime (UNODC) 118
United Nations Statistical Commission (UNSC) 22
United Nations Statistical Division (UNSD) 28, 117
Universal Declaration of Human Rights 110
UN Office of the High Commissioner for Human Rights (OHCHR) 110
UN Population and Development Inquiry 169
UN Population Division 28, 142
UN Principles on Personal Data Protection and Privacy of 2018 58
UN Statistical Division (UNSD) 138

UN World Data Forum 202
upper-middle-income countries 175
US Census Bureau 146
usual residence 20

voluntary migration 137
vulnerabilities 110

World Bank 26–27, 108, 147, 153, 173, 197
World Bank Development Data Partnership 92
World Bank Global Data Facility (GDF) 66
World Bank Global Data Facility and the Complex Risk Analytics Fund (CRAF'd) 127
World Development Report 2021 66, 197
World Development Report: Data for Better Lives 186
World Health Organization (WHO) 3, 157, 171, 173, 176, 191
World Health Survey 179
World Migration Survey 194, 195

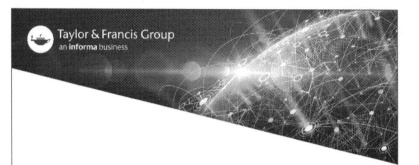

Printed in the United States
by Baker & Taylor Publisher Services